BOTHERING TO LOVE

BOTHERING TO LOVE

*James F. Keenan's Retrieval and
Reinvention of Catholic Ethics*

**Christopher P. Vogt
and Kate Ward, Editors**

ORBIS BOOKS
Maryknoll, New York 10545

Founded in 1970, Orbis Books endeavors to publish works that enlighten the mind, nourish the spirit, and challenge the conscience. The publishing arm of the Maryknoll Fathers and Brothers, Orbis seeks to explore the global dimensions of the Christian faith and mission, to invite dialogue with diverse cultures and religious traditions, and to serve the cause of reconciliation and peace. The books published reflect the views of their authors and do not represent the official position of the Maryknoll Society. To learn more about Maryknoll and Orbis Books, please visit our website at www.orbisbooks.com.

Library of Congress Cataloging-in-Publication Data

Names: Vogt, Christopher P., 1970- editor. | Ward, Kate, 1983- editor.
Title: Bothering to love : James F. Keenan's retrieval and reinvention of Catholic ethics / Christopher P. Vogt, Kate Ward, editors.
Description: Maryknoll, NY : Orbis Books, [2024] | Includes bibliographical references. | Summary: "Essays honoring the work of Catholic ethicist James F. Keenan"— Provided by publisher.
Identifiers: LCCN 2024004550 (print) | LCCN 2024004551 (ebook) | ISBN 9781626985957 (trade paperback) | ISBN 9798888660515 (epub)
Subjects: LCSH: Keenan, James F. | Christian ethics—Catholic authors.
Classification: LCC BJ1278.5.K44 B63 2024 (print) | LCC BJ1278.5.K44 (ebook) | DDC 241/.042—dc23/eng/20240308
LC record available at https://lccn.loc.gov/2024004550
LC ebook record available at https://lccn.loc.gov/2024004551

Contents

PART IV
ETHICS OF SEX AND GENDER

PART V
SPIRITUALITY AND MORALITY

Introduction

This volume honors James F. Keenan, SJ, a theologian, mentor, author, and teacher whose many and distinguished contributions to the church and the academy are almost impossible to evoke in a single phrase. We might summon Keenan's famous statement, "Mercy is entering into the chaos of another," noting the prominent role of God's mercy in his theology and the descent to the chaos of ordinary life in his practice of theological ethics. We might note his coinage of "Jesuit hospitality" as the hospitality that goes out to encounter the other on the road, and reflect on Keenan's intellectual and literal journeying, as a Jesuit and scholar, to accompany those on the margins.[1] "Bridgebuilder" is one of Keenan's own highest forms of praise, and one that could easily apply to Keenan himself, as his career is characterized by building bridges across cultures, disciplines, and misunderstandings, and creating community among those who long to have their voices heard. Or we could recognize his pioneering role in the establishment of both clergy ethics and university ethics, where Keenan exposes utilitarian thinking and practice in both fields by pointing to the simple alternative phrase, "But is it ethical?"

Instead, the title of our book in Keenan's honor riffs on another famous ethical definition of his, one which, like so much of his work, clarifies a rich insight of the Catholic theological tradition while making it accessible and new for modern believers. "Sin," Keenan tells us in his often-reprinted book *Moral Wisdom*, "is the failure to bother to love."[2] Catholics understand that sin is what separates us from God and one another, and Keenan's unforgettable framing helps us see how absolutely banal sin's presence in our lives can be, appearing when we feel most at ease, when we believe we have tamed sin and have it under control, when we forget or ignore our call to grow in love. For our title we take the mirror image

---

[1] James F. Keenan, "Jesuit Hospitality?" in *Promise Renewed: Jesuit Higher Education for a New Millennium*, ed. Martin R. Tripole (Chicago: Jesuit Way, 1999), 230–44.

[2] James F. Keenan, *Moral Wisdom: Lessons and Texts from the Catholic Tradition*, 3rd ed. (Lanham, MD: Rowman & Littlefield, 2017), 42.

of Keenan's insight, reminding us that God calls Christians to bother to love, to allow love to draw us out of our complacency to the side of the other who needs us. The Christian vocation is to love, a love that can be practiced in ten thousand places, amid the minutiae of ordinary life, in the distinct paths where God has called us. The call to bother to love reminds us that God calls us to grow, to change, to emerge into what we can be beyond what we currently are, and reminds us too that God does not call us to this difficult growth on our own, but remains present to us in empowering love and grace.

The many who have been privileged to be Keenan's students have seen, as we see, that for him the vocation of a moral theologian—of scholar, mentor, teacher, and leader—is a practice of bothering to love. Retrieving ancient theological traditions for contemporary believers; reinventing theological approaches to meet unforeseen contemporary needs; walking with those pushed to the margins whom the theological and ecclesial mainstreams ignore; giving voice to generations of scholars and building new communities for them to work together—we gratefully acknowledge these tireless achievements as evidence of Jim's practice of bothering to love the church, his brothers in the Society of Jesus, his students, and primordially Jesus, the Merciful Teacher. It is in reciprocal love and thanks that we offer this series of reflections on his theological accomplishments.

The subtitle of our book names what we see as two fundamental, interrelated dynamics that recur in Jim Keenan's scholarship: retrieval and reinvention. Much of his work entails an engagement of history and the Catholic moral tradition to unearth principles, concepts, and methods that have been forgotten or erased over time. At the same time, this retrieval does not seek to elevate an imagined past over the real claims of the present. Stewardship of the tradition requires a deep engagement of the world in which we find ourselves so as to provide a vision for how the riches of the past should be reimagined and reapplied in ways that fit the needs of the present moment. The ways Keenan's work is so often at once a retrieval and the creation of something new will become clear as we explore his many contributions to theological scholarship.

Retrieval

Keenan once shared a story of getting a telephone call from some Jesuits at Xavier High School in New York City who called to ask if he knew anyone who might have use for fifty volumes of manuals of moral theology published from the eighteenth to the early twentieth centuries. Keenan promptly jumped into a car with a Jesuit scholastic and drove over to Xavier to pick up all fifty volumes. The scholastic who had been drafted into service asked Keenan why he was so delighted to add these books to his collection. Keenan replied, "One of the tasks of a moral theologian is to be a keeper of the tradition. Now, I am getting some of that tradition before it gets lost."[3] While the divinity schools at Yale or the University of Chicago drew many of the most promising American graduate students in theology at the time, Keenan chose to pursue doctoral studies at the Gregorian in Rome because he wanted to learn the tradition. For Keenan, to be a keeper of the tradition entails much more than rescuing old books. Being a faithful steward requires a process of retrieval, interpretation, interrogation, and sometimes reimagination.

A sense of the importance of the tradition and the need for it always to be reinterpreted and renewed characterizes Keenan's work from the very beginning. The first academic article he published after taking his first tenure-track appointment as assistant professor of theology at Fordham University was "Taking Aim at the Principle of Double Effect: A Response to Khatchadourian."[4] A few years later, he published a second, more expansive article on double effect in *Theological Studies* that exemplified the dynamic of retrieval and renewal that would characterize so much of his work.[5] There, Keenan objected to using the principle as a formula for testing whether an action was right or wrong. To explain why, he turned to history and to how double effect emerged from the tradition of moral casuistry as a synthesis of insights gleaned from the resolution of paradigmatic cases. He showed that the principle is not some sort of universally applicable, magical formula for determining right and wrong, but only an aid to sound prudential reasoning. Investing the principle itself with authority only provides the illusion of moral objectivity. This was the first of many insights Keenan's retrieval of casuistry would contribute to ongoing debates in fundamental moral theology about freedom, conscience, and moral objectivity.[6]

Keenan's focus on the Catholic moral tradition is but one dimension of his vocation as a moral theologian and a Jesuit priest. He also has demonstrated a deep pastoral sensitivity and a profound sense of the importance of mercy for Christian theology and practice. His engagement of the tradition often has been guided by the pastoral needs of the moment. Some of the

---

[3] James F. Keenan, "Collaboration and Cooperation in Healthcare," *Australasian Catholic Record* 77, no. 2 (2000): 164.

[4] James F. Keenan, "Taking Aim at the Principle of Double Effect: A Response to Khatchadourian," *International Philosophical Quarterly* 28, no. 2 (1988): 201–5.

[5] James F. Keenan, "The Function of the Principle of Double Effect," *Theological Studies* 54 (1993): 294.

[6] James F. Keenan, SJ, and Thomas A. Shannon, eds., *The Context of Casuistry* (Washington, DC: Georgetown University Press, 1995).

most urgent questions facing the church and the world early in Keenan's career emerged in the context of the HIV/AIDS epidemic as the medical community struggled with how to treat and prevent the spread of the disease, and the church struggled with how to care pastorally for people who were HIV-positive (including members of many religious orders).

An especially heated controversy erupted after the administrative board of the United States Conference of Catholic Bishops published a pastoral letter on HIV/AIDS, in which the bishops maintained that Catholics should tolerate policies that allowed recommending condom use to HIV-positive patients who were insistent on being sexually active.[7] Keenan entered this debate by demonstrating that with the aid of the principle of cooperation (not tolerance), we can use prudential reason to conclude that it is morally licit for healthcare workers to advocate for condom use in certain circumstances.[8]

As the HIV epidemic raged on, many similar ethical and pastoral questions emerged. Keenan remained confident that the Catholic moral tradition was a rich, humane, and supple resource that could guide the church through these challenges. He turned again to the recovery of casuistry, proposing it as an ideal method for analyzing many new questions emerging in the face of HIV/AIDS. He favored an approach to casuistry that emerged in the seventeenth century, which did not seek to overturn principles but to be faithful to them while considering new cases—thereby offering solutions that are at once very traditional while also responsive to new circumstances and contexts.[9] This method was the centerpiece of a book Keenan edited with colleagues from the Catholic Theological Coalition on HIV/AIDS Prevention. It included essays by thirty-five Catholic theologians from around the world who used casuistry to analyze real cases that had come up in their local contexts.[10] Many of the book's chapters combined casuistry with the recovery of traditional principles of toleration, cooperation, and so on. The book demonstrated the value of the Catholic moral tradition and initiated a truly global theological dialogue. Lifting up the importance of

---

[7] Jon D. Fuller, SJ, and James F. Keenan, SJ, "Church Politics and HIV Prevention: Why Is the Condom Question So Significant and So Neuralgic?" in *Between Poetry and Politics: Essays in Honour of Enda McDonagh*, ed. Linda Hogan and Barbara FitzGerald, 158–81 (Dublin: Columba Press, 2003), 161.

[8] James Keenan, "Prophylactics, Toleration, and Cooperation: Contemporary Problems and Traditional Principles," *International Philosophical Quarterly* 29, no. 2 (1988): 205–21.

[9] James F. Keenan, SJ, "Applying the Seventeenth-Century Casuistry of Accommodation to HIV Prevention," *Theological Studies* 60 (1999): 500.

[10] James F. Keenan, SJ, "About This Book," in *Catholic Ethicists on HIV/AIDS Prevention*, ed. James F. Keenan, SJ (New York: Continuum, 2000), 13.

international, cross-cultural dialogue would become another of Keenan's important contributions to the field.

In addition to retrieving traditional principles and methods, Keenan also turned to history to set the agenda of Catholic moral theology at the start of the twenty-first century. In Aquinas, Alphonsus, and several influential twentieth-century moral theologians, Keenan found role models who embodied different aspects of his vision of what it means to do Catholic moral theology. He singled out St. Alphonsus Liguori as "the role model for the contemporary theologian," describing him as "the first major figure to combine ministry to the outcast with a vocation to shape the field of moral theology."[11] In both the theology and the pastoral practice of St. Alphonsus, what stands out is his appreciation of the importance of mercy. Alphonsus engaged in various ministries throughout his life that fit Keenan's definition of mercy as entering into the chaos of another person: as a member of a confraternity that attended to the needs of prisoners, especially those who were condemned to death; and later while teaching in Naples ministering to the poorest of the poor. Living at a time marked by moral rigorism, Liguori was known as a sympathetic confessor who encouraged penitents to trust in the mercy of God and the grace of the Eucharist and confession. As someone who spent a good deal of time among those most on the margins, he came to appreciate the complexity of the moral challenges they faced.[12]

We can see many of St. Alphonsus's theological priorities reflected in Keenan's work. In addition to serving as a leading scholar, Keenan consistently devotes considerable attention to addressing the pastoral needs of ordinary Christians.[13] He has raised up the moral issues of daily living as worthy of theological attention, and has done so in a way marked by a deep sense of the importance of mercy.[14] As a preacher and confessor, Alphonsus encouraged Christians to see themselves as called to strive for perfection. This was not an invitation to excessive scrupulosity. Alphonsus recognized that the most difficult answer is not always the right one but more typically lies somewhere between laxism and rigorism. The invitation to perfection was a reflection of God's loving call to each person to strive always for moral growth.

---

[11] James F. Keenan, "How Alphonsus' Ministry to the Margins Formed His Life as a Moral Theologian," *Studia Moralia* 59, no. 2 (2021): 277.

[12] Keenan, 281.

[13] James F. Keenan, *Virtues for Ordinary Christians* (Kansas City, MO: Sheed and Ward, 1996); James F. Keenan, *The Works of Mercy: The Heart of Catholicism*, 3rd ed. (Lanham, MD: Rowman & Littlefield, 2017).

[14] James F. Keenan, SJ, *Commandments of Compassion* (Lanham, MD: Sheed and Ward, 1999); Keenan, *The Works of Mercy*.

Similar themes and priorities can be found in the work of several theologians whom Keenan credits with dramatically reshaping the discipline in his careful work on the history of Catholic moral theology in the twentieth century.[15] That century began with a continuation of the manualist tradition—"books of moral pathology" focused on preparing priests to hear confessions.[16] The manualist tradition presented itself as timeless, claiming historical and universal consistency to such a degree that many at the time assumed it was only way that moral theology could be done.[17] Keenan documented the contributions of several early twentieth-century theologians he named as revisionists (Fritz Tillmann, Odon Lottin, Gerard Gilleman, among others) who transformed the discipline in ways we can see reflected in his own methodology. For their inaugural issue, the editors of the *Journal of Moral Theology* invited several leading moral theologians to write about a major figure who had influenced their own work and the discipline more broadly. Keenan chose to write about Bernard Häring, who, he believed, built successfully upon many of the advances of the earlier pioneers of moral theology in the twentieth century. Häring incorporated Tillmann's insights on the importance of scripture for moral theology and his framing the moral life in terms of a call to discipleship. He also drew upon Lottin's sense of the importance of focusing on conscience and the person as moral agent, and Gilleman's understanding of the centrality of charity for all the virtues and the moral life.[18]

Keenan characterizes Häring's writing as "invitational" and engaging, noting that one reason he was such an influential moral theologian was his conscious decision to write for general audiences in addition to his colleagues in the field. Häring did not write down to his lay audience, but rather "presumed the competency and the interest of the laity, in a way that no one else did."[19] Häring and his work were deeply formed by history and experience, especially his experience as a German who lived under the Nazi regime during the Second World War. His experience led him to conclude that responsibility—not obedience—should be at the center of Catholic

---

[15] James F. Keenan, *A History of Catholic Moral Theology in the Twentieth Century: From Confessing Sins to Liberating Consciences* (New York: Continuum, 2010).

[16] James F. Keenan, "From Teaching Confessors to Guiding Lay People: The Development of Catholic Moral Theologians from 1900–1965," *Journal of the Society of Christian Ethics* 28, no. 2 (2008): 142.

[17] James F. Keenan, "John Mahoney's *The Making of Moral Theology*," in *The Oxford Handbook of Theological Ethics*, ed. Gilbert Meilaender and William Werpehowski, 503–19 (New York: Oxford, 2007): 505.

[18] James F. Keenan, SJ, "Bernard Häring's Influence on American Catholic Moral Theology," *The Journal of Moral Theology* 1, no. 1 (2012): 24.

[19] Keenan, 31.

moral theology. His work emphasized the capacity of ordinary people to discern and to do good in response to God's invitation to discipleship.

The reformists of the twentieth century left a clear mark on Keenan's thinking, and many of his own contributions to contemporary moral theology can be seen as carrying forward the work they began. Like Tillmann, Keenan recognized the importance of integrating scripture into his work, especially as a means of connecting reflections on the moral life with the overriding theme of discipleship. With his longtime colleague at Weston Jesuit School of Theology, Daniel J. Harrington, SJ, Keenan wrote two books on scripture and ethics—first on Jesus and virtue ethics, and later, on Paul.[20] These books made helpful contributions to each field while remaining accessible to an educated lay audience. More recently, Keenan published the fruits of his career-long integration of history into moral theology with monographs on the history of Catholic moral theology in the twentieth century and a magisterial volume on the entire history of Catholic theological ethics.[21]

Like Häring, Keenan manages to be prolific and insightful in his writing both for academic audiences and lay readership. Throughout the 1990s he contributed monthly to the popular publication *Church* on discipleship, specific virtues, prayer, and spirituality, turning to the Ten Commandments in the latter half of the decade. His writing made clear that an important part of Keenan's vocation was to help ordinary people work through the moral issues that arose in their ordinary lives, and to invite his readers to see themselves as disciples of Christ who are called always to strive to grow in love and holiness. Woven throughout his popular and academic writing is the central importance of mercy. His engagement of the Ten Commandments was through the lens of compassion.[22] In the 2000s his writing for *Church* turned to the works of mercy; he later revised and published those columns as a book for a general audience.[23] Like his role models, Keenan's style of writing here was invitational, taking on a supportive, encouraging tone that conveyed a confidence in God's mercy and a desire for spiritual and moral growth in his readers.

As we turn to Keenan's reinvention of Catholic moral theology, one more note on the importance of retrieval is in order. The revisionists were

---

[20] Daniel J. Harrington, SJ, and James F. Keenan, SJ, *Jesus and Virtue Ethics: Building Bridges between New Testament Studies and Moral Theology* (Lanham, MD: Sheed and Ward, 2002) and *Paul and Virtue Ethics* (New York: Rowman & Littlefield, 2010).

[21] Keenan, *A History of Catholic Moral Theology in the Twentieth Century*; James F. Keenan, *A History of Catholic Theological Ethics* (Mahwah, NJ: Paulist Press, 2022).

[22] James F. Keenan, SJ, *Commandments of Compassion* (Lanham, MD: Sheed and Ward, 1999).

[23] Keenan, *The Works of Mercy*.

dissatisfied with the methods and focus of moral theology in their day. Each one turned to history and to forgotten parts of the tradition as resources for charting a new way of doing moral theology that was at once new and still faithfully Catholic. Lottin wrote his three-thousand-page study of the Scholastics on conscience and moral decision-making to demonstrate that what he was proposing—while seemingly new—was very traditional. Häring included a brief history of moral theology in *The Law of Christ* to show that his innovations on conscience and freedom were in fact in continuity with the tradition.[24] Against an ahistorical rendering of what is Catholic, a deep engagement with history and tradition is necessary to make clear that the immediate past is not "the way things have always been." The tradition is indeed richer, deeper, and more humane than that.

Reinvention

While retrieving key categories of ethical insight is a hallmark of Keenan's work, equally his legacy has been to approach ethical questions in a new way, or better, to reinvent our understandings of what constitutes an ethical question. His writings for general and scholarly audiences insist on the choices of ordinary life as the key ethical matter with which Christians should be concerned—from *Moral Wisdom* and *The Works of Mercy* to *The Moral Life: Eight Essays*, which discusses dispositions and resources for approaching the Christian moral life.[25] If this focus on ordinary life as distinct from the "quandary ethics" of the late twentieth century was not original enough, Keenan's reinvention of Catholic theological ethics has introduced whole new fields of inquiry to the lexicon, with church ethics, university ethics, and global Catholic ethics being just a few.

Keenan's work in church ethics extends from multiple edited volumes responding to the clergy sex-abuse crisis to articles probing the ethics of Jesuit formation practices. One of his earliest essays on clergy ethics raises moral issues with the practice of *informationes*, confidential internal reports, in the formation of Jesuits.[26] One of the most recent refines ethical criticism of the issue of clericalism in the Catholic Church to define and critique hierarchicalism, a vicious culture among bishops and church officials: "Hierarchy has a culture; when and where it is vicious in its elitism,

---

[24] James F. Keenan, SJ, "Notes on Moral Theology: Moral Theology and History," *Theological Studies* 62 (2001): 87.

[25] James F. Keenan, *The Moral Life: Eight Essays* (Washington, DC: Georgetown University Press, 2024).

[26] James F. Keenan, "Are *Informationes* Ethical?" *Studies in the Spirituality of Jesuits* 29, no. 4 (1997).

power, networking capability, and impunity is precisely what I mean by hierarchicalism."[27] Another significant contribution to clergy ethics is *Practice What You Preach: Virtue, Ethics, and Power in the Lives of Pastoral Ministers and Their Congregations*, which Keenan coedited with his student and contributor to this volume Joseph J. Kotva, Jr.[28] The volume gathers more than twenty contributions from an ecumenical group of theologians and pastoral ministers reflecting on ethical practice between ministers and their church communities. The volume appeared in 1999, three years before the *Boston Globe*'s Spotlight Team's initial report on the ecclesial coverup of clergy sex abuse reminded many Catholics that clergy ethics is an issue with which every religious community must contend.

Jesuits in formation and laity in a hierarchical church are relatively voiceless within complex structures built on history, tradition, and status. The contemporary university is another historically situated structure in which many groups, including students and contingently employed faculty, lack adequate power to defend their own dignity. Keenan pointed to an ethical vacuum in reflection on higher education as early as 2013, telling the Society of Christian Ethics that "in our own centers of higher learning, we have lived and worked wearing blinders to their lack of professional ethics. We have not asked 'but is it ethical?' when we should have, in part because we were not accustomed to see how ethically barren the academy's landscape is."[29] Rather than letting this omission stand, Keenan wrote *University Ethics*, in which he drew attention to precarious labor, lack of financial transparency, student hazing, and other glaring ethical concerns within higher education.[30] With ethicist and contingent scholar Matthew Gaudet, he coedited two special volumes of the *Journal of Moral Theology* focused on contingent faculty and on university ethics more broadly.[31]

Keenan's work on virtue ethics, one of his most prolific and influential areas of focus, certainly exemplifies retrieval. In many articles and edited volumes for general and scholarly audiences Keenan has raised up the

---

[27] James F. Keenan, "Hierarchicalism," *Theological Studies* 83, no. 1 (March 2022): 84–108.

[28] James F. Keenan and Joseph J. Kotva, eds., *Practice What You Preach: Virtues, Ethics, and Power in the Lives of Pastoral Ministers and Their Congregations* (Franklin, WI: Sheed and Ward, 1999).

[29] James F. Keenan, "A Summons to Promote Professional Ethics in the Academy," *Journal of the Society of Christian Ethics* 33, no. 1 (2013): 180.

[30] James F. Keenan, *University Ethics: How Colleges Can Build and Benefit From a Culture of Ethics* (Lanham, MD: Rowman & Littlefield, 2015).

[31] Matthew J. Gaudet and James F. Keenan, SJ, eds., *Contingent Faculty, Journal of Moral Theology* 8, special issue no. 1 (Spring 2019); and Matthew J. Gaudet and James F. Keenan, SJ, eds., *University Ethics, Journal of Moral Theology* 9, special issue no. 2 (2020).

legacy of Thomas Aquinas's theological virtue ethics to help believers today understand this context-sensitive, practical, growth-oriented method for living the Christian life.[32] One of his most influential contributions to virtue ethics may be "Proposing Cardinal Virtues," an article in *Theological Studies* that envisions the virtues on which the moral life "hinges" not through Aquinas's medieval psychology, but through the ways humans are relational—generally, specifically, and uniquely.[33] Keenan's framework retrieves Aquinas, reflecting the ways his virtue ethics points us toward practices of bothering to love and reinvents him in ways that can inspire moderns to such practices. For example, Aquinas's order of charity urges love for oneself as a gift from God (II-II q. 26 ad. 4). Keenan responds to this by elevating as a cardinal virtue self-care, the virtue through which we care for ourself, the relationship each of us has uniquely. Remaining firmly rooted in the tradition, his work viscerally connects with today's university students, who are concerned about finding self-worth outside the world's markers of success. Keenan uses virtue ethics not only to attend to the concreteness of moral lives, but also to make the Catholic ethical tradition vivid in a way that respects each person's call to growth. Uniting the down-to-earth elements of the manualist tradition with the concern for conscience and growth of postconciliar ethical approaches, virtue ethics in Keenan's hands is a tool for uniting believers struggling to do right and become good with the opportunities for moral action they see in the world around them.

Throughout his career Keenan has taught at universities around the world, including Loyola School of Theology in the Philippines, Dharmaram Vidya Kshetram in Bangalore, and his alma mater, the Gregorian. During his travels, when he realized that European ethicists, though only a brief train ride apart, did not know one another's work, he formed the idea that became Catholic Theological Ethics in the World Church (CTEWC). When Keenan founded the international organization in 2003, he unleashed an unprecedented wave of global intellectual energy. As of this writing, CTEWC has hosted nine international conferences on three continents, some involving hundreds of scholars; published fourteen books in three distinct series; funded scholars from Africa and Asia to complete their PhDs; and maintained a thriving international network of theological scholars through its directory, "virtual tables," publication projects, and newsletter. One of the greatest parts of Keenan's legacy, CTEWC helps Catholic ethicists see themselves as members of a global community, responding to global concerns. In his message to CTEWC in honor of its 2018 meeting in Sarajevo,

---

[32] For example, James F. Keenan, *Goodness and Rightness in Thomas Aquinas's Summa Theologiae* (Washington, DC: Georgetown University Press, 1992).

[33] James F. Keenan, "Proposing Cardinal Virtues," *Theological Studies* 56, no. 4 (1995): 709–29.

Pope Francis praised the group's "style of sharing which I trust you will pursue in a way that will prove fruitful for the entire Church."[34] When the Catholic Theological Society of America honored Keenan with its John Courtney Murray Award, CTSA president Paul Lakeland remarked that by recognizing Keenan, "the Society takes a step forward in recognizing much of what the future holds for the work of theological and ethical scholarship north and south of the equator."[35] Keenan's gift for elevating the voices of others means that his work as scholar and community-builder consistently points beyond himself to those often excluded by the church: voices of women, survivors of clergy abuse, LGBTQ+ persons, those experiencing street homelessness, and those in the global South.[36]

The work of an ethicist concerned with the practical experience of human suffering often requires courage. As Keenan became known for his research on HIV/AIDS, his promotion of the human dignity of people living with the virus drew slur-filled hate mail and attempts to threaten his ecclesial status and his employment. Following his conscience to defend the common good, he led Catholics for Obama in Massachusetts and spoke in favor of same-sex civil marriage in the Massachusetts State House. His political activism, which Michael Jaycox celebrates in his essay for this volume, drew another round of vitriol and hate. Here was a Jesuit priest acting as a moral leader, not presuming on his clergy status but drawing on his scholarly expertise to stand with the marginalized at a time of great import. This consequential entry into the public square was a reinvention of the ethicist's role as Keenan brought moral theology from the ivory tower to front-page news.

If the topics of Keenan's work speak of tireless reinvention, so too does his method. He continually works to overcome silos within academic theology, cowriting and teaching with the late biblical scholar Daniel J. Harrington, SJ; clearly outlining the links between spirituality and morality over decades of work; and advocating for the bridge-building character of virtue ethics. When his friend and doctoral student Lúcás Chan passed away at a tragically early age, Keenan completed his works in progress, enshrin-

---

[34] Pope Francis, "Message of the Holy Father to Participants in the Third International Conference of 'Catholic Theological Ethics in the World Church' [Sarajevo, 26–29 July 2018]," July 11, 2018.

[35] Michael Chovan Dalton, "James Keenan John Courtney Murray Award," video of Paul Lakeland's remarks, June 10, 2019, YouTube.

[36] See James F. Keenan, *Street Homelessness and Catholic Theological Ethics*, Catholic Theological Ethics in the World Church Series (Maryknoll, NY: Orbis Books, 2019); James F. Keenan, "The Gallant Rule: A Feminist Proposal," in *Feminist Catholic Theological Ethics: Conversations in the World Church*, ed. Linda F. Hogan and A. E. Orobator (Maryknoll, NY: Orbis Books, 2014), 219–31.

ing Lúcás's contributions in history as a last act of love for his friend.[37] Before it was fashionable for theologians to do interdisciplinary work, Keenan drew insights from psychology (Carol Gilligan), public health (Paul Farmer), literature (Graham Greene), and philosophy (Judith Butler), among other disciplines, to illuminate and communicate the insights of Catholic moral theology. Decades before *public theology* became a buzzword and academics learned to value clear, expert writing for general audiences, he broke open virtues, the works of mercy, the moral life, and other topics for non-scholarly readers with simplicity, clarity, and heart.[38]

Keenan's great gift for descending to the particular animates his scholarly contributions on innumerable painful topics of human life but might appear most memorably in his general-interest writings. His essay on love in the oft-reprinted general interest book *Moral Wisdom* is packed with unforgettable images, from the barbed-wire cross acknowledging German guilt in a Catholic church in Dachau to the aluminum-foil costumes Keenan's loving, hardworking parents created for their children. Insistently drawing our attention to the concrete reality of God's world and creatures, he concludes, "We cannot love our neighbors except for as they are."[39]

Keenan's work as theological mentor and editor respects this God-given call to attend to particularity, with the result that his legacy within theological scholarship is carried forward by a community of scholars noteworthy for their number, achievements, and diversity. His goal is not to form copies of himself, but to ensure that those scholars with whom he works are able to develop and refine the best possible version of their own voices and thoughts. As editor for a decade of the Moral Traditions series with Georgetown University Press, he shepherded the books of scholars who are now many of the leading voices of English-speaking moral theology. His work as editor of the Notes on Moral Theology section of the leading journal *Theological Studies* similarly guaranteed that readers would learn about concerns on the cutting edge of ethics, often at the hands of underrepresented or emerging scholars in the field. In the diversity of voices

---

[37] (Yiu Sing) Lúcás Chan, SJ, James F. Keenan, SJ, and Shaji George Kochuthara, CMI, eds., *Doing Asian Theological Ethics in a Cross-Cultural and an Interreligious Context* (Bangalore: Dharmaram, 2016); George Griener, SJ, and James F. Keenan, SJ, eds., *A Lúcás Chan Reader: Pioneering Essays on Biblical and Asian Theological Ethics* (Bangalore: Dharmaram, 2017); and Yiu Sing Lúcás Chan, SJ, James F. Keenan, SJ, and Ronaldo Zacharias, eds., *The Bible and Catholic Theological Ethics* (Maryknoll, NY: Orbis Books, 2017). See also the volume in tribute, *Bridging Scripture and Moral Theology: Essays in Dialogue with Yiu Sing Lúcás Chan, SJ*, ed. Michael B. Cover, John Thiede, SJ, and Joshua Ezra Burns (Lanham, MD: Lexington Books/Fortress Academic, 2019).

[38] Keenan, *Virtues for Ordinary Christians*; Keenan, *The Works of Mercy.*

[39] Keenan, *Moral Wisdom*, 18.

collected in this volume we see Keenan's students appreciating his work, building on it, jumping off from it, and even disagreeing with his insights, illustrating how one of his many remarkable gifts to the church as a scholar has been to help many theologians establish their own voice.

This Volume

As we envisioned this volume, we wanted it to reflect some of the breadth of the areas of moral theology to which Keenan has contributed over his long career. Fundamental moral theology, virtue and the virtues, and bioethics were obvious examples of areas where Keenan and many of his students have made noteworthy contributions. His recurring attention to the importance of discipleship, pastoral concerns of ordinary Christians, and his expansive writing on issues of religious life made a section on the intersection of spirituality and morality another natural choice. Although Keenan's own contributions on the ethics of sex and gender are comparatively modest, many of his students are among today's leaders in that subfield. The section featuring their work especially highlights how Keenan is a teacher and dissertation director who empowers his students to make the contributions they see as important rather than guiding them always toward his own priorities or producing a new generation of scholars cloned in his image.

Part I, "Fundamental Moral Theology," begins fittingly with an essay that combines attention to history and mercy. Inspired by Keenan's definition of mercy as "entering into the chaos of another," Eric Marcelo O. Genilo, SJ, calls moral theologians to practice mercy in order to "translate into the church's moral consciousness the experiences of chaos that have often been ignored or dismissed as unimportant." Mercy is a key ingredient in the development of doctrine, even though theologians may not always be successful in advocating for developments that respond to the chaos of concrete lives, as Genilo shows through examples from the twentieth and twenty-first centuries.

Osamu Takeuchi, SJ, examines the ways conscience is understood in contemporary Catholic moral theology, tracing key themes back to the thought of John Henry Newman. Takeuchi links conscience and the fundamental option to the importance of freedom, with particular attention to the ways that freedom is a gift of God's love and should be exercised responsibly as a response to that love.

Keenan's work often made clear the relevance of debates in fundamental moral theology for more practical issues. Christopher P. Vogt argues that the traditional concept of scandal is being overused and misappropriated in the development of diocesan and Catholic school policies on sex and gender. He describes how scripture and the broader moral tradition can yield a richer understanding of scandal, and he turns to casuistry to explain how focusing on specific persons and cases might make space for moral discernment on issues of sexuality and gender.

Kate Ward draws on Keenan's observation that virtues can conflict, pointing to material scarcity as a particular contributor to situations where "an opportunity for one virtuous choice is restricted by the equally good claim of another due to lack of resources." She turns to systematic theology and the parable of the father who had two sons to suggest that moral agency persists amid material scarcity because it is ultimately a gift of God's grace.

Finally, Mark Graham develops the concepts of moral goodness, sin, and the importance of love in Keenan's fundamental moral theology to give readers a deeper appreciation of the meaning of ecological conversion and its centrality for the Christian moral life.

Daniel Daly leads off Part II, "Virtue and Virtues," by sketching the key features of Keenan's approach to virtue ethics and examining the ways institutions influence the efforts of Christians to grow in virtue and the ability of all members of society to flourish and live good lives. He describes the ways that a virtue lens can enhance approaches to institutional and organizational ethics and concludes by pointing out how scholars might build upon Keenan's work on virtue and institutional ethics, especially by developing more precise, scientific accounts of the ways organizations shape individuals morally.

Kathryn Getek Soltis turns our attention again to Keenan's description of mercy as entering into the chaos of another, adding that it is a virtue that entails growing in solidarity with others and empowering them to act. She argues that Christians must resist a dangerous tendency of wanting to reserve mercy for the innocent and must instead enthusiastically enter into spheres of culpable chaos. Soltis calls for "a mercy that defies stigma and otherness, proclaiming that no one is beyond the scope of our concern," and explores some of the implications of a more expansive conception of mercy for addressing mass incarceration in the United States.

John Karuvelil, SJ, proposes the virtues of vulnerability and hospitality, consistent touchstones of Keenan's work, in response to the Indian government's profound violation of the rights of migrant laborers in response to COVID-19. In Keenan's definitions vulnerability is the capacity to be moral, and Jesuit hospitality goes out to meet those in need where they are. Karuvelil denounces the lack of these virtues in the Indian government's treatment of its migrant laborer citizens.

Following Keenan's lead as an early adopter of virtue ethics to address moral growth in ordinary life, Conor Kelly shows how virtue can provide a "theologically robust conception of the good life." Kelly proposes the virtues of humility, perseverance and mercy as necessary for addressing the ethical challenges facing twenty-first-century Christians in their ordinary lives.

Xavier Montecel finds in Keenan's work on spirituality, morality, and virtue a profound sense of the importance of the liturgy in the moral life. Delving deeply into Keenan's work and reflecting on the Christology implicit in virtue ethics, Montecel concludes: "The virtues . . . are more than just the good habits we carry from liturgy. Virtues are the means through which we sacramentally embody the presence and action of Christ for the life of the world."

Drawing upon his own experiences as a physician who has cared for vulnerable populations in Africa and his theological training, Vincent Leclercq, AA, begins Part III, "Bioethics," by analyzing how Keenan's response to the HIV/AIDS epidemic brought new methods and priorities to bioethics. Keenan's revival of casuistry, his focus on persons and virtue, and his insistence on examining the social and political dimensions of the epidemic had lasting effects on Christian bioethics and Catholic moral theology more broadly.

Joseph Kotva applauds Keenan's efforts to advance university ethics but challenges his assumption that medical education provides a model for it. He calls attention to problems in both the official and hidden curricula at medical schools that undermine the well-being of students and foster vice rather than virtue. Kotva recommends changes in institutional culture and systemic reforms that would address structural injustices in medical education while better protecting the mental health of medical students and enhancing their formation in virtues such as empathy.

Cristina Richie proposes practices for "integral bioethics," including lower carbon consumption in healthcare systems and applying the principle of proportionality when causing suffering to nonhuman animals. Integral bioethics is inspired by the principle of integral ecology and Keenan's radical inclusivity.

The section on bioethics concludes as Edwin Vásquez Ghersi, SJ, shows how the COVID-19 pandemic teaches us that global bioethics must broaden its gaze beyond the individual. He proposes relationality, vulnerability, cooperation and multilateralism, social justice, solidarity, and responsibility and care as "traits of affective wisdom" that assist bioethicists in this crucial task.

In Part IV, "Ethics of Sex and Gender," Michael Jaycox draws on his own experience to affirm Keenan's efforts to cultivate the distinctive priorities and voice of each of his students. He then leads us into the subfield of the ethics of sex and gender by reflecting on Keenan's ethical method to deduce anthropological, historical, and practical considerations for articulating a Catholic sexual ethic. A relational anthropology focused on the moral growth of the person and rigorous retrieval of historical sources are important tools for ethicists, whom Jaycox also calls to apply their ethical commitments in practical action on behalf of vulnerable persons as Keenan has done throughout his career.

Megan McCabe applauds Keenan's call to understand conscience as socially responsible but highlights the need to advance theologies of conscience even further in light of the fact that culture can form consciences in ways that ignore or accept the suffering of others, such as in the cultural construction of "rape myths." McCabe proposes the preferential option for the poor as a necessary normative principle to direct the social conscience's formation: "A socially responsible conscience formed by the preferential option is one that is able to wrestle with complicity in upholding the cultural scaffolding of rape in a wide variety of ways, including subtle and unconscious actions."

Animated by similar concerns, Craig Ford builds on Keenan's relational ethics to propose *eros* as an epistemological key to overcoming racism and heterosexism, products of sinful morally formative communities. Drawing on insights from queer thinkers and scholars of color, Ford extends relational virtue ethics in an eschatological direction, proposing we envision our consciences formed by exemplars from the future.

Ronaldo Zacharias observes that traditional Catholic sexual ethics forces homosexual persons into a problematic dichotomy between being and acting. Virtue ethics, led by a renewed understanding of the virtue of chastity, can help homosexual persons integrate their selves and their actions. Zacharias asserts, "An inclusive sexual ethic cannot make normative claims while disregarding that we all were created to be free in corresponding to God's love and in finding ways that allow us to integrate being and acting in just, faithful, and caring relationships."

Part V, "Spirituality and Morality," begins with Maria Cimperman, RSCJ, who finds vivid resonance between virtue ethics, the church's journey toward synodality, and insights and practices from religious community life. Articulating synodality as a virtue, she finds that the practices of sacred conversation used in religious life yield rich insights for growth in this personal and communal virtue, which the whole church can learn from members of consecrated communities.

Then, engaging the literature of disability studies, Mary Jo Iozzio provides a rich analysis of the meaning and significance of vulnerability for theological anthropology and our understanding of God's passibility. Finally, Ai Pham, SJ, describes Keenan's method as bridging moral teaching and pastoral practice centered on three themes of charity-love, conscience, and moral discernment. Pham finds such bridge-building alive in Australian

Catholics' reception of *Amoris Laetitia* as the church in Australia navigates between the ideal and the reality of family life.

We thank the contributors for their exceptional contributions, which advance the future of Catholic moral theology even as they demonstrate each author's gratitude to Jim Keenan for his mentorship, friendship, and leadership in the field. Thanks are due as well to many people whose generous help made the volume's publication possible. Steve Dalton, the head librarian at Boston College School of Theology and Ministry, combed the shelves of printed dissertations to ensure we were able to find and contact all of Jim's doctoral students. We are delighted to publish the volume with Orbis Books, where Jill Brennan O'Brien first welcomed the project, and Robert Ellsberg and Tom Hermans-Webster shepherded it home. Gregory Kalscheur, SJ, dean of the Morrissey College of Arts and Sciences at Boston College, provided funds to support the publication of this book. In addition to their contributions to this volume, Dan Daly and Mary Jo Iozzio conceived, planned, and raised funds for the celebratory conference where we will present it to Jim. We are grateful to Toni Ross for helping protect Jim's schedule for the conference, and we recognize her role as a sustaining partner in so much of Jim's important work in the theological community. Finally, Jim, we thank you. If this volume's editors and contributors have succeeded in retrieving and reinventing the Catholic theological tradition, lifting up the voices of others, and collaborating together in vulnerability, trust, and charity, it is because we have you as our exemplar.

PART I

FUNDAMENTAL MORAL THEOLOGY

1.

Entering into the Chaos of Another

Mercy and the Development of Moral Doctrine and Pastoral Practice

ERIC MARCELO O. GENILO, SJ

In his article "Mercy: What Makes Catholic Morality Distinctive," James Keenan defined mercy as the willingness to enter into the chaos of another.[1] Mercy requires a readiness to become vulnerable to and to be affected by the suffering of others. Mercy does not remain at the level of emotions but extends to solidarity and action in response to the needs of those experiencing chaos. In *The Works of Mercy: The Heart of Catholicism,* Keenan illustrates how the virtue is actively exercised in the Catholic Church's tradition of corporal and spiritual works of mercy.[2]

For Keenan, mercy is at the heart of the mystery of the incarnation and God's plan of salvation. Drawing from one of the meditations of the *Spiritual Exercises of St. Ignatius,* he describes the Trinity looking down from heaven at the chaos of human existence caused by sin and death. Moved by what they see, the Trinity sent the Son to be incarnated in our troubled world. Not only did Christ become "God with us," but by his saving words and actions he became our way out of chaos and our path to union with the Trinity. Keenan presents the parable of the Good Samaritan as an allegory of the Christian story of salvation, which is a story of divine mercy.

---

[1] James Keenan, "Mercy: What Makes Catholic Morality Distinctive," *Church* (Fall 2000), 41–43.

[2] James Keenan, *The Works of Mercy: The Heart of Catholicism* (Lanham, MD: Rowman & Littlefield, 2008), 9–71.

The parable also serves as a mandate to the church to extend mercy to all humanity placed under its care.

Keenan's definition of mercy has been applied to various situations of chaos that demand a compassionate response. Nichole Flores argues that mercy is a public virtue that needs to be urgently applied to the Syrian refugee crisis.[3] Valerie Smith writes about the necessity and risks of liturgical mercy that refuses to exclude from the Eucharist persons in sinful situations.[4] Meghan Clark describes the practice of mercy embodied in a primary school for street children and orphans in Kenya run by religious sisters.[5]

This essay explores the critical role of mercy in the work of moral theologians and pastoral leaders who seek to renew the church's norms and pastoral practices to address the chaos faced by persons experiencing difficult moral situations. Using examples of interventions by moral theologians and church leaders, this essay argues that the willingness to enter into the chaos of others is a necessary virtue for those who seek to move the Catholic moral tradition to a more faithful imitation of the mercy of Christ.

Mercy and the Development of Moral Doctrine

In his article "Experience and the Development of Moral Doctrine," John Noonan highlights the role of experience in the development of the church's moral teaching.[6] Using examples of shifts in the church's teaching on adultery, usury, capital punishment, the treatment of heretics, and slavery, Noonan shows how new experiences brought about by historical events and societal changes led to a reconsideration of church norms that were previously considered stable and unchanging.

Noonan describes two levels of experience: the experience of those who make the rules, and the experience of those who are affected by the rules. Those who suffer under existing rules are either voiceless (for example, enslaved people and condemned prisoners) or are not given attention because of their questionable moral or religious status (for example, adulterers, usurers, and heretics). While there may be public calls to change the

---

[3] Nichole Flores, "Mercy as a Public Virtue," *Journal of Religious Ethics* 48, no. 3 (2020): 458–72.

[4] Valerie Smith, "The Risk of Liturgical Mercy," *Studia Liturgica* 49, no. 1 (2019): 58–70.

[5] Meghan Clark, "Mercy in Chaos," *US Catholic* 81, no. 4 (April 2016): 8.

[6] John Noonan, "Experience and the Development of Moral Doctrine," *CTSA Proceedings* 54 (1999): 43–56.

rules, the rule makers can remain unmoved if they consider the current rules adequate and the difficulties of those subject to the rules to be insignificant. For a reconsideration of moral norms to happen, those who make the rules should be willing to be affected by the experience of those burdened by the rules and realize that their situation of chaos is unacceptable and must be alleviated.

Noonan highlights the unique role of individuals who can enter into the chaos of those affected by the rules and translate their experience in a compelling way into the experience of the rule makers. These translators are able to foster understanding, sympathy, and solidarity between the rule makers and those subject to the rules. These translators must have affective knowledge of the plight of those in chaos while having a certain stature or specialized training that will allow them access to the rule makers and credibility as experts on the matter.

In the history of the development of the church's moral doctrine, many persons have performed this crucial role of translator. Among these are moral theologians who have used their learning and professional status to give voice to the experience of those affected by the rules and to enable those who have the power to change the rules to gain a more complete and sympathetic understanding of chaotic situations. These theologians help move the moral tradition forward by proposing ways to revise or develop current norms and pastoral practices through the creative use of moral principles, casuistry, and the wealth of wisdom from the church's moral tradition.

It must be noted that not every attempt to act as a translator on behalf of those in chaos will be immediately successful in changing church rules, attitudes, and practices. The right conditions must be present before a change or development of moral doctrine can come to fruition. While initial attempts to address the chaos of others affected by church rules may fail, the ideas and pastoral solutions presented can reemerge and influence developments in moral teaching and practice in the future when the conditions are right. Acts of mercy may not always bring about the expected result, but their intrinsic value remains and can inspire and inform future acts of mercy.

Advocating for Those in Chaos

The impact of entering into the chaos of another upon the work of moral theologians can be illustrated by exploring the contributions of moral theologians Josef Fuchs and John Ford concerning specific ethical issues where they have advocated a change in church norms or pastoral practice.[7] Fuchs and Ford acted as translators for the experience of persons dealing with extraordinary situations that had not been adequately addressed by church teaching during their time. The examples presented also show how failure to bring about immediate change in church teaching does not prevent the possibility of developments in the future.

Josef Fuchs and the Birth Control Commission Majority Report

Josef Fuchs was one of the most influential moral theologians of the twentieth century. A professor of moral theology at the Pontifical Gregorian University since 1954, Fuchs taught in the manualist tradition until 1966, when he experienced an intellectual conversion during his participation in the Papal Commission on Population, Family, and Birth formed by John XXIII.[8] The commission was tasked to advise the pope on whether the teaching on contraception defined in *Casti Connubii* could be reformed in view of the advent of the birth-control pill and the growing global population.

During the commission's early meetings Fuchs defended the church's prohibition on contraception. His intellectual conversion came about during commission sessions when data from an extensive survey of married couples on the use of the rhythm method was presented. Married women who were members of the commission also shared their experiences in using the church-approved rhythm method for regulating births. The survey and personal testimonies revealed great dissatisfaction with the rhythm method because of its limited rate of success, its inadequacy to prevent life-threatening medical conditions related to pregnancy, and marital tensions caused by the difficulties of practicing the periodic sexual abstinence required by the method. The challenging experiences of Catholic couples struggling with the church's prohibition against contraception moved a majority of commission members, including Fuchs, to recommend to the pope that the teaching on birth regulation should be reformed. Writing the report on the majority opinion of the commission, Fuchs gave importance to the experience of the faithful as a basis for considering a change in the church's teaching: "Then must be considered the sense of the faithful: according to

---

[7] Josef Fuchs and John Ford had personal and professional connections with Keenan. Fuchs was Keenan's mentor and dissertation adviser at the Gregorian University, while Ford was Keenan's predecessor as professor of moral theology at Weston Jesuit School of Theology in Cambridge, Massachusetts.

[8] James F. Keenan, *A History of Catholic Moral Theology in the Twentieth Century: From Confessing Sins to Liberating Consciences* (London: Continuum, 2010), 120–21.

it, condemnation of a couple to a long and often heroic abstinence as the means to regulate conception, cannot be founded on the truth."[9]

Fuchs expressed confidence that married couples, aided by grace, are capable of developing well-formed consciences that will enable them to make prudent moral decisions on birth regulation that would provide the best possible good for their family, their future children, and their community. Fuchs stressed that the Holy Spirit does not only assist the magisterium, but it also assists married couples in their moral discernment and concrete application of norms in their marital life.[10]

Fuchs's intellectual conversion was a direct result of his willingness to enter into the chaos of couples raising their families in difficult circumstances. He responded with mercy by advocating for the primacy of conscience of married couples to decide the manner of family planning appropriate for them, guided by right reason. Fuchs sought to translate the experience of struggling couples into the theological language of the magisterium in order to convince the pope to reform the teaching on contraception.

Paul VI's encyclical *Humanae Vitae* was published in 1968, two years after the papal commission ended its work. While the encyclical introduced developments on the meaning and ends of Christian marriage, it retained the prohibition against the use of contraceptives. Fuchs's proposal was not endorsed by the church. In practice, however, many married couples have chosen to ignore the church's prohibition and followed their consciences in planning their families according to their unique circumstances. Demographic data show that a majority of Catholic women use a form of birth control other than natural family planning.[11]

New conditions and situations have led church leaders to reconsider the appeal to the primacy of conscience on the use of contraceptives as proposed by Fuchs. The HIV-AIDS pandemic has challenged the church to find ways to address the chaos experienced by persons, families, and communities affected by this deadly disease. While the hierarchy has not recommended condoms for preventing the spread of HIV, a number of bishops have advised their local churches that such preventive measures by an HIV-discordant couple can be a legitimate moral choice. For example, the bishops of South Africa, in their statement "A Message of Hope,"

---

[9] Robert McClory, *Turning Point: The Inside Story of the Papal Birth Control Commission, and How* Humanae Vitae *Changed the Life of Patty Crowley and the Future of the Church* (New York: Crossroad, 1995), 178–79

[10] McClory, 175–76, 183.

[11] Rachel K. Jones and Joerg Dreweke, *Countering Conventional Wisdom: New Evidence on Religion and Contraceptive Use* (New York: Guttmacher Institute, 2011), 8.

recognized the right of married couples affected by HIV to decide how to best prevent the spread of the disease:

> The Church accepts that everyone has the right to defend one's life against mortal danger. This would include using the appropriate means and course of action. Similarly, where one spouse is infected with HIV/AIDS they must listen to their consciences. They are the only ones who can choose the appropriate means, in order to defend themselves against the infection. Decisions of such an intimate nature should be made by both husband and wife as equal and loving partners.[12]

The bishops of Chad advised couples in a similar situation to use their conscience as "the ultimate moral rule" and reminded them that "no one is bound to do the impossible."[13]

While there is a difference in context between the cases of family planning and HIV prevention, Fuchs's insight that the couple concerned is in the best position to discern and decide what is best to prevent harm during their marital union applies in both cases. Fuchs's response of mercy to difficulties in family planning in the 1960s continues to be relevant in our present time when deadly viruses threaten married couples.

John Ford on Birth Control, Obliteration Bombing, and Alcoholism

Birth Control

John Ford is considered one of the leading moral theologians in the United States from the 1940s to the late 1960s. He was also a member of the papal birth control commission and authored the commission's minority report urging the pope not to change the teaching on contraception. Committed to preserving the authority of the magisterium to decide on moral matters, Ford disagreed with Fuchs's proposal to allow married couples to decide on birth-control methods. Ford argued that changing the teaching would irreparably damage the magisterium's authority to bind consciences.[14] This stance should not be interpreted as Ford's unwillingness to help couples

---

[12] South African Bishops Conference, "A Message of Hope," July 30, 2001.

[13] Bishops of Chad, "Statement on AIDS," October 2002.

[14] Eric Marcelo O. Genilo, *John Cuthbert Ford, SJ: Moral Theologian at the End of the Manualist Era* (Washington, DC: Georgetown University Press, 2007), 140–41.

who find the church's teaching difficult or impossible to follow. Ford preferred to offer pastoral solutions that recognized the diminished subjective culpability of those unable to follow the church's teachings because of impaired freedom or knowledge.[15] These solutions are consistent with Ford's manualist approach to moral cases.

While Ford's commitment to magisterial authority prevented him from challenging church norms that had been taught authoritatively, he showed greater creativity and initiative when dealing with areas of morality in which the church had been silent or had not given a definitive position.

Obliteration Bombing

A grave and urgent situation in World War II moved Ford to speak out on behalf of people experiencing deadly chaos. In 1944 Ford wrote "The Morality of Obliteration Bombing,"[16] one of the best moral critiques during World War II of a particular strategy of waging war against Germany. This article was considered to be "the most widely influential article that has ever appeared in *Theological Studies*."[17] The article's simple yet forceful application of moral reasoning to evaluate obliteration bombing went against the prevailing attitude, which was to end the war at all costs. The timing of the article was significant because World War II was still in progress. This article is referred to by writers on the just-war tradition as an example of a clear application of moral reasoning to the reality of war.

Moved by the suffering and death of German civilians in cities targeted for destruction, Ford challenged his fellow Americans to see these civilians not as enemy combatants but as ordinary people living ordinary lives. He created an extensive list of at least 109 different classes of persons who lived and worked in the targeted cities. In presenting this list Ford was appealing to his readers to recognize the humanity of these persons suffering Allied bombardment.

> Read the list below. If you can believe that these classes of persons deserve to be described as combatants, or deserve to be treated as legitimate objects of violent repression, then I shall not argue further. If, when their governments declare war, these people are so guilty that they deserve death, or almost any violence to person and property short of death, then let us forget the law of Christian charity, natural

---

[15] Genilo, 148.

[16] John Ford, "The Morality of Obliteration Bombing," *Theological Studies* 5 (September 1944): 261–309.

[17] John Langan, "Catholic Moral Rationalism and the Philosophical Basis of Moral Theology," *Theological Studies* 50 (1989): 34.

law, and go back to barbarism, admitting that total war has won out and we must submit to it. The list:

Farmers, fishermen, foresters, lumberjacks, dressmakers, milliners, bakers, printers, textile workers, millers, painters, paper hangers, piano tuners, plasterers, shoemakers, cobblers, tailors, upholsterers, furniture makers, cigar and cigarette makers, glove makers, hat makers, suit makers, food processors, dairymen, fish canners, fruit and vegetable canners, slaughterers and packers, sugar refiners, liquor and beverage workers, teamsters, garage help, telephone girls, advertising men, bankers, brokers, clerks in stores . . . all children with the use of reason, i.e., from seven years up.[18]

Ford used moral arguments and rhetoric to condemn the injustice being committed against German civilians and to urge those in power to respect the right of noncombatants to be exempted from military violence during wartime. While the destruction of cities remained a tactic of World War II up to the atomic bombings of Hiroshima and Nagasaki in 1945, Ford's critique of obliteration bombing in 1944 is considered one of the inspirations for the condemnation of attacks against civilians as a crime against humanity, expressed in *Gaudium et Spes* (no. 80) as the threat of nuclear war loomed during the Cold War.

Alcoholism

On a more personal level Ford used his own experience of chaos to contribute to a development of the church's pastoral approach to alcoholism. Ford's interest in alcohol studies came from his own experience of alcoholism and recovery. In 1946 Ford was invited to attend Alcoholics Anonymous (AA) meetings. The positive effect of Ford's participation in AA meetings on his recovery and his exposure to fellow alcoholics and their stories led him to work with the early pioneers of the alcoholism recovery movement.

Ford's approach to alcoholism is described as a combination of rigorous moral theology and attentive listening to the stories and experiences of alcoholics, which results in developing "a sophisticated understanding of freedom and responsibility regarding addiction to alcohol and other drugs."[19] Ford's significant contribution to the change in the church's pastoral approach toward alcoholism was his insight, drawn from experience, that alcohol addiction should be treated primarily as a disease rather than

---

[18] Ford, "The Morality of Obliteration Bombing," 283–84.

[19] Oliver J. Morgan, "'Chemical Comforting' and the Theology of John C. Ford, SJ: Classical Answers to a Contemporary Problem," *Journal of Ministry in Addiction and Recovery* 6, no. 1 (1999): 50.

simply a moral problem that can be resolved in the confessional. He warned priests not to address alcoholism by making an alcoholic penitent promise not to take another drink under pain of mortal sin. Ford reasoned that this would be an unreasonable and ineffective demand due to the compulsive nature of the penitent's alcohol addiction. Priests should instead lead penitents to a recognition of their addiction and urge treatment in order to move toward recovery.[20]

Ford personally understood the chaos of alcoholism, and he used his skill as a theologian and pastor to translate his and others' experience of alcohol addiction into the language of Catholic pastoral theology, leading to a development in the church's response to persons struggling with alcoholism. Ford's focus on the treatment and recovery for alcoholics resulted not only in the promotion of the Twelve Step program of Alcoholics Anonymous among Catholics but also in the endorsement of his approach and ideas in an interfaith consensus statement issued in 1966 by The Ecumenical Council on Alcohol Programs (TECAP). This consensus statement became the basis of many church-based alcohol treatment and prevention programs.[21] Ford also dedicated hours of his time to assisting individuals suffering from the chaos of alcoholism. He served for more than thirty years, until the age of eighty-six, as a telephone counselor for an alcoholism referral hotline.[22]

Responding with Mercy to Contemporary Situations of Chaos

The challenging work of theologians and pastoral ministers as agents of mercy continues today. Many persons in situations of chaos are still excluded or burdened by existing church norms and practices. People like Fuchs and Ford are needed today to translate into the church's moral consciousness the experiences of chaos that have often been ignored or dismissed as unimportant.

One area that needs a response of mercy from the church is the experience of transgender persons whose struggles with gender identity are often misunderstood or dismissed by others. The experience of gender dysphoria is not easily grasped by pastors and is sometimes confused with same-sex attraction. The church needs sympathetic and knowledgeable persons who can translate the experience of transgender persons into the language and experience of church leaders and pastoral ministers in different cultural settings. Finding a sensitive way to describe the inner struggle for personal

---

[20] John Ford and Gerald Kelly, *Contemporary Moral Theology*, vol. 1 (Westminster, Maryland: The Newman Press, 1960), 300–305.

[21] Morgan, "'Chemical Comforting' and the Theology of John C. Ford, SJ."

[22] Morgan, 57n18.

integration of transgender men and women is greatly needed in many local church contexts where conversations on sexual matters are often avoided. This service of translation can bring about a more understanding and caring pastoral approach toward persons struggling with gender identity that will help them move from marginalization to fuller inclusion in the life of the community.

The work of mercy also includes giving a voice to those who are unable to speak and are in dire need of rescuing from inhuman conditions. This is the plight of thousands of abandoned frozen embryos that are no longer needed for in vitro fertilization. In danger of being discarded or used for stem-cell research, these embryos can be saved through adoption. The church, however, does not support embryo adoption because it will require the use of technologies associated with in-vitro fertilization and embryo transfer, which the church prohibits. While it may be difficult to imagine or describe the experience of an embryo frozen indefinitely and not allowed to reach full personhood, it remains an experience unworthy of a human being. Theologians should speak on behalf of these embryos and argue for their adoption by appealing to the church's commitment to the sanctity of life.

We will continue to uncover chaotic experiences of vulnerable persons that have been missed or disregarded by church norms. The important task of translating these experiences into the language of the leaders of the church needs moral theologians and ethicists to facilitate and pursue a revision of our norms and pastoral practices for the good of God's people. Keenan, Fuchs, and Ford have shown us that moral theology practiced with mercy can truly make a difference in the life of the church and in the world.

2.

Conscience and the Fundamental Option

Osamu Takeuchi, SJ

God in the beginning created human beings and
   made them subject to their own free choice.
If you choose, you can keep the commandments;
   loyalty is doing the will of God. (Sir 15:14–15)

Most people would agree with this statement: I would like to shape my life by making choices and decisions based on my own free will. They agree with this because they have respect for the person making that statement. However, another factor that comes into play here is the reality that the decisions or choices the person makes must be for the good of other people as well. The fundamental question arising here is: What role does conscience play in guiding us to make choices and decisions that are not only free but also good? How do the decisions we make in conscience relate to what is known theologically as the fundamental option: our efforts to orient our very existence toward or away from our ultimate goal? This essay explores the relationship of conscience and the fundamental option inspired by James F. Keenan's pathbreaking work showing the role of the conscience in growth in love. As Keenan reminds us, "The call to grow, the call to move forward as disciples, the call to put on virtue is always a call heard in the Christian conscience."[1]

---

[1] James F. Keenan, *Moral Wisdom: Lessons and Texts from the Catholic Tradition* (Lanham, MD: Rowman & Littlefield, 2004), 30.

Conscience

Conscience occupies a particularly vital position in considering the relationship between God and humans. "Conscience is the most secret core and the sanctuary of the human person" (*Gaudium et Spes*, no. 16) where we discern the way we should go. "Do good and avoid evil"—this is what conscience requests of us. However, conscience is not merely a faculty of discernment and judgment concerning right and wrong, or good and evil. Rather, it reveals the fundamental disposition of human beings to live as human beings.[2] It ethically promotes the growth of personality. It is the ontological ground for human existence and where we see that human existence is a participation in God's existence.

The meaning of the word *conscience* can be confirmed by its etymology. The word is composed of *con* ("together," "whole") and *science* ("knowledge"), from which several connotations for the word *conscience* can be derived, including "knowing something together" and "common knowledge." The first thing we need to understand from these expressions is that conscience is communal in nature. In *con* we see the basis for a kind of common or hermeneutic horizon. At the same time we can also see in *con* the basis for the universality of conscience. On the other hand, *science* does not refer to mere intellectual or objective knowledge but to the ethical and existential knowledge of human beings. This kind of knowledge is confirmed in the scriptures: for the Israelites, knowing was not merely abstract knowledge, but an existential relationship with the subject.[3]

Conscience and Synderesis

The first use of the word *conscience* (*syneidesis*) in the New Testament is in Paul's Letters; it does not appear in the Synoptic Gospels. This

---

[2] *Conscience* is translated as *ryōshin* in Japanese. However, the two words do not have precisely the same meaning. "While conscience has been understood as a faculty of intellectual judgment on the distinction between good and evil, *ryōshin* has been understood as the basis of conscience in the Confucian tradition. *Ryōshin* is more deeply rooted in human nature than conscience understood too narrowly in intellectualist terms. In other words, *ryōshin* is regarded as a human disposition that transcends mere rational judgment. The main role of *ryōshin* is to determine how to cultivate oneself to become an authentic self." See Osamu Takeuchi, SJ, "Three Modes of the Embodiment of Conscience," in *Conscience and Catholicism: Rights, Responsibilities, and Institutional Responses,* ed. David E. DeCosse and Kristin E. Heyer (Maryknoll, NY: Orbis Books, 2015), 28–29.

[3] John Mahoney, *The Making of Moral Theology: A Study of the Roman Catholic Tradition* (Oxford: Clarendon Press, 1987), 185. I. Howard Marshall et al., eds., *New Bible Dictionary*, 3rd ed. (Downers Grove, IL: Inter-Varsity Press, 1996), s.v. "Conscience," by S. S. Smalley, 221.

understanding of *syneidesis* saw a new theological development in the Middle Ages. According to Thomas Aquinas, a human being is a person created in the image of God.[4] One of his greatest contributions to the understanding of conscience is his distinction between conscience and *synderesis*, which is "habitual knowledge of the first principle of practical reasoning."[5] According to St. Thomas, conscience is based on *synderesis* and is binding insofar as it is based on it. *Synderesis*, as the first principle of practical reason, requires our unconditionally "doing good and avoiding evil." Whereas *synderesis* can never be wrong in that first-principles are always right, conscience can be wrong. Conscience is the faculty that facilitates the judgment and application of ethical knowledge to concrete and individual acts.

According to John Henry Newman, when God commands us to do something through conscience, God does not simply command us to do a certain thing, but to do what we perceive subjectively to be right. Herein lies one of the possible ways that conscience can err. As Jerome stated, *synderesis* can be understood, as a "spark of conscience" or as a "little flame that gives light and warmth."[6] Although conscience is not straightforwardly the voice of God, *synderesis* can be seen as something that moves us to attempt to discern God's will for us.

The idea that conscience speaks to us as a voice can be considered in relation to natural law. Natural law is said to be *lex indita non scripta* (law inscribed in the human heart and not written down). Natural law is not created by society but is in some sense universally inborn in all human beings (cf. Rom 2:14–16). The Second Vatican Council states:

> Deep within their consciences men and women discover a law which they have not laid upon themselves and which they must obey. Its voice, ever calling them to love and to do what is good and to avoid evil, tells them inwardly at the right moment: do this, shun that. For they have in their hearts a law inscribed by God. Their dignity rests in observing this law, and by it they will be judged. Conscience is the most secret core and the sanctuary of the human person. There they are alone with God whose voice echoes in their depths. By conscience, in a wonderful way, that law is made known which is fulfilled in the love of God and of one's neighbor. (*Gaudium et Spes*, no. 16)

---

[4] *S.T.*, I-II, Prologue. Cf. *S.T.*, I, 93, 4.

[5] Richard P. McBrien, ed., *The HarperCollins Encyclopedia of Catholicism* (New York: HarperCollins Publishers, 1995), s.v. "synderesis."

[6] *Commentary on Ezekiel*, 1.7 (Latin Text in Migne, *Patrologia Latina*, vol. 25, col. 22).

Conscience as an Intersection of Ethics and Spirituality

Becoming a good human being (ethics) and becoming a holy human being (spirituality) are essentially the same in human beings and should be
integrated. "Be holy, for I, the Lord your God, am holy" (Lev 19:2; cf.
1 Pet 1:15). To that end God has given humans a conscience. The call to
be holy is, so to speak, an invitation from God to human beings, and the
duty of humans consists in responding to it. Conscience should not be
reduced to a mere ethical category but rather should be considered in relation to spirituality.[7] The encounter between ethics and spirituality can be
seen in two characteristics of conscience: embodiment and transcendence.
In other words, ethics reveals the embodiment of conscience as a norm of
human conduct, and spirituality reveals the transcendence of conscience as
a relationship between God and humans.

John Henry Newman was one of the first and most important theologians
to understand conscience as an intersection of ethics and transcendent
spirituality, an intersection Keenan develops in his own work. In the formation of conscience, love occupies a central position. The essence of love
is very concrete. It begins with God's gratuitous compassion for human
beings (transcendence of conscience), which manifests itself concretely
as self-love and love of neighbor (embodiment of conscience). In other
words, this is the reality of conscience as the intersection of spirituality
and ethics, the demand of conscience for us. Keenan speaks of this in the
following way: "Conscience 'demands' that we love God, ourselves, and
our neighbors. Conscience 'dictates' that we pursue justice." The demands
of conscience, according to Keenan, are developed through a close relationship with virtues. In this development, we respond to God, our neighbors,
and ourselves, based on love. "Virtuous practices become the exercises for
the formation of conscience."[8]

Keenan also stresses the importance of reconciliation in relation to mercy.
Speaking of the call from Christ, he says, "The Christian is called to do what
Christ did: reconcile." The very place where this call is heard is none other than
conscience. Hence, he continues, "This call to reconciliation, along with the call
to be vigilant about the spiritual needs of the other, eventually coalesced into the
spiritual works of mercy."[9] This reality is also an encounter between spirituality

---

[7] Mark O'Keefe, OSB, *Becoming Good, Becoming Holy: On the Relationship of
Christian Ethics and Spirituality* (New York: Paulist Press, 1995).

[8] Keenan, *Moral Wisdom*, 35.

[9] James F. Keenan, SJ, *The Works of Mercy: The Heart of Catholicism* (Lanham,
MD: Rowman & Littlefield, 2005), 63.

and ethics. Moreover, at the root of this reconciliation is the reconciliation of God and human beings by Christ.[10]

The discovery of conscience and the encounter with God are inseparable. It is often said that conscience is the "voice of God," but more accurately, it is the place where one can hear God's voice. Human beings hear the voice of conscience in its deepest sense when they hear it out of love for God, who is its source. This listening eventually becomes second nature or a habit for us. Hence, Newman calls conscience an "ethical sense." He does not regard it merely as an oracle independent of human reason, nor does he fall into a rationalism that reduces it to reason. It works healthily in the integrated interaction of human reason, emotion, and spirit.

According to Newman, conscience is the vicar of Christ.[11] Hence, obeying the commands of conscience means obeying the word of Christ and partici- pating in the fulfillment of God's will. Thus, for him, in its deepest sense, conscience is rooted in the religious dimension. Similarly, James Keating declares that to do the truth that conscience commands is also a sign of par- ticipation in the mission of Christ, who was sent into the world "not to do my own will but the will of the one who sent me" (Jn 6:38).[12] This dispensation through conscience is one of the features of Newman's understanding of conscience, which sees the heart at the center of the person.

A final basis for the transcendence of conscience is in the indwelling of the Holy Spirit. "Through the power of the Holy Spirit, conscience comes to know with Christ, and in Him with others."[13] It is none other than the Holy Spirit who nurtures and guides our conscience after Jesus has left this world (Jn 14:26). Vatican II speaks of God leading human beings to salva- tion through the indwelling of the Holy Spirit, even those "who, through no fault of their own, do not know the Gospel of Christ or his Church, but who nevertheless seek God with a sincere heart, and, moved by grace, try in their actions to do his will as they know it through the dictates of their con- science—these too may attain eternal salvation" (*Lumen Gentium,* no. 16).

The Religious Conscience and Knowledge of God

Newman's view of conscience is neither that of a natural scientist nor that of a metaphysician, nor is it based on the positivism of empirical science

---

[10] We may recall here the idea of "*anakephalaiōsis* (recapitulation) in Christ" of Irenaeus (*Against Heresies*, 3. 18. 7, 5. 21. 1).

[11] Cardinal John Henry Newman, *Certain Difficulties Felt by Anglicans in Catholic Teaching,* vol. 2 (London: Longmans, Green, 1891), 248–49.

[12] James Keating, "Newman: Conscience and Mission," *Irish Theological Quarterly* 67 (2002): 103.

[13] T. F. Torrance, *God and Rationality* (London: Oxford University, 1971), 174.

or the abstract understanding of intuitionism. Rather, it is based on a kind of phenomenological or psychological method.[14] He tends to emphasize the concept of conscience in terms of habit. In other words, he is interested in the origins and nature of conscience in human ethical life and how it is formed, rather than in a conscience riddled with doubt. He was interested in the psychological aspects of ethical conscience and its ascetical content, but he was even more interested in religious conscience, that conscience which informs us about how to believe. While the former is an anthropocentric conscience, the latter is a God-centered conscience.

In this religious conscience we can see the autonomy of conscience. This idea may be possible by understanding conscience as an intersection of ethics and spirituality. In terms of ethics, freedom has an important place. As we discuss in the next section, the fundamental option is closely related to freedom and person. The fundamental option also contributes to the establishment of a person as an ethical subject. In terms of spirituality, freedom is moved directly by God as the self-realization of the will that precedes the freedom to make choices among objects. In conscience, we form our *persona* or person in its deepest sense. This could be made possible by the fundamental option.

The Fundamental Option

The fundamental option is a choice or decision by which humans, as personal beings, fundamentally direct their existence or their entire life in relation to their ultimate goal.[15] In other words, the fundamental option is the free definition of oneself by oneself and in one's very being. Thus, the fundamental option is a human act that is deeply related to *persona* or person and freedom.

The Fundamental Option and Basic Freedom

Bernard Häring was interested in the ways that the fundamental option was both an expression of basic freedom and "at the same time an option for creative freedom and creative fidelity."[16] He also points out that the fundamental option is closely related to freedom and personality.

---

[14] F. James Kaiser, FSC, *The Concept of Conscience according to John Henry Newman*, STD diss. (Washington, DC: The Catholic University of America Press, 1958), 286.

[15] Eugene J. Cooper, "Notes and Comments: The Fundamental Option," *The Irish Theological Quarterly* 39 (1972): 383–92.

[16] Bernard Häring, *Free and Faithful in Christ: Moral Theology for Clergy and Laity*, vol. 1: *General Moral Theology* (New York: The Seabury Press, 1978), 167.

The least we can say here is that a fundamental option is the activation of a deep knowledge of self and of basic freedom by which a person commits himself. . . . Fundamental option is confirmed in its essence only when the person, as a person, commits himself to the Other, to the value person.[17]

Human beings, as personal beings, are endowed with basic freedom. The human spirit sees its own life as a whole and is aware of its ability and responsibility to direct it. This is nothing less than the awareness of basic freedom. Thus, the fundamental option accompanies the establishment of the person as an ethical subject and is also the exercise of basic freedom.[18] Basic freedom makes possible not only union with oneself but also with the world as a whole.

Fundamental decisions presuppose this basic freedom by which human beings carry out or reject their decisions. This basic freedom is nothing other than the personal freedom of the self. In Thomas Aquinas, this can be seen in the theory of the inner impulse (*instinctus*).[19] That is, in this impulse freedom is moved directly by God as the self-realization of the will that precedes the freedom to make choices among objects.

Fundamental Option and Persona *or Person*

The fundamental option cannot be reduced to individual acts.[20] Rather, each individual act is based on the fundamental option, which makes the act meaningful, that is, an ethical act. The parable of a Tree Known by Its Fruit (Lk 6:43–45) may be helpful in examining the relationship between persons and individual acts. Here, the tree represents the person. Hence, if the person is good, the actions (fruit) that come from that person will naturally be good. The reverse is also true. The expression "action follows being" is also helpful in this regard.

In the first place, the fundamental option is not, nor should it be, reducible to individual acts. Of course, this is not to say that individual mistakes and sins are unimportant. What is important is the solidarity of all peoples in the salvific work of Christ. This is the fundamental direction in which the fundamental option should aim.[21]

---

[17] Häring, 168.

[18] Häring, 168.

[19] Klaus Riesenhuber, *Kindaitetsugaku no Konponmondai [The Fundamental Problems of Modern Philosophy]* (Tokyo: Chisen Shokan, 2014), 138.

[20] Bernard Häring, *My Hope for the Church: Critical Encouragement for the Twenty-First Century*, trans. Peter Heinegg (Liguori, MO: Liguori/Triumph, 1999), 26.

[21] Häring, 26.

As Häring also says, the fundamental option is not a one-time decision, but one that should be repeated many times.[22] Certainly, the fundamental option must be made individually, but it must be understood fundamentally in terms of membership in a community, while retaining its content and dynamism.[23]

The attitude we should take is not an action-centered ethic but an agent (person)–centered ethic.[24] The former position is taken in *Veritatis Splendor* and the *Catechism of the Catholic Church*, in which the emphasis is on individual actions and on intrinsic and absolute evil. According to Häring the focus instead should be "on the decision for salvific solidarity in Christ and with all people. And this decision is not made once and for all but made over and over."[25] What is important is to ascertain where our fundamental direction is headed, and for this purpose we must locate the fundamental option on the horizon of salvation in Christ. To this Häring states: "But before and beyond focusing on individual acts, we find in a specifically Christian morality the basic intention and basic decision that must become increasingly better and more effectively rooted in continuous repentance. What counts are decisive convictions, basic attitudes (virtues), and character formation to match."[26]

When the ethicality of an act is questioned, a distinction is made between *actus hominis* (act of a human person *without* a moral dimension) and *actus humanus* (act of a human person *with* a moral dimension). The issue here is the question of what makes an act a human act. Here, the exercise of freedom occupies an important position. In other words, the person is the subject of the ethical act. Individual acts can also be thought of as the concrete embodiments of that person. The highest stage of human action is nothing other than the personal act.

To be free is an actively acquired self-existence.[27] Therefore, the subject in the concept of freedom is nothing other than the subjectivity of the person. The fundamental option is the purest self-realization of self-definition, and at the same time, it is also the mystery and mission of the person. This is because the fundamental option, being based on basic freedom, cannot be deduced.

Each free act of human beings is individual. Therefore, each individual act forms the concrete individuality of a person. Thomas Aquinas takes this

---

[22] Häring, 26.

[23] Häring, 66–67.

[24] Häring, 68.

[25] Häring, 26.

[26] Häring, 69.

[27] Klaus Riesenhuber, *Chusei niokeru Jiyu to Choetsu [Freedom and Transcendence in the Middle Ages]* (Tokyo: Sobun-sha, 2000), 82.

idea as his starting point in developing his concept of person.[28] According to him, the basis of the structure of action is one's ethical freedom and self-definition. As personal beings, human beings are free in the determination of their will, and they are the agents of their own action. In this sense we may be able to say that the will is the root of action.[29]

Call from the Ultimate Purpose

The fundamental option is made possible by a call from God as the ultimate purpose and a response to that call.[30] This call can be said to be both comprehensive as well as based on the unconstrained. This comprehensive call also forms the core of human freedom. Through moral and personal acts humans move toward the religious act of self-transcendence to the unconstrained or ultimate purpose. There, a transcendental and dialogical relationship is established between the comprehensive freedom of the unconstrained and the finite freedom of humans.[31]

Freedom is also, in itself, a call toward the ethical good. Therefore, the more closely freedom is united with the good, the richer its growth. Through such ethically good actions, faith as a theological virtue is soundly nurtured. In this sense, the fundamental option is of great importance for the possibility of human self-realization or salvation. The church speaks of this in the following way:

> Human dignity rests above all on the fact that humanity is called to communion with God. The invitation to converse with God is addressed to men and women as soon as they are born. For if people exist it is because God has created them through love, and through love continues to keep them in existence. They cannot live fully in the truth unless they freely acknowledge that love and entrust themselves to their creator. (*Gaudium et Spes*, no. 19)

Human beings can only make the fundamental option for the transcendent Other, and it is possible only because of the self-gift of the transcendent Other mediated by the Word. In this sense, this self-gift takes the form of a call. In other words, it takes the form of a decision to believe, mediated by the Word. This call from the good to human beings is a totally free act. It is rooted in the essence and will of God and thus embraces the unconditional

---

[28] *S.T.*, I, 29, 1.
[29] *S.T.*, I-II, Prologue.
[30] Häring, *My Hope for the Church*, 164–65.
[31] Riesenhuber, *Fundamental Problems of Moral Philosophy*, 130–31.

absoluteness that is God himself. When human beings respond freely to this call, they are invited into a true encounter with God.[32]

Response to the Good Itself through Love

The fundamental option is open to and aimed at the good itself. The good itself is the ultimate purpose to which our entire life is ordered,[33] but we are totally free to will or not will this ultimate end. Thus, the fundamental option is nothing more than the exercise of our basic freedom.

A person is not something that has already been completed, but rather something that is constantly being formed by choices and decisions based on the freedom given to each one of us.[34] This process is never ad hoc but rather has a certain direction and order within it. In other words, there is an ultimate purpose, which is called the good itself. This goodness itself gives meaning to our individual choices and decisions.

Freedom, in its essential sense, is self-determination. This self-determination is made possible by self-transcendence toward the goal, the unconstrained good. In other words, a free act is nothing but an "opening" to transcendence as the unconstrained good. Therefore, free acts determine human beings in terms of one's ultimate meaning.

As *Gaudium et Spes* (no. 19) states, the relationship between God as the good itself and human beings is based on love. In other words, love alone is the appropriate response to the good itself. Hence, we can say that the diversity of ethical obligations is supported by the prompting to love. The intrinsic tendency of the will is evoked by the good itself, and the intrinsic tendency of the will, which is the basis of the whole of natural law, also has its basis in voluntary love. In this way, human beings move toward the good itself.[35]

Love is nothing other than the very gift of freedom. This love is given by faith and can be integrated with life. Also, love is the true nature of the redeemed human being and is given its mission through Christ.[36] Love is a virtue of the virtues grounded in the mutual indwelling (*perichoresis*) among the persons of God.

---

[32] *S.T.*, I-II, 19, 10, ad. 1.

[33] Regarding the recognition of freedom and goodness in the fundamental option, Häring sees its basis in the Trinity of God. Bernhard Häring, *Frei in Christus: Moraltheologie für die Praxis des christlichen Lebens: Band I Das Fundament aus Schrift und Tradition* (Freiburg, Basel, Wien: Herder, 1989), 189.

[34] *S.T.*, I, 29, 1.

[35] Riesenhuber, *Freedom and Transcendence in the Middle Ages*, 360.

[36] Häring, *Frei in Christus*, 204–5.

Human nature completes itself only through free action. In other words, human beings realize themselves in action.[37] The base in this process is the intentionality toward transcendence. In practical life, this is embodied in human dignity and rights. These are essential to the human person. Dignity is the foundation of free self-determination.

Conclusion

Freedom is not the same as arbitrariness. Hence, with the exercise of freedom comes responsibility. This freedom is originally given to us in order that we may move toward true happiness. True happiness for us is nothing other than to participate in Life itself. It is essential that the exercise of such freedom be as orderly as possible, so that we may be led to true peace. What is required for this is conscience and a fundamental, consistent, and lifelong choice based on it.

> Set before you are fire and water;
>> to whatever you choose, stretch out your hand.
> Before everyone are life and death,
>> whichever they choose will be given to them.
>>>>> (Sir 15:16–17)

---

[37] Klaus Riesenhuber, *Choetsuni tsuranukareta Ningen: Shukyo-tetsugaku no Kiso-zuke [A Human Being Penetrated by Transcendence: Foundations for the Philosophy of Religion]* (Toyko: Sobun-sha, 2004), 175.

3.

Overcoming the Silence of Scandal

Creating Space for Discernment on Sex and Gender

CHRISTOPHER P. VOGT

James F. Keenan's contributions to fundamental moral theology and the broader field of theological ethics are innumerable. In this brief essay I identify and build upon three specific areas of Keenan's scholarship: the recovery of traditional concepts and principles from the Catholic moral tradition, the integration of insights from scripture into moral theology, and the use of casuistry as a method of moral reasoning. After highlighting examples of those distinctive features of Keenan's work, I demonstrate their ongoing relevance by offering my own recovery of a traditional concept, gleaning insights from scripture, and turning to moral casuistry to address a contemporary moral issue. More specifically, I show how the traditional concept of scandal is being overused and misappropriated, describe how scripture can give us deeper insight into our theological understanding of scandal, and explain how focusing on specific persons and cases might make space for moral discernment on issues of sexuality and gender.

Three Marks of Keenan's Work: Traditional Principles, Casuistry, and Scriptural Insights

Some of Keenan's most important early work in fundamental moral theology involved the recovery and careful interpretation of traditional principles from the Catholic moral tradition (cooperation, double effect, toleration, etc.).[1] This work had important applications in the field of healthcare ethics, especially for the 1995 revision of "Ethical and Religious Directives for Catholic Healthcare Services" and subsequent debates about how to interpret and apply them.[2] Keenan also drew upon traditional principles to engage emerging moral questions about HIV/AIDS prevention, such as whether it was licit for Catholics to recommend the use of condoms to HIV-discordant couples or to HIV-positive individuals with no intention of remaining sexually abstinent.[3]

Another area of scholarship where Keenan became influential centered on the recovery of casuistry from the sixteenth and seventeenth centuries. Keenan's historical research found that both the innovative high casuistry of the sixteenth century and the casuistry of accommodation of the seventeenth century had promising relevance for contemporary moral theologians.[4] He noted that high casuistry arose during the age of exploration (i.e., early European colonialism), a period of dramatic change when people began to doubt the adequacy of existing moral principles. The Catholic moral tradition risked irrelevance if it could not provide new insights to emerging questions that had never been asked before.[5] Casuistry allows theologians to reason through the logic of a specific case to find where beliefs converge and to come to a resolution without getting bogged down in theoretical disagreements.[6]

The era of high casuistry in the sixteenth century was marked by innovation, with authoritative cases moving the tradition forward and becoming the basis for moral decision-making. As the phase of innovation waned, authoritative cases were rearticulated as stable principles that guided moral reasoning. Keenan identified a second approach to casuistry that emerged

---

[1] James F. Keenan, SJ, "The Function of the Principle of Double Effect," *Theological Studies* 54 (1993): 294–315.

[2] James F. Keenan with Thomas Kopfensteiner, "The Principle of Cooperation," *Health Progress* 76, no. 3 (April 1995): 23–27.

[3] James Keenan, "Prophylactics, Toleration, and Cooperation: Contemporary Problems and Traditional Principles," *International Philosophical Quarterly* 29 (1989): 205–20.

[4] James F. Keenan, "The Casuistry of John Mair, Nominalist Professor of Paris," in *Context of Casuistry (Moral Traditions)*, ed. James F. Keenan and Thomas A. Shannon (Washinton, DC: Georgetown University Press, 1995), 85. James F. Keenan, "Applying the Seventeenth-Century Casuistry of Accommodation to HIV Prevention," *Theological Studies* 60 (1999): 492–512, esp. 493–501.

[5] James F. Keenan, "Moral Discernment in History," *Theological Studies* 79 (2018): 673.

[6] Keenan, "Applying the Seventeenth-Century Casuistry of Accommodation to HIV Prevention," 495.

in the seventeenth century as new principles became settled. This type of casuistry does not seek to overturn principles but rather to be faithful to them while considering new cases. It asks whether an exception should be made to a principle without compromising the principle itself, thereby striking a balance between maintaining moral order and addressing the messy chaos of reality.[7] It is this latter form of casuistry that was employed by Keenan and his colleagues who founded the Catholic Theological Coalition on HIV/AIDS Prevention to address moral questions related to that pandemic. The group recruited thirty-five Catholic theologians from around the world, asking them to use casuist methods on real cases from their local contexts to navigate tensions between certain moral positions adopted by church leaders and public-health measures favored by Catholic health workers on the front lines of the pandemic.[8] Many of the book's chapters combined casuistry with attention to the recovery of traditional principles of toleration, cooperation, and so on. Thus, in this book two of the hallmarks of Keenan's approach to Catholic moral theology came into wide and international use.

Keenan also contributed significantly to contemporary Catholic moral theology by engaging scripture and biblical studies. His approach to virtue ethics resonated with that of William C. Spohn, Stanley Hauerwas, and others who insisted that for virtue ethics to be Christian, it must be Christocentric and draw deeply on the New Testament in its account of the shape of the virtues. With his colleague at Weston Jesuit School of Theology, Daniel J. Harrington, SJ, Keenan published two coauthored books on virtue ethics and scripture that grew out of their popular team-taught courses on the same topic.[9] Keenan's teaching and mentoring of a new generation of theologians also influenced scholarship in this area, most notably through his doctoral directee, the late Yiu Sing Lúcás Chan, SJ who published two books and numerous essays on biblical ethics before his untimely death at the age of forty-six in 2015.[10]

---

[7] Keenan, 500.

[8] James F. Keenan, SJ, "About This Book," in *Catholic Ethicists on HIV/AIDS Prevention*, ed. James F. Keenan, SJ (New York: Continuum, 2000), 13.

[9] James F. Keenan, SJ, and Daniel Harrington, SJ, *Jesus and Virtue Ethics: Building Bridges between New Testament Studies and Moral Theology* (Lanham, MD: Sheed and Ward, 2002). James F. Keenan, SJ, and Daniel Harrington, SJ, *Paul and Virtue Ethics* (Lanham, MD: Sheed and Ward, 2010).

[10] Yiu Sing Lúcás Chan, SJ, *The Ten Commandments and the Beatitudes: Biblical Studies and Ethics for Real Life* (Lanham, MD: Rowman & Littlefield, 2012); Yiu Sing Lúcás Chan, SJ, *Biblical Ethics in the 21st Century: Developments, Emerging Consensus, and Future Directions* (Mahwah, NJ: Paulist Press, 2013).

The Use and Misuse of the Theological Principle of Scandal

In his work on the principle of cooperation and HIV prevention Keenan often encountered resistance from church leaders and other interlocutors who were concerned that hospital policies or methods of HIV prevention would cause scandal. For example, church leaders said that casuistry around condoms and HIV prevention was scandalous despite widespread theological agreement that the use of prophylactics to prevent the spread of disease was morally licit.[11] Similar concerns about causing scandal were raised regarding the involvement of Catholic healthcare systems in needle-exchange and safe-injection facility programs in the USA, Canada, and Australia despite strong evidence of their effectiveness and clear data that they do not promote illicit drug use.[12] Concerns about causing scandal persist in the field of healthcare today, but increasingly the imperative of avoiding scandal has been used to justify policies regarding sexuality and gender at church-affiliated agencies, especially schools. For example, Catholic school administrators have fired openly gay teachers citing the desire to avoid scandal. The frequent appeal to scandal to justify policy and personnel decisions demands scrutiny.

There is a difference between the theological concept of scandal and the broader use of the term in the public sphere. Most people understand scandal in a sociological sense, for example, when a public figure engages in alleged, apparent, or actual wrongdoing by behaving in a way that is contrary to the law, morality, social expectations, or all three.[13] Scandal ensues when the wrongdoing becomes public. People react to the shocking behavior, which often undermines their confidence in that individual and the institution the person led. A "family values" politician who gets caught having an adulterous affair would be an instance of this sort of scandal. However, theological scandal is something different.

The theological concept of scandal has deep roots. Aquinas named scandal as a sin against charity and defined it as "something less rightly said or done that occasions spiritual downfall."[14] Relying on St. Jerome, Aquinas noted the biblical roots of the term, with the Greek word *skandalon* meaning "obstacle" or "stumbling block." To give scandal is to place an

---

[11] Keenan, "Applying the Seventeenth-Century Casuistry of Accommodation to HIV Prevention," 503.

[12] Christopher P. Vogt, "Recognizing the Addict as Neighbour: Christian Hospitality and the Establishment of Safe Injection Facilities in Canada," *Theoforum* 35, no. 3 (2004): 317–42.

[13] Angela Senander, *Scandal: The Catholic Church and Public Life* (Collegeville, MN: Liturgical Press, 2012), 8.

[14] Aquinas, *Summa Theologiae* II–II 43.1.

obstacle on another person's path causing the person to fall into sin or to be harmed spiritually. A primary biblical reference point for understanding scandal is 1 Corinthians 8, where Paul considers whether it is acceptable to eat meat sacrificed to idols. He concludes that since Christians know that idols are not real there is no moral danger in eating meat sacrificed to them; however, he goes on to say that one should refrain from eating such meat if it would cause a weaker brother or sister in the faith to stumble (that is, to be scandalized).

The moral manuals developed many categories and classifications of scandal: direct (intentionally causing another to stumble), indirect (unintentional, even if possibly foreseen), scandal of the weak (stumbling out of ignorance or weakness on the occasion of another person's good or indifferent action), and pharisaical scandal (when a person is scandalized as a result of intentionally and maliciously misconstruing another person's actions).[15] Bernard Häring's treatment of scandal is notable because of the complexity of his analysis. He considered both those who might give scandal and the scandalized, arguing that one must not discount the moral agency even of people who are frail or weak.[16] One giving scandal might provide an occasion for one's neighbor to sin, but ultimately the neighbor retains some degree of freedom and responsibility. Following Aquinas, he also noted that education can be an important remedy for scandal, especially in situations where "the weak" are scandalized by a right action or by the truth.[17]

The *Catechism of the Catholic Church* (CCC) also treats scandal very briefly as a "failure to show respect for the souls of others." In contrast to Häring and Aquinas, there is no acknowledgment of the agency of the scandalized, focusing instead entirely on those who would give scandal. The CCC defines scandal as "an attitude or behavior that leads another to do evil." It adds that "scandal can be provoked by laws or institutions, by fashion or opinion. Therefore, they are guilty of scandal who establish laws or social structures leading to the decline of morals and the corruption of religious practice" (no. 2286). Including "attitudes" among those things that can cause scandal greatly expands its scope beyond its traditional parameters to include anything that those who fear scandalizing the faithful believe could cause a "decline of morals," even silent, internal dissent from church teaching.[18] Furthermore, this view of scandal ignores the possibility

---

[15] Thomas A. Nairn, "Ethics—Just because It Shocks Doesn't Make It Scandal," *Health Progress* (November–December 2012).
[16] Bernard Häring, *The Law of Christ*, vol. 2, trans. Edwin G. Kaiser, CPPS (Westminster, MD: The Newman Press, 1963): 479.
[17] Häring, *The Law of Christ*, 480; cf. Senander, *Scandal*, 27.
[18] Senander, *Scandal*, 22.

that someone might willfully and even maliciously misinterpret the actions of others in order to accuse them of causing scandal (pharisaical scandal).

Scandal, Sex, and Gender

Jillian Mulderig was fired from her position as softball coach at Camden Catholic High School after administrators were sent a video where she proposed marriage to another woman. Olivia Reichert and Christina Gambaro were fired from their teaching jobs at a St. Louis Catholic high school after school officials realized they were a lesbian couple.[19] There are over one hundred more examples of Catholic institutions summarily firing employees because of their LGBT identity.[20] Over the last decade Catholic school systems took steps to expand their ability to fire personnel who deviate from church teaching in their personal lives. More recently, Catholic dioceses have begun implementing new gender policies that apply in parish settings and Catholic schools.[21] While children struggling with gender dysphoria are not excluded from enrolling in a Catholic school, many of these policies (for example, in Omaha, Nebraska, and Lafayette, Louisiana) mandate that the name, pronouns, uniforms, bathrooms and other school facilities used by students must be those that correspond to their sex assigned at birth.

Although school and diocesan officials do not typically use the language of scandal in the articulation and execution of these policies, that is the principle that underlies these decisions. Teachers are fired to ensure there is no confusion about the church's stance on same-sex relationships, the inseparability of sex and gender, and so on. These policies should be interpreted in the context of contemporary American society, where ideas and norms about sex and gender are fiercely contested. The Congregation for Catholic Education's (CCE) 2019 statement "Male and Female He Created Them" makes its interpretation of the cultural landscape clear, calling the current situation an "educational crisis" in which "an ideology that is given the name 'gender theory'" that is based on "an anthropology opposed to faith and right reason" is causing cultural disorientation and confusion.[22]

---

[19] New Ways Ministry, "Employees of Catholic Institutions Who Have Been Fired, Forced to Resign, Had Offers Rescinded, or Had Their Jobs Threatened Because of LGBT Issues," online (updated September 21, 2021).

[20] New Ways Ministry.

[21] Katie Collins Scott, "Catholic Dioceses Release New Gender Policies," *National Catholic Reporter*, February 17–March 2, 2022.

[22] Congregation for Catholic Education, "Male and Female He Created Them: Towards a Path of Dialogue on the Question of Gender Theory in Education," Vatican City (2019).

Thus, strict policies on sex and gender are seen to be essential in addressing what magisterial authorities see to be grave error leading to moral decline.

Twenty years ago James Keenan argued that there was a need for robust dialogue about Catholic moral theology on sexuality that engaged the lives and experiences of gay men and women.[23] Today we could add that a similar dialogue is needed on issues of gender identity, but appeals to scandal are being used to short-circuit and delegitimate those questions and conversations.[24] Invoking scandal serves as a means of ignoring sociological data indicating that among everyday Catholics beliefs about sexual ethics, same-sex marriage, and so on are not resolved, or perhaps more accurately are resolving in opposition to official teaching (75 percent of US Catholics say society should be accepting of homosexuality and 61 percent favor legalized gay marriage).[25]

Another problem with the excessive use of scandal is that it risks causing what Lisa Fullam has called "opposite scandal."[26] By this, Fullam means that efforts to avoid scandal or confusion about church teaching can sometimes end up causing a different sort of scandal or confusion. For example, firing people because they are in a same-sex marriage might cause scandal by confusing parents and students about the church's clear teaching on the moral imperative to respect the full and equal dignity of all people regardless of sexual orientation. An excessive focus on clarity and consistency of message combined with a failure to acknowledge moral complexity can lead to "opposite scandal" and failures of charity. The proper motivation for seeking to avoid causing scandal is the spiritual and moral well-being of fellow Christians. Jesus's command to love God and neighbor is fundamental to Christian discipleship; attempts to avoid scandal should not result in failures to bother to love.[27]

Scandal in the New Testament

The present controversies around theological scandal can be enriched by turning to scripture for a fuller understanding of the concept. Our discussion

---

[23] James F. Keenan, "The Open Debate: Moral Theology and the Lives of Gay and Lesbian Persons," *Theological Studies* 64 (2003): 127–50.

[24] Here and throughout the remainder of the chapter, any reference to scandal refers to scandal in the theological sense.

[25] Jeff Diamant, "How Catholics around the World See Same-Sex Marriage, Homosexuality," Pew Research Center, online (November 2, 2020).

[26] Lisa Fullam, "Giving Scandal," *America*, November 1, 2010.

[27] Keenan defines sin as "a failure to bother to love." See James F. Keenan, *A History of Catholic Theological Ethics* (New York: Paulist Press, 2022), 22.

of scandal so far relies on the imperative to avoid scandal in the early church, but the primary catalyst of scandal in the New Testament is Jesus himself.[28] He preaches in the synagogue and temple precincts (Mk 6:3, Mt 13:57, Lk 20:1–2), he associates with sinners (Lk 19:1–10), he shows disregard for tradition (Mt 15:12), he tells Peter that the Son of Man must suffer crucifixion (Mt 16:21–23), and his death on a cross becomes a stumbling block (*skandalon*) for many (1 Cor 1:23). The fact that Jesus causes scandal tells us that people are sometimes offended by things that should not offend them. Offense can be necessary and valuable. Scandal or "stumbling" can be a moment of disruption that can lead people to recognize that they were wrong and that they need to change their thinking and their values. In the Gospels, Jesus confronts and offends people whose actions contradict the life to which God is calling them. He offers the people he offends an opportunity to reexamine their beliefs and embrace a new way of thinking and living.[29] Thus, a primary purpose of scandal in the New Testament is to disturb so as to lead people to conversion. Likewise, Christians today who refuse ever to be scandalized or shocked by Jesus Christ and the Gospels have missed the opportunity to be shaken in a way that would have opened their eyes to the truth.[30]

Let us turn to the familiar parable of the Good Samaritan to see how scandal and conversion are connected in the Bible (Lk 10:29–37). In its original context this parable is scandalous because it combines "good" with "Samaritan," which would have been seen as a contradiction, and also because the (presumably) good priest and Levite are cast as villains. Jesus tells the parable in response to a lawyer's question about the limits of who should be considered a neighbor. Instead of answering that question, he explains how one should go about being a neighbor. The lawyer in the story and the hearer of the parable today are both confronted with a challenge. Both must choose whether to harden their hearts and turn away or to live in a radically new way.[31] Rather than aligning the word of God with the established order and conventional expectations, this and other parables of Jesus disorient the hearer in order to reorient them toward a new way of seeing and living.[32] We can see this in the way Pope Francis uses the same parable to confront people with the challenge of the gospel today in *Fratelli Tutti*. This moment of being scandalized can lead us either

---

[28] Enda McDonagh, *Doing the Truth: The Quest for Moral Theology* (Notre Dame, IN: University of Notre Dame Press, 1979): 180.

[29] David McCracken, *The Scandal of the Gospels: Jesus, Story, and Offense* (New York: Oxford University Press, 1994), 7.

[30] Häring, *The Law of Christ*, 475.

[31] McCracken, *The Scandal of the Gospels*, 137.

[32] McCracken, 88.

to reject the assertion that no one lies outside the scope of the neighbor relationship, or we can be shaken out of our complacency by the story and "feel indignant, challenged to emerge from our comfortable isolation and to be changed by our contact with human suffering" (no. 68).

Turning to scripture helps us see that scandal is a much richer and more complicated concept than the current edition of the CCC would suggest. Like the people of Jesus's day, we must also be confronted by the strangeness of what he preached. We must not too easily assume that God's will and God's word align neatly with convention and our expectations. As Angela Senander puts it, "When faith is reduced to teaching and when dissent from any teaching becomes scandal one will miss the invitation of the Holy Spirit to communicate God's reign in new ways."[33] When something emerges that scandalizes the faithful, such as new understandings of the relationship between sex and gender, the normalization of same-sex marriage, and so on the church must discern whether we are scandalized because of our own weakness. Could this actually be a moment when God is shaking us out of our own blindness and complacency? Scandal must not be used to short-circuit the essential work of moral discernment.[34]

Casuistry and Moral Discernment

Casuistry can provide an important mode of moral discernment that should take place in response to questions that arise in the context of theological scandal. This is especially true in the current debates about sex, gender, and educational policies. Although the Congregation for Catholic Education has called for dialogue on these issues and officially embraced a policy of "listening, reasoning, and proposing," its recent document "Male and Female He Created Them" included no direct engagement with scholarship on sex, gender, and LGBT issues, or with any personal narratives of gay or transgender persons; instead it critiques "gender ideology."[35] As Craig Ford has observed, the danger in condemning ideologies and ideas rather than engaging people in dialogue is that you risk misunderstanding what people actually believe.[36]

Keenan's scholarship makes clear that casuistry is especially helpful when we are confronted by new questions and situations where traditional principles no longer seem convincing. Casuistry also affords the possibility

---

[33] Senander, *Scandal*, 46.

[34] McDonagh, *Doing the Truth*, 185.

[35] Congregation for Catholic Education, "Male and Female He Created Them."

[36] Craig A. Ford, Jr., "Transgender Bodies, Catholic Schools, and a Queer Natural Law Theology of Exploration," *Journal of Moral Theology* 7, no. 1 (2018): 76.

of staking out modest points of practical agreement where profound disagreements exist at a theoretical level between interlocutors.[37] Stories and cases provide narratives that can illuminate and clarify our beliefs, concerns, and points of agreement in ways that direct theoretical discussion sometimes cannot. Sometimes a good case can help us see something we might have missed or a point that needs to be engaged. The aim of a casuistry of accommodation is not revolutionary but rather modest and practical; it can forge limited consensus on policy even where theoretical agreement remains elusive.

Let us take very briefly the case of an adolescent transgender child, who might alternately be described as a child who expresses persistent, consistent gender dysphoria (that is, those with an awareness that their gender does not conform to the one assigned to them at birth). In this case, a student whose sex was male at birth seeks to be recognized as a girl at the Catholic school she attends. She is petitioning to wear a girl's uniform, to have teachers address her using she/her pronouns, to use bathrooms designated for girls, and to participate in sex-segregated PE classes and a school athletic team with girls. Should school leaders honor this request?

This case can be helpful for engaging the analysis and guidance put forward by the CCE. We might begin by asking whether this student's story fits with the CCE's statement's portrayal of how gender ideology manifests itself in transgender persons. The CCE asserts that adherents of today's gender ideology deny that any differences between men and women exist and seek a genderless society (no. 11). Furthermore, it asserts that gender ideology is attached to an inflated understanding of human freedom and radical views of autonomy that maintain that human identity and gender are matters of unlimited, free, individual choice and that all are free to manipulate the body as they please (nos. 19, 20).[38] But that depiction does not correspond to the student's own narrative (nor those of many transgender persons). She states that from very early in life she experienced a persistent, consistent sense that she is "really a girl." In that testimony there is no note of asserting radical autonomy over and against God or nature, nor some kind of whimsical playfulness around gender norms. There is a desire to be recognized and addressed "as who I really am."[39]

---

[37] Keenan, "Applying the Seventeenth-Century Casuistry of Accommodation to HIV Prevention," 495.

[38] Elizabeth Sweeny Block, "Christian Moral Freedom and the Transgender Person," *Journal of the Society of Christian Ethics* 41, no. 2 (2021): 331–47.

[39] I am aware that there is a plurality of modes of being transgender and objections raised to the "born this way" narrative, but there is not space to address that here. See Ford, "Transgender Bodies, Catholic Schools, and a Queer Natural Law Theology of Exploration," 97.

Lindsay Herriot and Tonya Callaghan analyzed public arguments around a case like the one described above and found that theological objections to accommodating the student's requests could be boiled down to two. First, gender is given by God and cannot be changed; to seek to transition to a gender differing from the sex of the body of one's birth would be to rebel against God. As one student reported: "[School administrators told me] God doesn't make mistakes and if he made me a boy then I would have to stay a boy."[40] A related objection is that the body reveals God's plan for us. We can see this argument reflected in "Male and Female He Created Them" when it asserts that as we mature as persons, we do so in a way that is specific to our sex and by doing so we respond to "the design of God according to the vocation to which each one is called."[41] The CCE and others consider these points to be irrefutable and leading to a self-evident conclusion that the student should be loved and respected but dissuaded from her desire to be recognized as a girl. But queer theology would lead us to ask why the student in our case should take her sex at birth as definitive. Why is it assumed that her claim that she "really is" a girl is not a discernment of something that is given by God and part of her vocation? Why can we not see seeking to transition as an effort to be true to herself as God made her?[42]

We have in this case an instance of theological scandal – a disruption and something new. Are we scandalized because this novelty is contrary to what we know to be true and revealed by God, or are we scandalized because of our weakness and inability to listen to the Holy Spirit? On the one hand, it appears that this student seeks to alter that which cannot and should not be altered, and yet we might ask whether you can be wrong about knowing whether you are a man or a woman.[43] The question is whether one can truthfully identify with a gender that is incongruent with one's sex, but another way to ask the question is whether our current understanding of gender actually conforms with reality. Do we have concepts adequate to the phenomenon of incongruent gender identities?[44]

The case has come up many times in many different contexts and has concluded in a variety of ways. Typically, school officials refuse the

---

[40] Lindsay Herriot and Tonya D. Callaghan, "Possibilities for a Trans-Affirming Policy Potential: A Case of a Canadian Catholic School," *Journal of Catholic Education* 22, no. 3 (2019): 73.

[41] This quotation, cited in "Male and Female He Created Them" (no. 4), is from the Congregation for Catholic Education (CCE), *Educational Guidance in Human Love* (November 1, 1983), no. 5.

[42] Herriot and Callaghan, 75.

[43] David Albert Jones, "Truth in Transition: Gender Identity and Catholic Anthropology," *New Blackfriars* 99 (2018): 765.

[44] Jones, 765.

student's request in the interest of maintaining the school's "Catholic identity," at which point the student typically enrolls somewhere else. However,
one case like this one was resolved differently and in a way that required
considerable compromise. The Archdiocese of Vancouver instituted a policy
that allowed parents to request accommodations on a case-by-case basis,
allowing students to be called by their chosen name and affirming pronouns,
to wear alternate uniforms, to use a private, single-person restroom and
changing room, while refusing the option for transgender students to use
gendered restrooms and locker rooms.[45] The policy emphasized the fact
that an important part of Catholic identity is to be an inclusive community that respects the dignity of all persons. By offering accommodations
rather than new universal policies, the school maintained its commitment
to Catholic doctrine. The solution is not a monumental breakthrough, but
it facilitated a deeper sense of the complexity of the issue and afforded the
opportunity to recognize the student's personal experience and narrative
as morally relevant.

Casuistry could be helpful on this issue in other ways. For David Albert
Jones, intellectual humility in the face of the possibility that our grasp of
gender may be inadequate to reality calls for entertaining a number of
different cases and analogies that can enrich our understanding of what it
means to transition and whether it is morally licit. Conflict and controversy
around sex, gender, and identity will persist far into the future. Keenan's
method of recovering traditional concepts, turning to scripture, and employing casuistry will serve us well as we continue to engage in dialogue
and discernment.

---

[45] Herriot and Callaghan, "Possibilities for a Trans-Affirming Policy Potential," 69.

4.

Moral Agency in a World of Scarcity

KATE WARD

This essay explores how material scarcity shapes and conditions moral agency. Attending to moral agency amid scarcity not only honors the Christian ethical call to listen to the marginalized, but it also illuminates how it is a common human experience. These inquiries are enabled by James F. Keenan's many pathbreaking contributions to the field of moral theology, most particularly his proposal of cardinal virtues that illustrate how the multi-relational nature of human responsibility almost requires that virtues will conflict.[1] This essay attempts to honor Keenan's conviction that moral theology must attend to concrete living by exploring material scarcity as a situation where persons may confront inability to pursue cardinal virtues at the same time.

I begin with theological and experience-based accounts of scarcity and its impact on the moral life. Material scarcity shapes material agency, but only indirectly shapes moral agency when it provides or removes the wherewithal for acts and practices of virtue. This said, material scarcity never completely removes moral agency. Moral agency's persistence in situations of extreme material scarcity is explored through theological accounts of enslaved and imprisoned US women developed, respectively, by M. Shawn Copeland and Cara Curtis. Despite profoundly constrained material agency, these women capably demonstrate moral agency, honoring their relationships with self, others, and God.

Christians can regard the ability to exercise moral agency amid scarcity as evidence of God's grace. This insight is explored through Jessica

---

[1] James F. Keenan, "Proposing Cardinal Virtues," *Theological Studies* 56, no. 4 (1995): 709–29.

Coblentz's account of "small agency," developed through theological analysis of the experience of persistent depression. "Small agency" enables acts that did not previously seem possible to the sufferer of depression, and this "small agency" is experienced as God's grace amid the scarcity of possibility and well-being that depression imposes. Inspired by Lúcás Chan's biblical virtue ethics, I close with an analysis of the Lucan parable of the Father of Two Sons (Lk 15:11–32).[2] Focusing on the younger son sheds light on agency amid scarcity, God's involvement in our agency, and the role of community in responding to material scarcity.

How Scarcity Shapes and Conditions Material Agency

Economists view scarcity as a defining feature of human life that gives rise to markets and human behavior within them. But how can we reconcile this view of scarcity as commonplace and morally neutral with Christian faith in an all-powerful, loving God who desires this-worldly flourishing for all creation? Economist and theologian Albino Barrera brilliantly reconciles the two realities, writing that scripture suggests that God "envisions and intends the created world to be one of material sufficiency, if not abundance, *although one that is merely conditional*—contingent on human need and human response."[3] Thus, inequalities in the goods needed for dignified life "stem from moral evil and the contingency of social processes and outcomes," from human failure to achieve God's creative design of sufficiency for all creatures.[4] Though humans clearly fail in our divine call to care for one another by distributing the world's goods to ensure sufficiency for all, Barrera suggests that "God permits a world of material want in order to imbue humans with even greater perfections. . . . Unconditional material sufficiency . . . would have removed or dulled the efficacy of these venues for growth in perfection."[5]

While resolving the question of how systemic scarcity persists in a world beloved by God, Barrera omits important aspects of human moral response to scarcity. By depicting "growth in perfection" as the result of redistributing surplus goods, Barrera implicitly envisions a Christian ethics focused

---

[2] Biblical scholars typically avoid giving a title to this parable, traditionally known as the Prodigal Son. My focus on the younger son's experience is not meant to forestall other interpretations, for example, of the father's compassion or the older brother's anger.

[3] Albino Barrera, *God and the Evil of Scarcity: Moral Foundations of Economic Agency* (Notre Dame, IN: University of Notre Dame Press, 2005), 74.

[4] Barrera, 33.

[5] Barrera, 34–35.

on the moral experience of those with considerable material agency, by which I mean control over their material environment and the ability to move within material space. The Christian tradition recommends particular attention to those who are poor or in prison, and to others experiencing profound scarcity of material agency.[6] Where are their opportunities for growth in perfection—perhaps by advocating for a more just distribution of worldly goods, or doing their heroic best to pursue virtue within the current, unjustly distributed system? Barrera doesn't tell us.

Attending to the experience of scarcity produces insights for understanding growth in virtue as well as moral agency. The Christian tradition consistently insists on the ascetic qualities of poverty, even unchosen poverty, to support personal growth in holiness. Those who experience poverty—struggling to survive—with equal consistency report that their material lack promotes growth in certain virtues even while denying goods needed for pursuit of others.[7] As two brief examples, Linda Tirado and Stephanie Land are US authors who write from their experience raising children in working poverty. Tirado shows that the knowledge of how easily life can be tipped off balance encourages those in poverty to demonstrate solidarity by supporting one another through difficulties.[8] For her, poverty imposes a practice of solidarity due to the need to assist others who can then be relied on in a tight spot. In contrast, Land movingly writes of the moral anguish of an impoverished parent who cannot provide ordinary good things, like fruit, for her child.[9] Since virtues are formed through practices—repeated acts—scarcity impedes the development of virtue when it removes access to practices.

Ethicists often discuss the best moral uses of material agency, recommending charitable use of money, temperate use of food and drink, and ecologically conscious or even sacramental use of resources. While virtuous use of material goods is important to the moral life, it is crucial to understand that moral agency and material agency are not coextensive; even where material agency may be almost nonexistent, moral agency remains present. Nor should we make the opposite mistake of assuming that those

---

[6] This preferential concern is as ancient as the Christian tradition of the works of mercy: James F. Keenan, *The Works of Mercy: The Heart of Catholicism*, 3rd ed. (Rowman & Littlefield, 2017).

[7] I develop this argument more fully in Kate Ward, *Wealth, Virtue, and Moral Luck: Christian Ethics in an Age of Inequality* (Washington, DC: Georgetown University Press, 2021), chap. 6.

[8] Linda Tirado, *Hand to Mouth: Living in Bootstrap America* (New York: Putnam Adult, 2014), 24–25.

[9] Stephanie Land, *Maid: Hard Work, Low Pay, and a Mother's Will to Survive* (New York: Hachette Books, 2019), 130–31.

whose material agency is consistently curtailed experience identical moral agency with those whose material agency is practically limitless.[10]

Recently, theologians have taken up critical realist social theory to explain rigorously how social structures such as economic inequality shape human choice. Social structures, "systems of human relations among social positions," do not determine human action, but provide the field of play for its exercise through the menu of opportunities, restrictions, and incentives offered within the structure.[11] Poverty does not take moral freedom away from the poor, but it places restrictions on its exercise—for example, when material scarcity removes access to practices.

A social structure might encourage virtue by incentivizing and offering opportunities for virtuous choices and restricting vicious ones.[12] By contrast, people beset by material scarcity frequently encounter situations where an opportunity for one virtuous choice is restricted by the equally good claim of another due to lack of resources. As I explain elsewhere:

> Many contemporary virtue theorists agree with James Keenan that the vicissitudes of human life introduce conflict into our virtue pursuit. . . . Everyone faces conflicts between virtues, but scarcity often forces those living in poverty to make difficult choices between good ends while wealth enables others to pursue multiple goods simultaneously. For example, poverty can force tough choices between caring for self and family, or between caring for self or family and pursuing justice for others. These tough choices cause lasting harm. . . . Because poverty increases the likelihood that virtues will conflict, it poses a particular risk of burdened virtue that harms moral selves.[13]

Ethicists must take seriously the moral impact of material scarcity on those experiencing it, an impact rarely felt by those with more than enough. Scarcity's interference with virtue pursuit is another way our sinful failure to distribute earthly goods so that all have enough keeps our fellow human beings from enjoying God's plan that they flourish abundantly.

---

[10] Researchers who study scarcity note that while material scarcity is unique in influencing every area of life, everyone will at times experience scarcity in ways that place some limits on cognitive decision-making power—scarcity of time or mental health, for example. Sendhil Mullainathan and Eldar Shafir, *Scarcity: Why Having Too Little Means So Much* (New York: Times Books, Henry Holt and Company, 2013).

[11] Daniel K. Finn, *Consumer Ethics in a Global Economy: How Buying Here Causes Injustice There* (Washington, DC: Georgetown University Press, 2019), 66, 68–74.

[12] See Daniel J. Daly, *The Structures of Virtue and Vice* (Washington, DC: Georgetown University Press, 2021), chap. 6.

[13] Ward, *Wealth, Virtue, and Moral Luck*, 175–76.

Moral Agency Persists amid Scarcity

While scarcity's impact on the moral life can be profound, material scarcity never takes away moral agency. People living in the most inhuman circumstances can and do act morally and pursue virtue despite options profoundly constrained by scarcity. We might imagine enslavement or imprisonment as examples of situations where constrained material agency all but vitiates moral responsibility. But that belies the real moral agency demonstrated by human souls in those conditions.

M. Shawn Copeland identifies moral agency amid the devastating suffering experienced by enslaved US Black women. She writes, "These and so many other women were caught, but not trapped. . . . These Black women wade through their sorrow, managing their suffering, rather than being managed by it."[14] For enslaved US people, tactics of resistance to evil included religious practice—even questioning God—and maintaining memories of loved ones and of the possibility of freedom.[15] An important tool of resistance for enslaved Black women was sass: audacious, disrespectful, and witty language that enslaved women used "to guard, regain and secure self-esteem; to obtain and hold psychological distance; to speak truth," and to articulate their own human dignity and moral norms.[16] With no legal right to their own possessions or autonomy over their own bodies, enslaved Black women exercised moral agency to nurture relationships with God, others, and self: practicing religion and questioning God; sustaining stolen relationships through memory and story; and using sass for self-defense at the service of self-love.

Along similar lines, ethicist Cara Curtis described the moral agency exercised by incarcerated women in the ethic of care they practice to honor relationships with one another and voice their own moral norms in a prison system that denies human dignity and vitiates material agency. These women practice an ethic of interpersonal care that also resists the systemic injustices that constrain their lives. For example, the food and personal-care items provided in the US prison system are frequently inadequate to human dignity, so these incarcerated women organize supply drives for others less able to provide for their material needs.[17] "The motivating context for their

---

[14] M. Shawn Copeland, "'Wading Through Many Sorrows': Toward a Theology of Suffering in Womanist Perspective," in *Womanist Theological Ethics: A Reader*, ed. Katie Geneva Cannon, Emilie Maureen Townes, and Angela D. Sims (New York: Westminster John Knox Press, 2011), 147.

[15] Copeland, 147–50.

[16] Copeland, 150–51.

[17] Cara E. Curtis, "'No One Left Behind': Learning from a Multidimensional Ethic of Care in a Women's Prison in the US South," *Journal of the Society of Christian Ethics* 41, no. 1 (2021): 28.

caring actions is a systematically uncaring environment," Curtis writes. "They care at least partly in response to this systematic uncaring . . . in contexts of violence and control, care acts can be diagnostic of particular areas of neglect and exposure."[18] Spicy, Kharisma, Daring, Ilillana, and the other "everyday ethicists" Curtis met in prison have their material agency profoundly constrained: their actions are limited by scarcity of material resources and bodily autonomy. However, as Curtis shows, they exercise moral agency to care for one another and to practice care for moral selves by articulating community moral norms.

What enables humans, material creatures that we are, to exercise moral agency when material agency is profoundly constrained or totally absent? As so often in theological ethics, we must look beyond human will to God's loving engagement with human life.

Agency amid Scarcity
Is a Gift of God's Grace

Jessica Coblentz has defined "small agency" as an experience of God's grace that allows persons to act when taking action feels impossible. Coblentz reflects theologically on depression, which can be experienced as scarcity of many of the goods of life. Sufferers describe the loss of a sense of possibility and promise, of being at home in the world, and even of God's loving presence.[19] Among the goods of life that depression renders scarce can be the sense of agency for even the most minor, life-enabling actions. For example, sufferers experience getting out of bed or taking a shower as literal impossibilities.[20] When this felt potential for action has been experienced as scarce, its return is no less than an "emergent possibility for survival."[21] The "life-giving expansion of possibility" that is small agency represents "an avenue of connection to others . . . as well as a reminder of [one's] dignity. . . . Small agency introduces change into an experience of suffering wherein the possibility of change—and thus, hope—has often largely diminished."[22] Authors reflecting on depressive experience reveal that small agency

---

[18] Curtis, 30.

[19] Jessica Coblentz, *Dust in the Blood: A Theology of Life with Depression* (Collegeville, MN: Liturgical Press, 2022), chaps. 1–2.

[20] Coblentz, 190.

[21] Coblentz, 189.

[22] Jessica Coblentz, "The Possibilities of Grace amid Persistent Depression," *Theological Studies* 80, no. 3 (September 2019): 564–66.

does not occur in an instant, and it often never manifests as a complete restoration of how a sufferer previously experienced her agency in the world. Rather, this recovery of possibility often unfolds over the course of many months and even years, and for some, it includes additional diminishments in agency as well as recoveries of it. And when it does occur, it cannot be reduced to the will of sufferers themselves. Depression memoirs reveal that this is, at least in part, a gift, just like other instantiations of grace and its effects.[23]

For Coblentz, we can regard small agency as an example of grace, one of the "gratuitous, elevating, and healing effects of God's loving presence."[24] Small agency may not be identical to the agency of the enslaved or imprisoned, just as the experience of depression is not identical to those circumstances, but Coblentz points us toward an overarching truth: when we witness acts of agency that seemed humanly impossible, we can regard that agency as a gift of God's grace.

Another example of God's grace enabling agency amid extreme scarcity can be found in Luke's parable of the Father of Two Sons.[25] The story accords with Coblentz's account of divine grace providing small agency in a situation of scarcity and provides clues to the purpose for which God's grace empowers human agency.

The parable highlights the agency exercised by the younger son at his lowest point, when, having freely spent everything he found himself in dire need in a famine-stricken country, with no remaining right to any help from home. His scarcity of material resources, community support, and physical health are highlighted by the Lucan author: "He longed to eat his fill of the pods on which the swine fed, but nobody gave him any. . . . 'Here am I, dying from hunger,'" the desperate son thinks (Lk 15:16–17).[26] Biblical scholar Amy-Jill Levine explains the structural inaction behind the younger son's need: he spent all his money in "a region where love of strangers was

---

[23] Coblentz, 565.

[24] Coblentz, 571.

[25] James F. Keenan often turns to this parable as he heralds mercy as the constitutive feature of the Catholic moral life: Keenan, *The Works of Mercy; Moral Wisdom: Lessons and Texts from the Catholic Tradition* (Lanham, MD: Rowman & Littlefield Publishers, 2010), 58–59; and "The World at Risk: Vulnerability, Precarity, and Connectedness," *Theological Studies* 81, no. 1 (March 2020): 132–49.

[26] Levine and Witherington note that the family discussed in the parable is quite wealthy; such scarcity would be an unpleasant novelty to the younger son. Amy-Jill Levine and Ben Witherington III, *The Gospel of Luke*, New Cambridge Bible Commentary (Cambridge: Cambridge University Press, 2018), 419.

not in the law code."[27] Out of options, without even animal fodder to eat, he experiences an instance of small agency leading to moral agency and, finally, the promise of material agency restored.

A pivotal point in the story occurs when the younger son "comes to his senses," compares his dire straits with the fortunate lot of "hired workers" in his father's house, and resolves to return home and beg to join their ranks (Lk 15:17–19). Biblical scholars find rich insights in the text's description of the younger son's experience. Like many, Luke Timothy Johnson translates the verb as "coming to himself."[28] Melissa Harl Sellew doubts that "the words mean something suggestive of their modern psychological import, that the prodigal has regained his true nature"; rather, "coming to himself" indicates "inner debate" but not repentance.[29] Levine concurs that the mere presence of interior monologue, a common narrative device in Luke, does not indicate a morally good character or action.[30] In contrast, Grant Osborne finds a consistent theme of repentance in the younger son's actions throughout the story.[31]

To harmonize these distinct views, we could read the story as depicting a positive moral change without imputing that change to the younger son's own choice. As Keenan comments, "The Christian tradition has always taught that the first sign of God's presence is an ability to see in a way that we never before could."[32] Perhaps this experience of "coming to himself" is an experience of Coblentz's small agency, an encounter with God's grace, for the younger son.

Having experienced God's illuminating grace, the younger son is able to persist in moral agency amid scarcity. He formulates a plan for action, resolving "to get up" (Lk 15:18), a verb repeated two verses later to show that he did exactly as he had planned. His moral agency enables him to assess accurately both his current prospects and his own character ("I have sinned. . . . I no longer deserve to be called your son" [Lk 15:18–19]). Some commentators read the son's repeated speech to his father as a "rehearsed legal confession" that

---

[27] Amy-Jill Levine, "A Parable and Its Baggage: What the Prodigal Son Story Doesn't Mean," *The Christian Century* 131, no. 18 (September 3, 2014): 21.

[28] Luke Timothy Johnson, "Narrative Criticism and Translation: The Case of Luke-Acts and the NRSV," in *Scripture and Traditions: Essays on Early Judaism and Christianity in Honor of Carl R. Holladay*, ed. Patrick Gray and Gail R. O'Day, 387–410 (Leiden: Brill, 2008), 387–409; see also Levine and Witherington, *The Gospel of Luke*, 421.

[29] Melissa Harl Sellew, "Interior Monologue as a Narrative Device in the Parables of Luke," *Journal of Biblical Literature* 111, no. 2 (1992): 246.

[30] Levine, "A Parable and Its Baggage."

[31] Grant R. Osborne, *Luke: Verse by Verse*, Osborne New Testament Commentaries (Bellingham, WA: Lexham Press, 2018), chap. 15:1–32.

[32] Keenan, *The Works of Mercy*, 121–22.

"gives the impression of being calculated."[33] To me, the identical repetition emphasizes the congruence of plan and action: the strategy devised amid the younger son's "dire" scarcity has come to pass. Just as he planned, he "got up" and returned home to clearly acknowledge his relationship with his father and his own sinful status. Action followed on thought and was sustained.

Rather than attributing the younger son's change of heart and circumstances to his own will, the parable throughout points to God's grace enabling human action. The verb used for "get up" in both instances, *anistēmi*, is used in Luke for Jesus's resurrection and for the miraculous healings of Simon Peter's mother-in-law and Jairus's daughter.[34] The younger son's "getting up" is not a rugged, individualist, up-by-his-own-bootstraps model of agency, but an agency enabled by God's empowering grace. The merciful father confirms that God is responsible for his son's return when he twice joyfully proclaims that his younger son "was dead and has come to life again" (Lk 15:24, 32).[35] Of course, just as the vivifying verb suggests, returning the dead to life can only be the action of God.

God's gift of small agency does not bend the laws of nature, science, or society. It does not empower the younger son to turn pods into fattened calves, nor does it magically restore him to economic self-sufficiency. Rather, it enables him, in Barrera's terms, to move toward God's desire of sufficiency for all by requesting help from someone who has a surplus to distribute, his father. Many biblical scholars mention that the younger son could have sought material assistance among the Jewish community where he found himself but did not do so.[36] The gift of small agency enables him to acknowledge vulnerability and request assistance. All humans are, for at least some time, dependent on others for material needs. The younger son's restoration to enough moral agency to ask for help is a clear reminder that

---

[33] F. Scott Spencer, *Luke*, The Two Horizons New Testament Commentary (Grand Rapids, MI: Eerdmans Publishing Company, 2019), 393; Levine and Witherington, *The Gospel of Luke*, 424.

[34] Pablo T. Gadenz, Peter Williamson, and Mary Healy, eds., *The Gospel of Luke (Catholic Commentary on Sacred Scripture)* (Grand Rapids, MI: Baker Academic, 2018), 246, 94, 151.

[35] Levine and Witherington challenge the traditional identification of the parabolic father with God, noting that "God certainly does not have slaves in contradistinction to two sons" (424). I suggest that allegorical interpreters as well as those who hold with Levine and Witherington that the parable is about a human family could both agree that restoring the dead to life is divine work and that the parable links this work with the son's return.

[36] In addition to being co-religionists with the younger son, a Jewish community had the religious expectation of assistance to strangers, which appears not to have been the case for the majority group in that "distant country." Levine and Witherington, *The Gospel of Luke*, 420; David E. Garland, *Luke*, Zondervan Exegetical Commentary Series on the New Testament, vol. 3 (Grand Rapids, MI: Zondervan, 2011), 625–26.

moral agency need not be, and for none of us will always be, premised on material self-sufficiency.

Conclusions

Attention to moral agency amid material scarcity recommends at least four goals for theological ethics. The first is an awareness that, while moral agency always remains present, material scarcity may significantly curtail access to particular acts. Theologians and pastors should do all we can to understand and articulate when performing a particular act may require uncommonly heroic moral effort.[37] Equally, we should proceed with extreme humility when recommending particular acts for a given situation. Second, we must recognize that material scarcity increases the chance that acts of virtue may be out of reach or may conflict with other equally virtuous acts, so that material scarcity is not simply a material problem but can have long-lasting moral impacts.

Third, we must understand that moral agency can be exercised anywhere along the spectrum of material agency, from the wealthy father commanding others to prepare a lavish feast to incarcerated women with few possessions inviting friends to contribute to needier peers. Some moralists worry that providing needy people with material goods takes away their agency, while well-intentioned community activists proclaim that allowing recipients of food assistance to choose their own groceries restores autonomy. Both positions oversimplify the relationship between material and moral agency. Moral agency is a gift of God, not within human power to take or give. However, as Barrera clearly shows, God does call us to help others achieve material agency for the good of their bodies and, as I have shown, their pursuit of virtue. Finally, as we learn from Coblentz and the younger son, attention to scarcity reminds us of the truth that applies to all of us: that agency and progress in the moral life ultimately depend on God's grace.

Correctly understanding the role of scarcity in the moral life helps accomplish two tasks that Jim Keenan describes as foundational for moral theology in the twenty-first century and beyond: responding to suffering and descending to the particular.[38] This has been a brief attempt to give a particular account of how the suffering of scarcity shapes moral lives.

---

[37] *Amoris Laetitia*'s movement to allow divorced and remarried Catholics to discern receiving the Eucharist demonstrates the humility about prescribing acts that may be difficult to carry out which I am envisioning here.

[38] James F. Keenan, *A History of Catholic Theological Ethics* (Mahwah, NJ: Paulist Press, 2022), chap. 8.

5.

James Keenan's Fundamental Moral Theology and Catholic Environmentalism

MARK GRAHAM

Each of us has cause to think
with deep gratitude of those who have
lit the flame within us.
—ALBERT SCHWEITZER

Pope Francis's call to ecological conversion for the world's 1.3 billion Catholics in *Laudato Si'* (2015) represents one of the most urgent and consequential undertakings in church history. We stand at an unprecedented moment in which one species—*Homo sapiens*—has become so successful at developing technologies, controlling natural forces, subduing threats, and refashioning our world to satisfy our desires that virtually every usable ecosystem has been colonized. According to Francis, this process of colonization has resulted in a massive fouling of our planetary nest, with degradation, pollution, and destruction of natural capital occurring on an almost unimaginable scale today. Not only have we "disappointed God's expectations" (*Laudato Si'*, no. 61) by our environmentally nefarious behavior, but we have also created widespread unsustainability in which we are incrementally undermining the natural systems upon which all life on Planet Earth depends.

If Pope Francis's call to ecological conversion in *Laudato Si'* is successful,[1] Catholics could become a beacon of light to the larger Christian and human communities and provide an impetus to make an intentional commitment to environmental goals, which could be just the infusion of energy and knowledge needed to begin reversing the environmental destruction caused during the past several centuries. If the pope is unsuccessful, though, our once fecund planet could be reduced to little more than a barren rock surrounded by lifeless oceans, hostile to every form of life and a sad reminder of an episode of prodigious divine grace and creativity thwarted by the callousness of one species.

The work of the inimitable James F. Keenan, SJ, might be critical to the success of Pope Francis's agenda of ecological conversion, even though environmentalism is not a major focus of his work. Keenan's fundamental moral theology provides important conceptual clarity on several necessary prerequisites for the success of ecological conversion. If it is similar to the concept of moral conversion in Catholic moral theology, an ecological conversion will typically not occur in a dramatic fashion—like St. Paul being struck by lightning and hearing the voice of Jesus on his way to Damascus—but incrementally through a persistent resolve to strive to become more environmentally benign every single day.[2] Moreover, in order for Catholics to embrace the process of ecological conversion, we will have to be convinced that ecological conversion is well grounded theologically, that it is a necessary ingredient in accepting God's gracious gift of salvation, and that it will help further God's handiwork in bringing our part of creation to fruition. To this end, let me develop key elements of Keenan's fundamental moral theology and then show how they further *Laudato Si's* goal of making ecological conversion theologically rich and persuasive.

Moral Goodness, Sin, and Love

Moral Goodness

Keenan's early study of Thomas Aquinas[3] led to a direct repudiation of the synthesis attained by the neo-Thomist manualists on the way in which a person becomes good morally. Both Keenan and the neo-Thomist manualists

---

[1] For a discussion of *Laudato Si's* strengths and weaknesses, see Mark Graham, "Pope Francis's *Laudato Si'*: A Critical Response," *Minding Nature* 10, no. 2 (May 2017): 57–64.

[2] William C. Spohn, *Go and Do Likewise: Jesus and Ethics* (New York: Continuum, 1999), 110–12.

[3] James F. Keenan, SJ, *Goodness and Rightness in Thomas Aquinas's* Summa Theologiae (Washington, DC: Georgetown University Press, 1992).

agreed that God's gracious gift of salvation requires a moral response, and the neo-Thomist manualists maintained that this response entails an agent cooperating with the promptings of divine grace and performing morally right actions conforming to the objective moral order. In their minds the only path to personal moral goodness is through morally right behavior, and there is a direct transference of the moral quality of one's actions to the texture of a person's moral goodness or badness. As Thomas Slater states succinctly, "By performing good actions a man becomes a good man morally, and he is a bad man if he performs bad actions."[4]

Keenan's reading of Thomas Aquinas's *Summa Theologiae* led him to a very different conclusion about the connection between actions and moral goodness. According to Keenan, goodness is antecedent to any action an agent performs, and while it is connected to the rightness or wrongness of actions, insofar as a good person will always be concerned with acting rightly, moral goodness is not directly reducible to or created by acting rightly. In other words, acting rightly does not necessarily make one a better person morally. Instead, Keenan argues that Aquinas locates moral goodness in a consistent pattern of striving to become a better person and to act rightly: "We no longer call people good if they do good actions. Rather, we call people good who strive to realize rightness in their lives and in their world."[5]

For Keenan, then, Thomas's notion of moral goodness requires a significant conceptual shift: While trying to figure out what is morally right in practical situations is still important and necessary, moral goodness requires attention to one's character and underlying dispositions, and the real formation that must take place is striving every day to become a better person by cultivating character traits such as love, compassion, and empathy. With this shift the focus in Catholic moral theology is not simply an intellectual exercise of knowing both theoretically and practically the right thing to do, but in becoming a certain kind of person who is habituated in the correct way and who is consistently committed to striving to become a better personal morally.

Sin

From its inception,[6] Catholic moral theology was envisioned as a discipline necessary to understand and control sin and to standardize penances

---

[4] Thomas Slater, *A Manual of Moral Theology*, vol. 1, 3rd ed. (New York: Benzinger Bros., 1908), 41.

[5] Keenan, *Goodness and Rightness in Thomas Aquinas's* Summa Theologiae, 7.

[6] James F. Keenan, SJ, *A History of Catholic Theological Ethics* (Mahwah, NJ: Paulist Press, 2023). See also John A. Gallagher, *Time Past, Time Future: An Historical Study of Catholic Moral Theology* (Eugene, OR: Wipf and Stock, 2003), chap. 1.

for specific sins. Catholics who have used the sacrament of confession to seek forgiveness know how sin is conceived in the Catholic tradition: from young children whose confessions might focus on mistreating siblings, lying to parents, and disobeying household rules; to adolescents whose sexual indiscretions, experimentation with alcohol or drugs, or poor treatment of classmates and friends are likely fodder for the confessional; to adults who might confess a wide range of offenses from minor to extraordinarily grave. All these share one common trait; these sins are discrete, individual acts that deviate from acceptable standards. In other words, they are pieces of behavior that fall short of norms that regulate human life. Furthermore, these moral failings are usually manifestations of a chronic weakness, which means that most people will have ongoing problematic behavioral areas in which the destructive behavior is repeated over and over again, even though they might be accompanied by full knowledge of their dastardly ramifications and of a sincere desire to change their behavior. In many ways we typify St. Paul's insight that we are so weak that we can grasp the right thing to do and yet not do it, preferring instead to act wrongly and to wallow in evil (Rom 7:19).

For Keenan, there is no disputing that sinning out of weakness is a reality that everyone faces: "Where you and I are weak, messy, and broken, we believe we sin."[7] Yet he also insists that it is easy to trivialize and domesticate sin in this manner, as it causes us to focus on those isolated areas of our lives that prove to be chronic nuisances. In this way we can package sin "into nice, discrete, manageable categories" and we can regularly confess them and receive forgiveness, thereby containing sin and restraining its destructiveness.[8]

Or so we think. According to Keenan, this is the convenient lie we tell ourselves to avoid the uncomfortable truth that sin is uglier and far more pervasive than this sanitized account admits and that "we have deep within us some incredible, hidden sinfulness."[9] Cold-heartedness, meanness, pettiness, resentfulness, anger, a propensity to violence—given the right circumstances, all of these damaging qualities will readily come to the surface. Yet this is a pill far too bitter to swallow, so we tell ourselves stories that reinforce our innate goodness, remain convinced that we really are good people underneath our occasional moral transgressions, and we cheerily conduct our lives as if we simply need to create the right circumstances for the full expression of our goodness to shine forth and the kingdom of God will be right around the corner.

---

[7] James F. Keenan, SJ, *Moral Wisdom: Lessons and Texts from the Catholic Tradition* (Lanham, MD: Rowman & Littlefield, 2004), 52.

[8] Keenan, 53.

[9] Keenan, 54.

Keenan suggests that we understand sin as a failure to bother to love, which is illustrated over and over in scripture, from the rich man who ignores Lazarus, the beggar outside his gate (Lk 16:19–31), to the angry people who fail to feed the hungry and clothe the naked and are thereby consigned to eternal perdition in the parable of the Sheep and Goats (Mt 25:31–46), to the priest and Levite in the parable of the Good Samaritan who pass by the beaten man in the ditch without stopping to render aid (Lk 10:25–37). In this account, sin lurks in our apathy, in not caring enough to lift a finger, in not asking difficult questions that might stir up trouble, in choosing a safe path rather than a loving path. It also lurks, according to Keenan, in precisely those spots in which we feel comfortable and self-assured, which are typically in our personal strengths. This might seem very counterintuitive, as most of us probably feel that individual strengths represent our best parts, where a combination of sustained attention and the intentional cultivation of native talents results in recognized excellence. Yet these areas of strength are precisely where we become complacent and unloving: "Our sin is usually where you and I are comfortable, where we do not feel the need to bother, where . . . we have found complacency, a complacency not where we rest in being loved but where we rest in our delusional self-understanding of how much better we are than others."[10]

Love

With few notable exceptions for the past century the singular trajectory in Christian ethics has been to regard *agape* as the highest and purest form of love.[11] In contradistinction to *eros* and *philia*, which are respectively understood as fiery and romantic love and love for the sake of a friendship, *agape* is distinguished by the fact that it requires no emotional attachment, seeks nothing in return, has only another's well-being in mind and, perhaps most importantly is willing to suffer and sacrifice for another. Similar to the love that Jesus showed on the cross, *agape* is self-abnegating love that only cares for the other's good, regardless of the personal costs to oneself.

While Keenan has no interest in disputing that *agape* is a noble form of Christian love, he claims that even to begin to understand *agape* or any of the other forms of love requires an analysis of the prior dynamics of attachment and the deepest human longings. For Keenan, union is what every human desires, with God and other human beings, at every moment of our lives, from the trivial to momentous occasions in our lives. We crave to feel

---

[10] Keenan, 57.

[11] Gene H. Outka, *Agape: An Ethical Analysis* (New Haven, CT: Yale University Press, 1972).

connected, to bond with others, to form relationships, to create families and friendships, to feel part of a group that cherishes and honors our contribution to and importance within the group.

Moreover, this craving for connection is not something socially constructed or an optional part of our constitution that can be ignored blithely. To the contrary, it represents the most primordial and urgent need we have as humans, and we will go to almost any length to feel connected to others. As Keenan writes, "I tell . . . stories because when theologians start talking about love, it often loses its visceral sense. If we take the visceral sense out of love, we sap it of its energy. We need to feel that sense of union. Union has a very deeply felt, passionate, emotionally invested, human meaning. Union is what we all seek."[12]

Mother Teresa famously said that the greatest disease in the West is not tuberculosis or leprosy or any other medical malady; it is the debilitating loneliness of being unwanted, unloved, and uncared for. Keenan would readily agree. Humans were created to love and to be loved, to feel the deep desire for connection with God and others, and to work actively to ensure that nobody needs to feel lonely or abandoned—and it is our job as Catholics to radiate to others the union that God seeks with each of us, every moment of our lives.[13]

Jim Keenan's Fundamental Moral Theology and Catholic Environmentalism

While environmental ethics has not been a significant focus of Jim Keenan's corpus, his fundamental moral theology identifies necessary elements for the ecological conversion envisioned by Pope Francis in *Laudato Si'*. Keenan's fundamental moral theology presents a notion of moral agency that places a premium on consciously striving every single day to detect and overcome our subjective limitations and our sinfulness in order to be able to achieve greater levels of intimacy and union with others. Phrased a little differently, the moral life for Keenan is about unleashing the passionate, visceral love at the heart of our human nature and striving every day to figure out how our individual sinfulness holds us back from remaking our planet into an embodiment of this love.

The field of environmental ethics typically struggles with two significant epistemological hurdles compared to other areas of ethical deliberation.

---

[12] Keenan, *Moral Wisdom*, 12.

[13] James F. Keenan, SJ, *The Works of Mercy: The Heart of Catholicism* (Lanham, MD: Rowman & Littlefield, 2005).

First, it is often difficult to know the relevance of individual actions that contribute to large-scale environmental problems, and in many cases individual actions are not terribly relevant morally compared to patterns of behavior.[14] One act of driving a car and emitting pollution into the atmosphere, for instance, is not likely to injure anyone. Yet driving a car day after day and year after year releases a significant amount of pollutants into the atmosphere, including carbon dioxide, which might not only contribute to medical maladies like asthma, bronchitis, and lung cancer but also to pernicious, long-term threats to every living being on the planet via global climate change. So unlike individual acts in which perpetrators and victims are typically known, along with the negative fallout of those sinful acts, the effects of patterns of behavior are far more opaque and are highly diffuse spatially and temporally to the point that it is virtually impossible to know who is affected and in what ways by one's pattern of behavior. The psychological effect of this opaqueness is to regard these side effects as morally trivial and inconsequential since their full moral import can never be known precisely. Phrased differently, they disappear from our moral radar screen, even though we know on some level that they contribute to larger environmental problems.

Second, the world's economic elite (and if you are reading this essay, you are almost assuredly part of this class) are largely insulated from the more adverse effects of our environmentally damaging patterns of behavior, insofar as our economic clout allows us to foist off unwanted circumstances on others. So, for instance, Americans ship our electronic waste to Asian countries, where the poor have to deal with the heavy metals and toxins inside those electronic devices;[15] we enjoy the comfort and convenience provided by a steady supply of cheap fossil fuels, and leave future generations of poor people highly vulnerable in an unpredictable world affected by climate change;[16] and our rapacious appetite for meat is causing deforestation in some of the most valuable hotspots for biological diversity on Earth and desertification of agricultural land in some of the poorest areas of human habitation.[17] The world's economic elite have erected an almost consequence-free system that allows them to satisfy the widest range of desires while foisting off all the negative consequences of the satisfaction

---

[14] Mark Graham, "Catholic Act Analysis and Unintended Side Effects: Time for a New Tradition," *Studies in Christian Ethics* 18, no. 2 (2005): 67–88.

[15] Colin Lecher, "American Trash: How an e-Waste Sting Uncovered a Shocking Betrayal," *The Verge* (December 4, 2019).

[16] Intergovernmental Panel on Climate Change (IPCC), *Climate Change 2023: Synthesis Report: Summary for Policymakers* (IPCC, 2023).

[17] Victor Roy Squires and Ali Ariapour, eds., *Desertification: Past, Current and Future Trends* (New York: Nova Science Publishers, 2018).

of those desires on either poor people or on future generations, neither of which typically has a robust voice in policy circles nor is able to mount any effective political resistance.

This virtually consequence-free system typifies what Keenan calls sinning out of our strengths. The world's economic elite have erected a system in which power is exercised in such a way as to benefit them and to make the weaker and less fortunate bear the brunt of the negative environmental consequences of the economic elite satisfying their consumptive habits. Add to this stark power differential the fact that those bearing the brunt of large-scale environmental problems are typically nameless and faceless people living half a world away, and there is little incentive for those who control this system to want to change it any time soon. Having our moral psychology co-opted by a seductive, consequence-free system that encourages wallowing in apathy and embracing a casual nonchalance about behavioral patterns that contribute to some of the most nefarious long-term environmental threats identified in *Laudato Si'* is literally soul killing. The long-term pattern of accepting such willful ignorance and harms to others would be called, in Keenan's terms, moral badness.

Remember, for Keenan, moral goodness, which is directly connected to a person's soteriological status, is indicated by a consistent pattern of striving to know and to do what is right. So morally good Catholics will read *Laudato Si'*, be honest about the ways in which they contribute to pernicious environmental problems, think creatively and innovatively about ways to reduce their negative footprint, and then pledge to make a daily commitment to tread down a new and more environmentally benign path.

The success of this incipient ecological conversion and its ability to reap long-term benefits depends on two things. First, we must accept that the inescapable reality of sin will cause us to rationalize, engage in self-deception, justify our preferred behavior, trivialize the unintended side effects of our behavioral patterns, overlook important data, develop nearly intractable blind spots, and greenwash[18] our personal habits. Most of us denizens of economically fortunate countries will do almost anything psychologically to avoid taking a hard, honest look at the environmental consequences of our lifestyles. We do not ask the right questions, are incurious about the environmental import of our patterns of behavior, revel in our good intentions, and uncritically acquiesce to the typical greenwashing propaganda that is rampant among corporations, major media organizations, and American universities—yes, even Catholic universities! Sin is highly seductive and often masquerades as normalcy today, and the best policy for dealing with

---

[18] Greenwashing is the practice of making a policy, activity, or product appear more environmentally benign or less environmentally damaging than it actually is.

sin is honesty about ourselves, our behavior, and the typical ways in which we avoid uncomfortable truths.

Third, the only solution for overcoming sin is love and the intentional expansion of our zone of affection, according to Keenan, which also happens to coincide with Pope Francis's antidote to environmental destruction in *Laudato Si'*. For Pope Francis, St. Francis of Assisi exemplifies the love that ought to characterize our ecological conversion, as he regarded "every creature [as] a sister united to him by bonds of affection. That is why he felt called to care for all that exists." Absent this affection, we will almost assuredly treat God's creation in a hostile, callous manner:

> If we approach nature and the environment without this openness to awe and wonder, if we no longer speak the language of fraternity and beauty in our relationship to the world, our attitude will be that of masters, ruthless exploiters, unable to set limits on their immediate needs. By contrast, if we feel intimately united with all that exists, then sobriety and care will well up spontaneously. (*Laudato Si'*, no. 11)

Keenan concurs with Pope Francis: Love is union, or becoming one, with another, replete with feelings of tenderness and care, which in turn leads to showing mercy to another. Indeed, in the parable of the Good Samaritan (Lk 10:25–37), which Keenan thinks is the prototype for character formation in the New Testament, Jesus "teaches us not to look for a neighbor to love, but rather to *be* a neighbor who loves."[19] Just as the darkness of crucifixion is overcome by God's love in the resurrection, so too the power of love is the only thing that can overcome our wallowing in sin and all the callousness, indifference, and self-deception it engenders.

Keenan's fundamental moral theology, then, offers three important lessons that are critical to realize Pope Francis's agenda of promoting widespread and enduring ecological conversion in the church. First, it is really not a question of whether we are sinful, but how we are sinful, and we need continually to be honest with ourselves that a significant trajectory of our lives is an expression of this sinfulness, even though a genuine sense of moral superiority is never far beneath the surface in our moral psychology.

Second, we crave union with others and ought to let those inner promptings of affection have freer rein in our everyday lives. Pope Francis claims that everything on our planet—humans, animals, plants, ecosystems, rivers and streams, mountains and plains, those born and generations to be birthed far into the future—is interconnected and that our personal destinies are

---

[19] Keenan, *A History of Catholic Theological Ethics*, 20.

intimately intertwined (*Laudato Si'*, nos. 89–92). So not only should we consciously expand the zone of affection that we feel toward other humans, but we should also strive daily to cast our net of love farther and wider and to be a neighbor to those in need, whether human or not.

Third, becoming morally good and accepting God's gift of salvation entail improvement and striving every day to become a better person morally, which requires that we continually envision new and creative ways to pollute less, to be more sparing in our use of resources, and to sculpt patterns of behavior that are more environmentally benign. "Creation" has always been a theological way of describing human connection to nature. Today, the destiny of our small parcel of creation on Planet Earth is dependent upon the choices and self-control of one species, which in turn will have a direct effect on God, who takes delight in a universe that produces beings capable of knowingly and lovingly relating to God and one that continues to generate prodigious amounts of newness and variation among creatures who relate to God in unique ways.[20] Given this tight link between the flourishing of Earth and God's happiness, it is impossible to be a good Catholic today without being committed to environmental goals, and Keenan's fundamental moral theology provides a helpful blueprint for an ongoing ecological conversion that must occur in order to accept God's gracious offer of salvation and to fall passionately in love with God and God's creation.[21]

---

[20] Mark Graham, "Thomas Berry and the Reshaping of Catholic Environmentalism: From Human Well-Being to Biodiversity," *Worldviews* 24, no. 2 (2020): 156–83.

[21] Thanks, Jim, for everything that you have done for me, your students, and the church! Much love and gratitude.

PART II

VIRTUE AND VIRTUES

6.

Pathways of Holiness

Institutions, Moral Formation, and the Virtues

DANIEL J. DALY

In his 2022 book *A History of Catholic Theological Ethics* James Keenan provides a key corrective in the narrative of the development of moral theology by arguing that "Christians were not simply interested in avoiding sin; rather, they were from the beginning pursuing pathways of holiness."[1] Here, and elsewhere in his corpus, Keenan corrects John Mahoney's widely accepted claim that the moral tradition emerges from a preoccupation with sin, arguing instead that the moral life consists in striving for God through living the virtues.[2] The virtuous life is not a solitary endeavor, however. Keenan's pathways metaphor suggests symbolically that Christians walk together on well-trodden roads to God. Also in 2022 Keenan presided over the annual meeting of the Society of Christian Ethics, where scholars considered his chosen theme: "Examining the Ethics of Our Institutions: The Academy and the Church." Keenan is one of only a handful of Christian ethicists to develop a research trajectory in institutional ethics, seen especially in his work on ecclesial and university ethics. This short essay considers Keenan's contributions in each of the above areas. After highlighting critical aspects of his virtue theory, the chapter turns to Keenan's account of how Christians acquire and practice the virtues in community, and more specifically to how culture and social structures influence Christians' moral agency and

---

[1] James F. Keenan, *A History of Catholic Theological Ethics* (New York: Paulist Press, 2022), 208.

[2] John Mahoney, *The Making of Moral Theology: A Study of the Roman Catholic Tradition* (New York: Oxford University Press, 1987).

character, and either promote or thwart the human person's integral flourishing. Keenan has ethically analyzed social institutions in what he often calls the "key" of virtue. The chapter closes with a call for further research that explores and develops Keenan's insights on the relationship between social institutions and virtue and vice.

Keenan's Virtue Theory

Keenan continues to contribute significantly to the post–Vatican II revision of moral theology with his work in virtue ethics. His writing on virtue is prolific, with an astonishing forty-five articles that include the word *virtue* or *virtues* in the title. I do not attempt a comprehensive sketch here, but I develop five marks of Keenan's virtue theory pertinent to the current essay.

First, Keenan's virtue ethics focuses on moral striving and character growth that is capacitated by God's grace.[3] In his first book he writes, "The call to respond to grace in charity is the call to seek the increase of charity through striving to love God, oneself, and one's neighbor."[4] Second, Keenan provides a practice-based account of the virtues, regularly citing formational, iterative practices, such as feeding the hungry, to ground the virtues in tangible realities. Because "we become what we do," he argues that we need to morally "exercise."[5] Third, he develops an embodied virtue ethics based on moral exemplars, such as the Good Samaritan and, as I show below, his Boston College colleague, M. Shawn Copeland.[6] Fourth, Keenan recasts the virtues as excellences of human relationality. Because we are "beings in relationship," the virtues perfect our relationship to self, particular others, and humanity in general.[7] Fifth, Keenan consistently

---

[3] James F. Keenan, "Catholic Moral Theology, Ignatian Spirituality, and Virtue Ethics: Strange Bedfellows," *The Way* 88, no. supplement (1997): 36–45. When writing on the connection of Ignatian spirituality and virtue, he notes that "virtue ethics in this context is always subsequent to God's movement" (41).

[4] James F. Keenan, *Goodness and Rightness in Thomas Aquinas's Summa theologiae* (Washington, DC: Georgetown University Press, 1992), 140.

[5] James F. Keenan, *Virtues for Ordinary Christians* (New York: Sheed and Ward, 1999), 13.

[6] James F. Keenan, *Moral Wisdom: Lessons and Texts from the Catholic Tradition* (New York: Sheed and Ward, 2004), 173–74. The Good Samaritan is a common exemplar in his writings due to his focus on mercy as a distinctive virtue in Catholicism. Keenan mentions Copeland as a moral exemplar in his Society of Christian Ethics presidential address, "Social Trust and the Ethics of Our Institutions," *Journal of the Society of Christian Ethics* 42, no. 2 (2022): 254–56.

[7] James F. Keenan, "Proposing Cardinal Virtues," *Theological Studies* 56, no. 4 (1995): 704–29.

emphasizes the importance of mercy and prudence in the Catholic moral life. These play significant roles in his work analyzing institutions through the lens of virtue. Keenan contends that mercy is the distinctive mark of Catholic morality.[8] His now oft-cited definition of mercy is "the willingness to enter into the chaos of another."[9] Additionally, through the exercise of prudence, the person rightly "pursues ends and effectively establishes the moral agenda for . . . growing in [the] virtues."[10] Prudence directs moral action and integrates each moral act into the whole of a person's moral life.[11] Now that I have delineated several marks of his virtue theory, I turn to Keenan's account of the relationship of agency, moral character, and social institutions.

Institutions and Moral Formation

Keenan's account of virtue reflects the insight that multiple institutions and communities form an individual's moral character. A thread that binds together *The Works of Mercy: The Heart of Catholicism* is Keenan's attention to the institutionalization and communal practice of the works of mercy. Throughout the book he references the confraternities of the sixteenth-century "lay associations" that "wedded spiritual growth and devotion with the practice of mercy."[12] These and other similar organizations had an enormous influence on the moral formation of Catholics.[13] The moral and spiritual growth of members emerged from the structured practice of alleviating the suffering of others. For example, the Confraternity of Misericordia in Portugal was dedicated to all fourteen works of mercy, while the Confraternity of Divine Love nursed and cared for people with syphilis. Keenan emphasizes that the virtuous life for an individual emerges from his or her participation in institutions that "train" members to be virtuous.

---

[8] James F. Keenan, *The Works of Mercy: The Heart of Catholicism* (New York: Sheed and Ward, 2005), chap. 1.

[9] Keenan, 3. See also Thomas Aquinas, *Summa Theologiae* (Allen, TX: Christian Classics, 1981), I 21.4. Keenan derives his definition from Aquinas's account, which holds that the merciful person is "affected with sorrow at the misery of another as though it were his own," and "he endeavors to dispel the misery of this other."

[10] Keenan, *Moral Wisdom*, 151.

[11] James F. Keenan, "The Virtue of Prudence," in *The Ethics of Aquinas*, ed. Stephen J. Pope (Washington, DC: Georgetown University Press, 2002), 259–71.

[12] Keenan, *The Works of Mercy*, 12. Gervase Rosser, "The Ethics of Confraternities," in *A Companion to Medieval and Early Modern Confraternities*, ed. Konrad Eisenbichler (Boston: Brill, 2019), 94–95.

[13] Keenan, *A History of Catholic Theological Ethics*, 209.

For Keenan, institutions provide the explicit coaching needed to improve one's moral practice progressively. He argues that St. Ignatius's spiritual exercises, as a series of practices, form the exercitant in virtue. Here spiritual exercises are also simultaneously moral exercises.[14] In order to persevere in the exercises, the exercitant requires a prudent director.[15] The prudent director is not unlike the "anamchara" or "soul friend" with whom a monk could confess his sins for the purpose of recognizing one's vices and transforming them into virtues.[16]

Institutions also provide opportunities to encounter moral exemplars. In an autobiographical moment Keenan holds up his colleague, M. Shawn Copeland, for her "vulnerable style," patience, and perseverance.[17] Copeland provided Keenan with a peer exemplar upon whom he could model his action.[18] Institutions often raise up moral exemplars for their members to emulate. The Catholic church canonizes saints, and even the National Hockey League annually honors "the player adjudged to have exhibited the best type of sportsmanship and gentlemanly conduct combined with a high standard of playing ability."[19] In sum, Keenan consistently emphasizes that acquiring the virtues is a relational, often institutionally based, endeavor.

Institutions not only cultivate virtue, but they can also deform moral character. Consider Keenan's work on *hierarchicalism*, a term he developed to conceptualize the "vicious culture" that infects the Catholic episcopate.[20] Keenan argues that a culture of hierarchicalism forms bishops to reject the Christ-inspired "virtue of servant leadership" and instead facilitates the acquisition of vices in bishops that insulate them from accountability in all of its forms.[21] He maintains that although the ecclesial structures that give bishops immunity from punishment should be transformed, the deeper problem is cultural. Following the Center for Advanced Research in Language Acquisition, Keenan defines *culture* as "the shared patterns of behaviors and interactions, cognitive constructs, and affective understanding that are learned through a process of socialization."[22] Ultimately, the culture of the

---

[14] Keenan, *Virtues for Ordinary Christians,* 10.

[15] Keenan, "Catholic Moral Theology, Ignatian Spirituality, and Virtue Ethics."

[16] Keenan, *A History of Catholic Theological Ethics,* 86.

[17] Keenan, "Social Trust and the Ethics of Our Institutions," 254–56.

[18] On peer-exemplars' effectiveness, see Hyemin Han et al., "Attainable and Relevant Moral Exemplars Are More Effective Than Extraordinary Exemplars in Promoting Voluntary Service Engagement," *Frontiers in Psychology* 8, no. 1 (2017): 1–14.

[19] "NHL Lady Byng Memorial Trophy Winners," NHL.com, National Hockey League, June 26, 2023.

[20] James F. Keenan "Hierarchicalism," *Theological Studies* 83, no. 1 (2022): 85.

[21] Keenan, 87, 107.

[22] Keenan, 90n22.

episcopate is vicious insofar as it endorses behavioral patterns and cognitive categories that shield bishops from accountability. These patterns and ideas malform bishops and cripple their capacity to cultivate virtues like prudence and justice. Keenan proposes that a culture of accountability needs to be created within the episcopate to enable and require bishops to protect vulnerable laypersons, especially children and women. Keenan finds hope in the recent actions of Pope Francis, who, he contends, is slowly building a culture of accountability in the episcopate. Francis now requires all potential candidates for the episcopate to be vetted according to their actions regarding sexual abuse claims.[23] Francis is building an institution in which bishops are rewarded for demonstrating virtue.

Institutions and Human Flourishing

In addition to analyzing how institutions shape the moral character of their members, Keenan also evaluates the social effects of institutions through the lens of virtue. Virtuous institutions promote flourishing, while vicious institutions prevent it. Keenan's work on institutions, virtue, and flourishing has focused on the church and the academy.

Keenan emphasizes the power of naming institutions as virtuous and vicious in relation to their social effects. Categorizing institutions as virtuous or vicious illumines a hidden reality that alerts the community to the influence that institutions exercise in society. Consider, again, his work on the episcopal culture of impunity and secrecy. This vicious culture has devastated the lives of thousands of children in the United States alone. A culture of truthfulness and accountability is required to protect minors from the "soul murder" that is child sexual abuse.[24] The institutional church will protect minors from predation when the "vice of hierarchicalism" is transformed to the "virtue of servant leadership."[25]

In addition, Keenan suggests that a parish "can assess itself in terms of the virtues."[26] His focus is on the parish as an institution, not primarily on the individuals who have roles within the parish. He asks: "Does it pos-

---

[23] Keenan, 98–99.

[24] Leonard Shengold, *Soul Murder: The Effects of Childhood Abuse and Deprivation* (1989). The back cover of the book provides the clearest definition of the term: "To abuse or neglect a child, to deprive the child of his or her own identity and ability to experience joy in life, is to commit soul murder. Soul murder is the perpetration of brutal or subtle acts against children that result in their emotional bondage to the abuser and, finally, in their psychic and spiritual annihilation."

[25] Keenan, "Hierarchicalism," 107.

[26] Keenan, *Virtues for Ordinary Christians*, 100.

sess the quality of mercy? Is it a center of justice and is it identifiable for its fidelity? Do prudence, humility, and a reconciling spirit animate the parish council?"[27] Here "the virtues become the conduits for the parish's self-understanding, and growth, and greater service."[28] A virtuous parish is a sign of the kingdom of God by structuring itself to promote the flourishing of individuals and the common good of the larger community. For Keenan, institutions are only metaphorically virtuous, just as structures are only metaphorically sinful. His use of this metaphor has moved the field to consider how institutions habitually promote or undermine human well-being.

Keenan's pathbreaking 2015 book *University Ethics: How Colleges Can Build and Benefit from a Culture of Ethics* analyzes universities in terms of virtue. The book's thesis is that a culture of ethics is lacking in universities and that *any* culture of ethics will improve upon the status quo. However, it soon becomes clear that Keenan favors a virtue-centered approach to assess and guide the university as an institution. Consider his claim that higher education has a caste system. Drawing on the work of Pablo Eisenberg, Keenan argues that universities have "untouchables"—contingent faculty and service staff—who are victims of structural injustices.[29] The ethical solution is for tenure-stream faculty to enter into solidarity with those in the underclass to transform the vicious structures that harm the well-being of these vulnerable workers.[30] Later he argues that the academic culture of a university needs to be suffused with the virtue of integrity to transform the culture of dishonesty and cheating that is rife on college campuses today.

In the book's concluding section, entitled "If I Were a University President," Keenan suggests that he would convene a "University Ethics Committee." This committee would be charged with asking questions such as: What is "the climate of the culture: Is it chilly, racist, homophobic, inhospitable, or predatory?" Further, it would be charged with naming "the practices that harm the flourishment of the university."[31] Essentially, Keenan would deploy a committee to develop an organizational ethics audit in light of the virtues.

---

[27] Keenan, 100.

[28] Keenan, 100.

[29] James F. Keenan, *University Ethics: How Colleges Can Build and Benefit from a Culture of Ethics* (New York: Rowman & Littlefield, 2015), 72. See Pablo Eisenberg, "The 'Untouchables' of American Higher Education," *Huffington Post*, June 29, 2010; Pablo Eisenberg, "The Caste System in Higher Education," *Huffington Post*, September 4, 2012.

[30] Keenan, *University Ethics*, 78–79.

[31] Keenan, 214.

Key Contributions

Keenan's work on the relationships among institutions, virtue, and flour-ishing yields three key insights. First, he emphasizes that the pathways to holiness (or vice) are often institutionalized. We become what we do, and what we do is enabled (or constrained) by the organizations and institutions to which we belong. Put differently, we often become what our institutions enable us to become. Those who enter monastic life are enabled to grow in temperance and are constrained from lust and gluttony. Although not every nun or monk develops temperance, the cloistered environment and simple and limited foods render it difficult to enact and acquire these vices. Second, in a practical sense, Keenan's work is a not-so-subtle invitation to create and join a school of virtue. Here he decisively rejects the contem-porary tendency to discuss moral agency and development independently of social institutions. He supports a school of virtue approach by recalling the historical efficacy of institutions, like confraternities, to aid in the moral development of lay Christians, as well as by showing how contemporary institutions, such as the church and the academy, enable or constrain their members to acquire the virtues. Third, he distinguishes between culture and structure when ethically scrutinizing institutions. Although he contends that structures must be changed, ethical structures will only emerge when a com-munity has "an ethical culture that inspires and initiates those structures."[32] For Keenan, cultural change is primary. His prioritization of culture is remi-niscent of the Latin American bishops and Pope Francis, both of whom have contended that social structures emerge from a society's culture.[33] Keenan, the bishops, and Francis each contend that a society's culture and structure either enables or constrains its members from developing and flourishing.

The Work Ahead:
Institutional Pathways to Virtue and Flourishing

In this section Keenan's work serves as a point of departure for a call for further research on the interplay of structure, virtue, and flourishing. To do this well, Christian ethics should discuss social structures, such as

---

[32] Keenan, 79.

[33] Latin American Bishops Conference, *Evangelization in Latin America's Present and Future: Final Document of the Third General Conference of the Latin American Episcopate,* in *Puebla and Beyond,* ed. John Eagleson and Philip Scharper; trans. John Drury (Maryknoll, NY: Orbis Books, 1979), 438. Pope Francis, *Evangelii Gaudium,* no. 189, and, *Laudato Si',* no. 114 .

institutions and organizations, with greater sociological precision.[34] Official Catholic social teaching, for example, has been accused of operating as "not an exercise in social analysis, but a sermon."[35] Although critical realist social theory has emerged as a school that many Catholic ethicists, including Keenan, have appealed to for its account of social reality, the fact remains that the guild will significantly strengthen its analyses if its members appeal to one of the many such accounts that exist in social theory.[36] I, for one, eagerly await a time when theological ethicists define their accounts of structure, organization, institution, and culture in a manner informed by social science. Just as theological ethicists who investigate medical ethics are required to draw on medical science and use precise clinical terms, ethicists who investigate the relationship of moral agency and social structures are required to draw on social science.

To that end, for the remainder of this essay I discuss social bodies such as churches and universities as a special kind of social structure, an organization. A social structure is a web of relations among social positions.[37] American higher education is a social structure composed of multiple relations among preexisting social positions: professors and students; professors and deans; students and deans, and so on. When individuals assume the position of professor, they encounter prescribed and proscribed practices. The structure enables and rewards professors for publishing books, and constrains and punishes them for failing to submit grades on time. An organization is a complex social structure containing well-defined positions that have authority over other positions.[38] For example, Boston College is an organization within the social structure of American higher education that has a president, deans, and faculty members, among many other positions of authority.

---

[34] See the 2020 volume by Christian ethicists on the usefulness of critical realist social theory: *Moral Agency within Social Structures and Culture: A Primer on Critical Realism for Christian Ethics*, ed. Daniel Finn (Washington, DC: Georgetown University Press, 2020).

[35] Denis Goulet, "The Search for Authentic Development," in *The Logic of Solidarity: Commentary on Pope John Paul II's Encyclical "On Social Concern,"* ed. Gregory Baum and Robert Ellsberg (Maryknoll, NY: Orbis Books, 1990), 130.

[36] For an account of four of the most prominent social theories see Douglas Porpora, "Four Concepts of Social Structure," in *Critical Realism: Essential Readings*, ed. Margaret Archer, Roy Bhaskar, Andrew Collier, Tony Lawson, and Alan Norrie (New York: Routledge, 1998), 339–56.

[37] Douglas Porpora, "Who Is Responsible? Critical Realism, Market Harms, and Collective Responsibility," in *Distant Markets, Distant Harms: Economic Complicity and Christian Ethics*, ed. Daniel Finn (New York: Oxford University Press, 2014), 14.

[38] Dave Elder-Vass, *The Causal Power of Social Structures: Emergence, Structure and Agency* (New York: Cambridge University Press, 2010), chap. 7.

Keenan's emphasis on the importance of practices, exemplars, and schools of virtue invites greater attention among ethicists and practitioners to the structural and cultural pathways to holiness and virtue. Catholics, and all people of good will, require organizations that enable virtue and constrain vice. For example, the Jesuit Volunteer Corps and St. Vincent de Paul Society are well-established pathways of virtue for the average Catholic. However, the church should consider if new forms of spiritual and moral community are needed to practice the faith and the virtues. Does the church need new and decidedly very different confraternities? For example, given the current refugee crisis, there is a need for Catholics to develop a confraternity dedicated to "welcoming the stranger" (Mt 25:35). Such an organization would simultaneously promote the well-being and flourishing of the refugees who suffer and cultivate virtues in the members who serve.

In addition, it will be necessary for ethicists to continue to consider how lay Catholics can critically assess the organizations to which they already belong. Because members of organizations often "act differently than they would do otherwise,"[39] agents need to critically assess their ongoing participation in organizations related to their work, leisure, civic, and political lives. Do those organizations provide pathways to virtue through the promotion of the common good, or do they impose barriers to these positive moral goods? For example, does participation in the carbon economy vitiate those who have little recourse to carbon-free forms of energy?

Keenan has blazed a pathway of virtue himself. He envisioned and founded the Catholic Theological Ethics in the World Church (CTEWC) association and created "organizational structures . . . for solidarity."[40] The mission of the CTEWC is to engage "in cross-cultural conversations motivated by mercy and care."[41] It is an organization designed to cultivate intellectual and moral virtues in its members. More such organizations are needed.

A third area in dire need of further theological research is organizational ethics. Christian ethicists have ceded organizational ethics to the secular business ethics community. The former guild tends to focus on macro-level structural issues, like the economy, or micro-level issues related to personal moral decision-making. Keenan's work notwithstanding, the meso, or organizational, level has received far less scholarly attention. His focus on the moral impact of organizations serves as a call to develop ethical analyses

---

[39] Elder-Vass, 124.

[40] James F. Keenan, "Introduction: The Conference at Padua," in *Catholic Theological Ethics in the World Church: The Plenary Papers from the First Cross-Cultural Conference on Catholic Theological Ethics*, ed. James F. Keenan (New York: Continuum, 2007), 6.

[41] Keenan, 3.

of specific kinds of organizations in light of Christian values and virtues. Although Keenan has focused on the church and the university, there are many other areas, such as healthcare, economics, politics, and family life, in which structures influence human flourishing and moral character. Joseph Kotva's analysis of medical-education ethics in this volume is one example of this sort of scholarship, which is urgently needed.

Undertaking such studies with greater sociological precision will sharpen the ethical analyses and conclusions that ethicists make. Detailed explanations of the actual structures of an organization, through understanding the "org chart" and the enablements and constraints encountered by position-holders within the organization, will yield a finely grained account of the pathways or obstacles to virtue that real people face daily. For instance, how are people who inhabit social positions, such as university professors, enabled or constrained from developing virtues? Likewise, how are they enabled or constrained from promoting the flourishing of others? The more ethicists descend into the fine-grained reality of an organization, the less their analyses are pious and sermonic and the more trustworthy and accurate they become.

Further, following Keenan's desire to create a "University Ethics Committee," ethicists should collaborate with organizational administrators in various fields to develop theoretical and practical tools for organizational ethics audits. I contend that organizational ethics audits should be compulsory for Catholic organizations. Such an audit operationalizes the organization's Catholic values and virtues. In fact, ethics audits already exist in Catholic healthcare facilities. Many Catholic hospitals regularly perform audits to assess compliance with the United States Conference of Catholic Bishops' "Ethical and Religious Directives for Catholic Healthcare Services" (ERDs). The ERDs audit focuses on the facility's procedures over the previous twelve months. A hospital's organizational ethics audit would not focus on clinical medical procedures but, instead, would assess the organization's structure and culture according to how it forms its members' character and influences the larger community's flourishing.

Organizational ethics audits require a normative framework, necessitating the development of an account of organizational virtues. As I noted above, Keenan has called for specific virtues to be present in certain organizational contexts. However, he does not flesh out how an organizational virtue would differ from a traditional virtue. New research in this area should respond to two questions. First, what is an organizational virtue? Currently the concept is a vague metaphor incapable of guiding or assessing organizational decision-making because it needs an account of what an organization is. I have argued that "an organizational virtue is a web of relations among positions that enable position holders to promote human dignity, human wellbeing, and the common good."[42] Although this account is an improvement over previous accounts, more work in organizational virtue theory is needed. Second, are there cardinal organizational virtues that every organization should embody, or are such virtues unique to each kind of organization? Keenan's 1995 article "Proposing Cardinal Virtues" may provide guidance.[43] He argues that self-care, fidelity, justice, and prudence are universal cardinal virtues, but these are "skeletal." He notes that each culture gives "flesh to skeletal cardinal virtues."[44] Further, each of these virtues perfects how the person is relational. Each virtue, respectively, perfects the relation one has with oneself, specific family and friends, and humanity in general. I contend that an organization is related to three constituencies: its members, specific persons who are directly affected by its activities, and the larger world. Following Keenan's logic in "Proposing Cardinal Virtues," each relation would be guided by an organizational virtue. As Elizabeth Anscombe argues, virtue terms are thick, unlike deontological terms such as *right* and *wrong.*[45] So, while a skeletal theory of cardinal organizational virtues may help begin the conversation about what an organizational virtue is, a thick account could ultimately offer more robust normative guidance. Virtue ethics is a compelling methodology because it offers a content-rich account of the moral good. Therefore, in addition to developing an account of cardinal organizational virtues, ethicists require thick, context-specific accounts of organizational virtues if such concepts are to guide and assess the actions and policies of an organization.

This chapter has argued that Keenan's work on the relationship of institutions, virtues, and human flourishing teaches that organizational structures and cultures need to pave pathways to virtue so that, in the words of Dorothy Day, it is "easier for men to be good."[46] Following Keenan's lead, theological ethicists increasingly should scrutinize the social realities that influence moral agency, shape moral character, and promote or thwart the common good.

---

[42] Daniel J. Daly, "The Virtuous Hospital: A Catholic Organizational Healthcare Ethics," *The Journal of Healthcare Ethics and Administration* 8, no. 2 (Fall 2022): 7.

[43] Keenan, "Proposing Cardinal Virtues."

[44] Keenan, *Moral Wisdom*, 154.

[45] Elizabeth Anscombe, "Modern Moral Philosophy," *Philosophy* 33, no. 124 (1958): 7.

[46] Dorothy Day, *On Pilgrimage* (Grand Rapids, MI: Eerdmans, 1997), 151.

7.

The Virtue of Mercy
and Culpable Chaos

KATHRYN GETEK SOLTIS

Over the years I have attended numerous mandatory trainings to work as a prison chaplain or to volunteer in such facilities. One memorable session was a CPR lesson. Before any chest compressions or breaths, we were instructed to make sure that it was not a setup, not some manipulative ruse masquerading as a call for help. I was deeply disturbed. To be clear, I was not disturbed by the possibility of deception. After all, I have lived among human beings a long time now. But I was quite troubled by this insertion of deep-seated suspicion and fear into a life-saving protocol. General CPR instructions tell you to check for safety and use personal protective equipment, but this was different. This training taught us that before we attend to the unconscious person, we must remind ourselves that the person cannot be trusted. Prior to any act of mercy, we must recall the guilt and danger of those we encounter behind bars. It is a lesson that must be resisted, and can be, by exploring the work of Fr. James Keenan, SJ, on mercy.

James Keenan On Mercy

Keenan defines mercy as "the willingness to enter into the chaos of another."[1] It is a definition that has found widespread resonance among his readers, audiences, and students. Just one example is the 2020 issue of

---

[1] James F. Keenan, SJ, *The Works of Mercy: The Heart of Catholicism,* 2nd ed. (Lanham, MD: Rowman & Littlefield, 2008), xvii.

the *Journal of Religious Ethics* featuring multiple essays on mercy. The symposium that served as the genesis of this focus issue took Keenan's *The Works of Mercy* as one of its common texts. As editor Darlene Fozard Weaver notes, "Keenan's wonderful description of mercy as 'entering into the chaos of another' permeates these essays."[2] Part of the brilliance of the definition is its movement of solidarity. Keenan's mercy reveals a very active solidarity, assuming the literal burdens of the suffering other. As Nichole Flores observes, Keenan's definition requires "concrete, situation-changing actions," emphasizing not only heartfelt sympathy but also the social dimension of the corporal works of mercy.[3] Moreover, despite mercy's vulnerability to dynamics of condescension and subordination, Keenan anchors mercy in a commitment to the other as an equal, as a sister or a brother. Indeed, reflecting on the early Christian community, Keenan finds that in practicing the works of mercy, Christians "empowered the people they welcomed, not treating them as objects of beneficence but as siblings in the Lord."[4] The empowerment that Keenan mentions here is significant. It demonstrates that the goal of mercy is not simply to meet another's needs but to promote that person's capacity to act.

The power of Keenan's definition comes additionally from its thoroughly theological character. He affirms that mercy is "*above all* the experience we have of God."[5] In creation, God enters the chaos of the universe. In the incarnation, God enters the chaos of human existence. In redemption, God enters the chaos of our slavery to sin.[6] Keenan often turns to Aquinas to highlight the transcendent character of mercy. While charity is the greatest virtue, because it unites us in love to God, Aquinas also names mercy as the greatest because, through it, we become like God, exemplifying God in God's actions.[7]

Of particular interest for this essay is Keenan's wisdom in using the language of *chaos*. It is a term that suggests disorder and unpredictability. In the midst of chaos, a person may lack clear orientation and struggle to be at peace, but only in some situations is there moral fault. Thus, chaos beckons a response but not necessarily chastisement. On one hand, one's life may be in chaos because of one's own sinful choices (for example,

---

[2] Darlene Fozard Weaver, "The End(s) of Mercy," *Journal of Religious Ethics* 48, no. 3 (September 2020): 390.

[3] Nichole Flores, "Mercy as a Public Virtue," *Journal of Religious Ethics* 48, no. 3 (September 2020): 463.

[4] James F. Keenan, "The Evolution of the Works of Mercy," in *Mercy* (*Concilium 2017/4*), ed. Lisa Sowle Cahill, Diego Irarrázaval, and João Vila-Chã (London: SCM Press, 2017), 40.

[5] Keenan, *The Works of Mercy*, 9.

[6] Keenan, 4.

[7] Keenan, "The Evolution of the Works of Mercy," 33n1.

acts of racial discrimination leading to the losses of employment and relationships) or from the sinful choices of others (for example, life-altering injuries from being subjected to knowingly dangerous work conditions). On the other hand, a person may be in chaos where no sin is involved (for example, loss of housing from a natural disaster). Regardless of the presence of sin, the one who willingly enters into another's chaos shows mercy. The expansiveness of Keenan's chaos is key. Indeed, even where culpability does exist, the language of chaos guides us away from oversimplifying the moral responsibility. While terms like *harm* or *offense* might compel us to seek out guilty individuals, the language of *chaos* gestures toward a more complex web of blame and complicity. With an imagination for chaos, we can entertain the realities of social sin.

Despite the fact that Keenan's chaos provides a flexible moral context for another's suffering, I argue that presuppositions about innocence typically animate our enthusiasm for the virtue of mercy. As the first round of vaccines was rolled out in response to the COVID-19 pandemic, there was full support for prioritizing high-risk congregate settings when they were nursing homes, but controversy emerged over incarcerated persons receiving the vaccine before others.[8] In reflecting on HIV/AIDS, Keenan notes a similar dynamic. Despite comparable loss of life, other catastrophic events prompt a more sympathetic and supportive response since the condition of those with HIV/AIDS "is in many cases presumed to be their own fault."[9] Although mercy emphasizes need and not merit, the virtue—empirically— seems less persuasive when another's suffering is perceived to be of his or her own making. Might we unconsciously align those who are "most in need" with those who are "most innocent"? Can the virtue of mercy still do its work in the face of culpable chaos?

Our attraction to innocent suffering is telling. For example, in discussions of mercy a passive voice is often favored to speak of those in need: the marginalized, the excluded, those made vulnerable, and so on. There is a tendency to emphasize the diminished agency of those in need (for example, the voiceless) and to leave unidentified those whose agency is responsible for creating neediness and diminishment. Powerful images also lead us away from culpable chaos. In *The Principle of Mercy*, liberation theologian Jon Sobrino speaks of "the crucified people."[10] While important and legitimate, this language relies on the paradigmatic Christian symbol of *innocent* suffering. Marcus Mescher notes that "tenderness" is Pope

---

[8] David Montgomery, "Prioritizing Prisoners for Vaccines Stirs Controversy," *Stateline*, January 5, 2021.

[9] Keenan, *The Works of Mercy*, 128.

[10] Jon Sobrino, *The Principle of Mercy: Taking the Crucified People from the Cross* (Maryknoll, NY: Orbis Books, 1994).

Francis's shorthand for a theological and moral understanding of mercy, and then Mescher refers to the pope's explanation of tenderness: the analogy of parents who respond to the incomprehensible babbling of a baby.[11] Analogies have their limits, but it is significant that a babbling baby is free of any blame. Indeed, Mescher himself seems to focus on blameless chaos when identifying practices of mercy.[12] In an essay on mercy as a public virtue, Nichole Flores focuses on refugees identified as victims of violence.[13] To be clear, none of these thinkers suggests mercy is to be reserved for the innocent. In explaining mercy Pope Francis notes, "You can deny God, you can sin against him, but God cannot deny himself."[14] However, the rhetorical power of language and images that focus on blameless suffering can reinforce underlying presuppositions that some people are deserving of mercy and others are not. Mescher rightly chastises US Christians who are twice as likely as non-Christians to blame the poor for their state in life, suggesting that this judgment reflects a lack of mercy.[15] Yet the problem here is not only the *inaccuracy* of the blaming, but the *idea* that blame matters for how we treat others in need.[16] A full appreciation of Keenan's use of *chaos* is essential.

On one hand, it seems odd to suggest there is reluctance to exercise the virtue of mercy with and for those in culpable chaos. The theological tradition is clear that God's mercy is directed toward sinners. Yet I propose there are really two different kinds of sin in the conversation: unifying sin and differentiating sin. Unifying sin is the one we most often reference in the context of mercy. This is our sinfulness, our brokenness, which points to general realities of humanity (for example, deception, abuse of power, self-centeredness, judgmentalism, and so forth). We are in the habit of

---

[11] Marcus Mescher, "Mercy: The Crux of Pope Francis's Moral Imagination," *Journal of Catholic Social Thought* 16, no. 2 (2019): 254–55.

[12] "Mercy is realized through concrete practices like taking time to bask in the tenderness of God, drawing near others and listening to their perspectives and experiences, exercising imagination through empathy to understand other people across differences, and accompanying and collaborating as coequals in cultivating inclusive relationships" (Mescher, 270).

[13] Flores, "Mercy as a Public Virtue," 458–72.

[14] Pope Francis, *The Name of God Is Mercy: A Conversation with Andrea Tornielli*, trans. Oonagh Stransky (New York: Random House, 2016), 10.

[15] Mescher, "Mercy," 266.

[16] Philosopher Martha Nussbaum explicitly articulates the idea in question here, albeit in reference to compassion rather than mercy. Deriving her account from Aristotle, she argues that a judgment of nondesert is one of several key elements of compassion: "Compassion requires the judgment that there are serious bad things that happen to others through no fault of their own." Martha C. Nussbaum, *Upheavals of Thought: The Intelligence of Emotions* (New York: Cambridge University Press, 2001), 405.

assenting to this sinfulness that binds us together as flawed human beings. No one is righteous. Thus, unifying sin provokes no scandal and costs us little to admit. It does not render us vulnerable to exclusion or stigma. On the other hand, differentiating sin points to specific sources of guilt or culpability, often but not always involving egregious harm. This is sin that invites the conclusion that some persons are righteous while others are wicked. Mercy is less easily invoked here; instead, we veer toward talk of judgment and just compensation. Differentiating sin renders the sinner vulnerable to hatred, abandonment, and all matter of loss. It is the culpable chaos born of differentiating sin that threatens to eclipse our practice of mercy.

The Good Samaritan

The parable of the Good Samaritan (Lk 10:25–37) figures prominently in Keenan's writings on mercy.[17] He notes that it would seem the answer to the question posed to Jesus by the expert in the law—"And who is my neighbor?"—would be the man lying in the ditch. However, the surprise ending of the parable is that the neighbor is the one who shows mercy. Tracing the historical, christological meaning of the parable, Keenan clarifies it is not only the Samaritan entering into the chaos of the man in the ditch, but also Christ entering into the chaos of sinful humanity (Adam). Thus, the Good Samaritan is not one among many parables for Keenan, but a foundational explanation of the Christian call to love, revealing "the mercy of Jesus that makes possible our mercy."[18]

Pope Francis also turns to the parable of the Good Samaritan as a central text and devotes an entire chapter to it in his encyclical *Fratelli Tutti*. In this scriptural "encounter of mercy" he finds an urgently needed fraternal spirit of care and love that goes beyond boundaries and social groups (no. 83). He employs the parable to challenge widespread indifference to the suffering of others, especially the suffering caused by neglect and violence in the pursuit of power and gain. Pope Francis thus finds in the Good Samaritan the criterion for our time: "The decision to include or exclude those lying wounded along the roadside can serve as a criterion for judging every economic, political, social and religious project" (no. 69).

Sobrino also points to this parable as essential. In his opening chapter he explains the parable as a presentation of what it is to be human:

---

[17] For example, Keenan, *The Works of Mercy*, 2–3; and Keenan, "The Evolution of the Works of Mercy," 34–35.

[18] Keenan, "The Evolution of the Works of Mercy," 35.

The ideal human being, the complete human being, is the one who interiorizes, absorbs in her innards, the suffering of another—in the case of the parable, unjustly afflicted suffering—in such a way that this interiorized suffering becomes a part of her, is transformed into an internal principle, the first and the last, of her activity. Mercy, as re-action, becomes the fundamental action of the total human being.[19]

Ultimately for Keenan, Pope Francis, and Sobrino—despite slightly different emphases—the parable illuminates how we ought to respond (and how God responds) to suffering.

At first glance this powerful parable seems to be yet another example of a tendency to imagine mercy around innocent suffering. The man lying in the ditch has been beaten and left for dead. He is a blameless victim. His chaos is undeserved and unjust.[20] Certainly most readers conclude this—and Sobrino has explicitly done so above. Yet the parable is actually not conclusive on this point. The man, traveling from Jerusalem to Jericho, has been cruelly brutalized by thieves; this we know. However, there is no explicit mention of the man's innocence or the reason behind the assault. The man in the ditch could have, at some point, been among the band of thieves himself. He could have stolen from his thieving companions their share of the profits so that when they found him along the road they took it back, beat him, and left him for dead. The chaos could be culpable. Despite our desire to read innocence into grave suffering, we do not actually have the facts to come to that conclusion. And what is particularly striking about the parable is that the Samaritan does not try to figure out whether that bloodied man in the ditch may have deserved his fate. Might that be reckless on the Samaritan's part? What if, having been nursed back to health on the supreme generosity of a stranger, that half-dead man returns to his old ruthless and thieving ways? Why does the Samaritan not establish the man's innocence before restoring him? Let us return to Keenan's wise language to reply. Chaos is chaos, culpable or not. Mercy cannot be arbitrated on sin—even differentiating sin. Mercy seeks to bring the half-dead back to life, and does this without being contingent on moral fault, even the fault of egregious harm to others.[21] Until we recognize the absurd,

---

[19] Sobrino, *The Principle of Mercy*, 17.

[20] Since the road to Jericho was known to be dangerous, it could be argued that the wounded man was partially responsible for his fate. Still, few would conclude his assault was deserved.

[21] A version of this argument can be found in Kathryn Getek Soltis, "Can Justice Demand Prison Abolition?" *Church Life Journal*, McGrath Institute for Church Life, University of Notre Dame (March 12, 2019).

reckless extravagance of the Samaritan (and so our God), we risk missing the radicality of the virtue of mercy.

Encountering chaos is the *sole criterion* for practicing mercy. In the quotation above Sobrino implies this by naming "unjustly afflicted suffering" as only one possible version of suffering. He is explicit when he later describes mercy as "maximal," such that nothing comes before mercy and nothing goes beyond mercy to relativize it.[22] Keenan highlights these reflections of Sobrino in an essay arguing for the radicality and comprehensiveness of mercy.[23] For both Keenan and Sobrino, mercy conveys the essence of God's action. The chaos can be culpable or not: "God hears the cries of a suffering people, and *for that reason alone* determines to undertake the liberative activity in question" (italics added).[24] In Margaret Farley's reflections on mercy she also speaks of radicality, suggesting forgiveness is more radical than any other work of mercy because it requires truly loving those in need. She goes on to note that forgiveness from God involves being accepted "even without becoming wholly innocent."[25] The practice of mercy is one of radical inclusion. Indeed, despite our inclinations to make innocent suffering the norm for mercy, the theological model is irrefutably built on culpable chaos. Keenan's emphasis on the christological reading of the Good Samaritan makes this apparent. If the man lying in the ditch is Adam, it is his own sin that has left him half dead.

Mass Incarceration and the Virtue of Mercy

The virtue of mercy, especially as it is practiced toward people experiencing culpable chaos, is urgently relevant for mass incarceration in the United States. More human beings are incarcerated in the United States than any other nation—far beyond historical and comparative norms.[26] This scandalous reality is worsened through the systematic, disproportionate imprisonment of groups of the population, particularly along lines of race and class.

---

[22] Sobrino, *The Principle of Mercy,* 18.

[23] James F. Keenan, "Radicalizing the Comprehensiveness of Mercy: Christian Identity in Theological Ethics," in *Hope and Solidarity: Jon Sobrino's Challenge to Christian Theology,* ed. Stephen J. Pope (Maryknoll, NY: Orbis Books, 2008), 187–200, esp. 189–90.

[24] Sobrino, *The Principle of Mercy,* 16.

[25] Margaret A. Farley, "Mercy and Its Works: If Things Fall Apart, Can They Be Put Right?," *CTSA Proceedings* 71 (2016): 38–39.

[26] International comparisons, for example, are discussed in Emily Widra and Tiana Herring, *States of Incarceration: The Global Context 2021,* Prison Policy Initiative (September 2021). Historical data is included, for example, in Ashley Nellis, *Mass Incarceration Trends,* The Sentencing Project (January 25, 2023).

The relevance of mercy for all of this is regularly questioned by those who perceive it to be incompatible with justice and more appropriate for private, interpersonal matters. However, Nichole Flores has argued for mercy as a public virtue and finds that "Keenan's account of mercy . . . challenges Christian approaches to the refugee crisis that prioritize safety and security over solidarity with those who suffer."[27] While incarceration is distinct from the refugee crisis, they involve parallel discourses that perceive mercy as a threat to security. And mercy has long spoken to the reality of prisoners and captives. In fact, Keenan has highlighted key historical examples of visiting the prisoner, one of the corporal works of mercy, showing that it has not just been about visiting but about liberation and release.[28] Of course, the function of prisons and attitudes toward prisoners have shifted considerably over time. What can the practice of mercy mean for our contemporary reality of mass incarceration?

Mercy illuminates the way that mass incarceration is a crisis of social justice. The culpable chaos of those who have committed harm typically exists at the intersection of external and internal needs, and thus at the intersection of the corporal and spiritual works of mercy. Food and housing insecurity (feed the hungry, shelter the homeless) is often related to acts of harm (admonish the sinner, bear wrongs patiently). The poverty of those who find themselves behind bars in the United States is vastly disproportionate to the rest of the population.[29] Moreover, in the way it admonishes offenses, our criminal legal system actually drives poverty, creating debt and ruining opportunities for employment. While an incarcerated person may bear responsibility for a specific act that landed the person in the chaos of incarceration, that act is preceded by the chaos of an unjust society and then compounded by the constructed chaos of a broken, inhumane system. When we practice mercy and enter into these realities, we come to see that the culpability for the chaos of mass incarceration is far, far bigger than just the incarcerated person's agency.

Mercy is a movement of solidarity, and yet mass incarceration operationalizes profound barriers to that solidarity. Both racial hostility and racial indifference are key dynamics. By questioning the humanity of incarcerated persons, the criminal legal system lays bare the legacy of its precursor institutions, namely slavery and Jim Crow segregation. Indeed, the Thirteenth

---

[27] Flores, "Mercy as a Public Virtue," 464.

[28] James F. Keenan, SJ, *Moral Wisdom: Lessons and Texts from the Catholic Tradition*, 3rd ed. (Lanham, MD: Rowman & Littlefield, 2017), 98–100.

[29] For example, in 2014 dollars incarcerated people had a median annual income that was 41 percent less than nonincarcerated people of similar ages. Bernadette Rabuy and Daniel Kopf, *Prisons of Poverty: Uncovering the Pre-Incarceration Incomes of the Imprisoned*, Prison Policy Institute (July 2015).

Amendment to the US Constitution still affirms criminal punishment as the one exception to the prohibition of slavery. Our nation has accepted all sorts of affronts to basic goods for currently and formerly incarcerated persons. Life itself is attacked by capital punishment and life sentences (that is, death by incarceration). There is forced separation from families, rendering those families vulnerable to economic hardship and trauma and even causing changes in children on the genetic level similar to the profound effects from the death of a parent.[30] There is widespread voter disenfranchisement and legalized discrimination in employment and housing. It is all too clear that mass incarceration functions through the lens of differentiating, not unifying, sin. As Michelle Alexander remarks, "Criminals are the one social group in America that nearly everyone—across political, racial, and class boundaries—feels free to hate."[31] Resisting this is the mercy practiced by the Good Samaritan, a mercy that defies stigma and otherness, proclaiming that no one is beyond the scope of our concern.

Mercy also calls for empowerment and inclusion, and thereby opposes essential features of mass incarceration. As exorbitant numbers of men and women are locked in prisons or cycled through jail doors, the warehousing of human beings follows the logic of incapacitation, purporting to control crime through physical removal and the severe diminishment of the capacity to act. Danielle Sered, founder of an alternative-to-incarceration and victim-service program called Common Justice, observes that the "prison takes away the very power people should be obligated to use to make things right."[32] While society may be reluctant to empower those who have previously used their power to harm, the virtue of mercy confirms that such empowerment is necessary to live out our siblinghood.[33] In addition, mass incarceration's myths of differentiating sin and permissible marginalization are opposed by the radical inclusion of the virtue of mercy. Prison and its post-release consequences are legally and culturally approved vehicles of exclusion and stigma, implying that marginalization can be both beneficial and permissible. However, Catholic tradition is clear that exclusion is a grave threat; individual flourishing relies on relationality and participation in the community. As Pope Francis has made clear in his frequent critique of "throwaway culture," no member of society is ever disposable.

---

[30] Colter Mitchell et al., "Father Loss and Child Telomere Length," *Pediatrics* 140, no. 2 (August 2017).

[31] Michelle Alexander, *The New Jim Crow: Mass Incarceration in the Age of Colorblindness* (New York: New Press, 2012), 216.

[32] Danielle Sered, *Until We Reckon: Violence, Mass Incarceration, and a Road to Repair* (New York: The New Press, 2019), 94.

[33] Keenan, "The Evolution of the Works of Mercy," 40.

The exclusion of an individual cannot protect the community but always impoverishes and injures it.

Keeping in view the social injustices, the obliteration of human bonds that ought to keep us connected, and the disempowerment and marginalization, it is incredibly challenging to practice mercy. Our tendency to shy away from culpable chaos makes sense as a coping mechanism, if nothing else. And yet, an enthusiastic embrace of culpable chaos is demanded. Margaret Farley identifies one work of mercy—forgiveness or bearing all injuries—as especially relevant for the twenty-first century. She describes this as a highly active work that involves a decision "to accept anew the ones by whom we have been harmed."[34] Farley confronts the difficult questions directly, asking about situations when the injury continues to be perpetuated, when no remorse is present, and when oppressors consider their actions justified.[35] Her answer is what she refers to as "anticipatory forgiveness." In situations of "ongoing humanly inflicted evil and suffering, there is a call to forgive those who you also must continue to resist."[36] This aptly captures how the virtue of mercy can begin a response to mass incarceration. In fact, the only resistance against harm that is likely to be effective is the one enacted while standing in solidarity within the chaos.

Through practicing the virtue of mercy, we may arrive at the conclusion that punishment itself is unacceptable. To this end, there are instructive categories offered by Thomas Aquinas from his reflections on fraternal correction. Aquinas suggests that fraternal correction is an act of charity when it considers sin as harmful to the sinner, but that such correction is an act of justice when it considers sin as harmful to others and to the common good.[37] It is noteworthy that punishment is not recommended for the first type of fraternal correction, a correction that aligns itself with goals of rehabilitation and successful reentry. As an act of charity, the sinner is only to be addressed with warnings. Punishment is only viable for the second type of correction, which seeks to address the harm done to others since punishment deters through fear.[38] Punishment is impotent, it seems, to address the sinner's self-inflicted chaos. And so, the practice of mercy reveals the inadequacy of punishment. If we enter into the chaos—the culpable chaos—of another, our task is to respond to the suffering found there. We cannot decline to take action through the convenient conclusion that suffering is simply good for the person. As Sered argues, punishment cannot actually provide the transformation of behavior and healing of harm

---

[34] Farley, "Mercy and Its Works," 38.
[35] Farley, 39.
[36] Farley, 39.
[37] Aquinas, *Summa Theologiae*, II-II.33.1.
[38] Aquinas, *Summa Theologiae*, II-II.33.3.

that we seek—only accountability can do that.[39] At the end of the day, punishment—mass incarceration—abandons people to chaos and heaps more chaos on top. To hold another person accountable is a correction born of charity; it is an act of mercy that can only be accomplished by entering into chaos and fearlessly taking on its horrors.

There are several ways that it is dangerous to appeal to mercy as a response to mass incarceration. Yet Keenan's take on mercy can address all of these. First, the language of mercy (often heard as an alternative to justice) can make its hearers *more likely* to see the world through the lens of the deserving and undeserving. The wisdom of Keenan's chaos language is essential. Mercy is a willingness to enter and respond to problems and chaos simply because they are problems and chaos. Mercy insists that questions of fault can only be addressed after we have an intimate understanding of the needs. This means institutions and policies must be driven by humanity rather than guilt or innocence.

Second, there is a risk that mercy will invite responses to immediate needs and focus less on uncovering and dismantling unjust systems that create those needs. Indeed, Mescher notes that the documents of Catholic social teaching do not consistently connect mercy to work for social justice.[40] Yet Keenan suggests that in real merciful engagement we will come to face what causes the chaos of another.[41] Not only will we come to see and understand systemic causes, but we will be led to try to articulate and implement alternative structures. The felt human solidarity that prompts merciful action is in fact the underlying principle of the works of justice.[42]

Third and finally, appeals to mercy can distract us from our own complicity in creating chaos for others. Mercy tempts us when we seek our own righteousness as bestowers of mercy (likely in situations of differentiating sin). Yet a true movement of solidarity demands self-reflection. Self-reflection leads us to recognition of unifying sin where no one is righteous. Keenan emphasizes that it is knowing oneself as a sinner that makes it possible to admonish the sinner and endure wrongs without arrogance or moral superiority.[43] In entering the chaos and seeing it for what it is, we will not only be able to acknowledge our complicity but also begin to resist it.

Moving around a huge prison cell block one Ash Wednesday, I simply offered a warm smile and the ashes from which we were all made and to which we will all return. My movements and activities were not unusual for a lay Catholic chaplain. But the officers kept warning me to be more careful,

---

[39] Sered, *Until We Reckon,* 59.

[40] Mescher, "Mercy," 254.

[41] Keenan, *Moral Wisdom,* 103.

[42] Keenan, "Radicalizing the Comprehensiveness of Mercy," 197.

[43] Keenan, *The Works of Mercy,* 77.

less trusting. Should I have had more fear in my eyes, more chastisement, more condescension? It was as if safety could be found by holding back on another's full humanity. The officers preferred the hermeneutic of suspicion prior to the hermeneutic of siblinghood. Over the years some incarcerated people did attempt to manipulate me (though far less often than I experienced on the outside), but my desire to encounter the incarcerated person as person *did not* make me especially vulnerable to that manipulation. Privileging humanity doesn't mean one is naive about human brokenness or the reality of deception and harm. However, to perceive a human being *in the first place* as a threat, to place menace *before* all other identifiers, to put fear *out ahead* of the outstretched hand—that is the surest recipe for dehumanization. In teaching countless students, audiences, and readers about mercy, Fr. Jim Keenan has given a lesson in how to become more human and how to imitate our God. It is a lesson that reveals the nonsense of speaking of being worthy or unworthy of mercy. Mercy enters, acts, rescues, and empowers. And nothing short of this can address the chaos of mass incarceration.

8.

Vulnerability and Hospitality

Ethical Reflections on Forced Migration during the COVID-19 Pandemic in India

John Karuvelil, SJ

Introduction

On the evening of March 24, 2020, at 8 pm, the government of India ordered a three-week nationwide lockdown of the country—starting at midnight[1]—as prevention against the spread of the COVID-19 pandemic. There was just four hours for people to get back to their homes and villages, because at midnight everything would come to a standstill. After midnight people and vehicles were not to venture out, except for emergencies. The announcement was a bombshell for the more than sixty million migrant laborers in India who move from state to state for their livelihood.[2] A huge majority of them were thousands of miles away from their homes. They were not prepared for this, for they had neither the means to stay on where they were, in the far-flung cities and states, nor the means to travel back home. What happened after the lockdown order will remain as one of the most painful and dark periods in the history of Independent India, a period "reminiscent of the Partition exodus in 1947, minus pervasive communal

---

[1] Jeffrey Gettlman and Kai Schultz, "Modi Orders 3-Week Total Lockdown for All 1.3 Billion Indians," *The New York Times*, March 24, 2020.

[2] David N. Gellner, "The Nation-State, Class, Digital Divides and Social Anthropology," *Social Anthropology* 28, no. 2 (2020): 270.

massacres, but with random and callous police harassment"[3] and numerous avoidable deaths.

Reading the horrid stories of the migrants struggling to sustain their very lives—fighting hunger and thirst, the brutality of the police, the callous attitude of many state governments toward allowing their own migrant workers back, the dead silence of the central government and even the courts, and at the same time the few overstretched, concerned humanitarian nongovernmental organizations (NGOs) and volunteers with their limited means—what struck me were two words. Rather, they were virtues proposed by the world-renowned moral theologian James F. Keenan: *vulnerability*[4] and *hospitality*,[5] virtues that we all need to develop, especially those in authority. This essay analyzes the situation of the migrant laborers, describes the pain and suffering they had to undergo, and then proposes these two virtues of vulnerability and hospitality to help avoid such human-made catastrophes in the future.

Migrants during COVID-19 in India

People take the risk of migrating when they are left with no options to advance their lives where they live. They migrate to seek new opportunities and welfare for themselves and their families. Migrants can be categorized as voluntary migrants or forced migrants (refugees), and as internal migrants or international migrants. According to the 2011 census, India has approximately 455 million migrants.[6] The 2017 Economic Survey of India estimated there to be 60 million interstate migrants in India.[7] A majority of these migrant laborers come from the poorest states in the country, Uttar

---

[3] Gellner, 270.

[4] See James F. Keenan, "Linking Human Dignity, Vulnerability, and Virtue Ethics," *Interdisciplinary Journal for Religion and Transformation in Contemporary Society* 6 (2020): 56–73; Keenan, "The World at Risk: Vulnerability, Precarity, and Connectedness," *Theological Studies* 81, no. 1 (2020): 132–49; and Keenan, "Vulnerability and Hierarchicalism," *Melita Theologica* 68, no. 2 (2018): 129–42.

[5] Keenan speaks of "Jesuit hospitality," which is different from traditional understanding of hospitality. See James F. Keenan, "Jesuit Hospitality?," in *Promise Renewed: Jesuit Higher Education for a New Millennium*, ed. Martin R. Tripole, 230–44 (Chicago: Loyola Press, 1999).

[6] Shailendra Kumar and Sanghamitra Choudhury, "Migrant Workers and Human Rights: A Critical Study on India's COVID-19 Lockdown Policy," *Social Sciences and Humanities Open* 3, no. 1 (2021).

[7] Asma Khan and H. Arokkiaraj, "Challenges of Reverse Migration in India: A Comparative Study of Internal and International Migrant Workers in the Post-COVID Economy," *Comparative Migration Studies* 9, no. 49 (2021): 1.

Pradesh (23 percent) and Bihar (13 percent).[8] The other North Indian states—Jharkhand, Orissa, Assam, and others—also have huge migrant populations working in major cities of the country, like Delhi, Mumbai, Pune, Bangalore, and Chennai, and in well-off states, like Kerala.

The migrant laborers are the backbone and the prime movers of the country's economy, working in rural farms and as daily wage earners in cities at construction sites, hotels, restaurants; as delivery personnel; at hair-cutting salons; making or repairing automobiles; plumbing; delivering newspapers; and so on.[9] Escaping poverty in their native villages, they migrate to the cities or to better-off states, where they often live in ghettos or in congested urban slums, aspiring to upward mobility and saving their far-off families from the clutches of hunger. This workforce of millions is, unfortunately, neither organized among its members nor counted or taken seriously by any government agency, leaving these workers without any protection from any level of government or the legal system. The majority have had no formal education or training and belong to the most deprived communities. Since they have neither the protection of unions nor of any level of government, they are employed without work contracts and are denied the basic minimum wages stipulated under the Minimum Wages Act[10] that protects employees from exploitation by employers.[11] They are forced to work under hostile and unfavorable working conditions and lack access to all social and worker-welfare schemes.[12] In the 2020 lockdown, these approximately sixty million internal migrant workers bore the brunt of the completely ill-conceived, arbitrary and inhuman decision of the democratically elected government.[13]

---

[8] Chitranjali Negi, "Human Rights Violations of Migrant Workers in India during COVID-19 Pandemic," *SSRN Publications*, June 18, 2020.

[9] Soutik Biswas, "Coronavirus: India's Pandemic Lockdown Turns into a Human Tragedy," *BBC News*, March 30, 2020.

[10] Negi, "Human Rights Violations of Migrant Workers in India during COVID-19 Pandemic."

[11] For details on minimum wage, see "What Is the Minimum Wages Act?" *Legal India*, May 21, 2022.

[12] Sanjib Kumar Das, "COVID-19: The 'Invisible' Indians: Story of the 'Great Migration,'" *Gulf News*, May 20, 2020.

[13] Unfortunately, for some years now India's government refuses to give out data in matters that can affect its image, and what data is shared is often manipulated. Private agencies, which normally do a better job at collecting data, give varying figures. What I have provided here comes after consulting many reports. See Udit Misra, "Explainspeaking: What 2020 Taught Us about India's Internal Migration," *The Indian Express*, February 18, 2021; and J. Jesline et al., "The Plight of Migrants during COVID-19 and the Impact of Circular Migration in India: A Systematic Review," *Humanities and Social Sciences Communications* 8 (2021): 231.

India's Sudden Lockdown

The central government's sudden announcement of the three-week lock-down shocked the nation, especially the migrants. A fourteen-hour voluntary curfew had already been declared on March 22, 2020. Many business establishments, factories, eateries, and so forth, where many migrant workers were employed, had already closed down. The contractors, and other employers who had employed them had left the sites, and the workers, who were already living hand to mouth, were not paid, some for days and others for weeks. The instant lockdown across the country placed the people and the government in conflict. Researchers reported that "the agony, abandonment, worry, rage, suffering, frustration and adversities experienced and felt by the migrant workers are beyond conception."[14] As workplaces and transport services were shuttered, people were literally on roads, unable to stay back in their own shacks in slums and construction sites, with no money in their pockets, no food, no security of any sort, because they had not been paid and had no other savings or income. They could not go back to their own homes and villages because all transportation had come to a standstill. The outcome was an unprecedented humanitarian disaster where millions of poor migrants were stranded in cities at abandoned bus terminals and railway stations or forced to walk, cycle, bribe truck drivers, or to hitchhike home, often very dangerously at exorbitant fares, sometimes over distances of more than twelve-hundred miles, and on empty stomachs. The basic human right to get back to their homes unhindered was denied to them.

Insensitivity of the Government Administration

The ruthless enforcement of the lockdown was flawed from beginning to end. But what was unimaginable in a democratic society like India was the coming together of the legislative, judicial, and executive arms of government, supporting one another in unjust policy decisions. As the poor, hungry, exhausted migrants died like flies on the way, either from sheer hunger and exhaustion, or in accidents or from police brutality, the government not only enforced the ill-conceived, thoughtless, and unscientific lockdown, where police thrashed, harassed, and ill-treated thousands of migrants for

---

[14] Sakshi Sahni and Rawal Aulakh, "Impact of COVID-19 on Rural Migrants in India," in *Impact of COVID-19 on Rural India*, ed. R. K Sinha (New Delhi: Kalpaz Publications, 2020). Originally from G. R. Poornima and M. N. Kumar Suresh, "Corona India and Mass Migration: Unfolding Implications for the Present and the Future," *Mukt Shabad Journal* 9, no. 6 (2020): 1514.

daring to be on roads and attempting to cross state boundaries, but also remained a mute spectator even in the face of numerous avoidable deaths.[15]

The migrants were often left to the whims of police who mercilessly beat even disabled people.[16] In many parts of the country, police committed unspeakable crimes against the migrants. People were beaten to death, made to hop and crawl on roads in the hot summer heat and many were forced to commit suicide.[17] Most of those who bore the brunt of this brutality were the Dalit and Tribal migrants, those at the bottom of the socio-politico-economic ladder.[18]

Even more disheartening was the silence of the courts on grounds of noninterference in government policy matters.[19] Even the Supreme Court of India refused to entertain public interest litigation on the migrants' plight. Only after constant criticism from social activists, lawyers, and even retired judges did the Supreme Court recognize the plight of the migrant workers and ask the government to open up transportation for them. As a former chief justice said: "By effectively not granting any relief, the [Supreme] Court [was] denying citizens of the most fundamental right of access to justice, ensured under the Constitution. In doing so, it has let down millions of migrant workers, and failed to adequately perform as a constitutional court."[20]

Government Apathy and Loss of Lives

Fearing the brutish police force on highways, state entry points, and other roads, many migrants started walking on railway tracks to reach their destinations. When they were tired, they rested on the tracks, believing trains would not run because of the lockdown. As they dozed off on the railway tracks, dozens were run over by cargo trains and killed. Of the nearly one-thousand non-COVID deaths that happened during the lockdown, most were due to exhaustion, starvation, rail and road accidents, police brutality,

---

[15] Maria Abi-Habib and Sameer Yasir, "India's Coronavirus Lockdown Leaves Vast Numbers Stranded and Hungry," *The New York Times*, March 29, 2020.

[16] Abi-Habib and Yasir.

[17] C. Shastri, "Coronavirus Update: MP Tribal Beaten to Death by Police during Lockdown, Alleges Family," *Hindustan Times*, April 5, 2020. Negi, "Human Rights Violations of Migrant Workers in India during COVID-19 Pandemic"; and Abdul Alim Jafri, "UP: Dalit Youth Found Hanging from Tree after Allegedly Being Beaten Up by Cops," *News Click*, April 2, 2020.

[18] See B. Sivakumar, "Half of India's Dalit Population Lives in 4 States," *The Times of India*, May 2, 2013.

[19] Kumar and Choudhury, "Migrant Workers and Human Rights."

[20] Ajit Prakash Shah, "Failing to Perform as a Constitutional Court," *The Hindu*, May 25, 2020.

denial of timely medical care, and suicides.[21] As Kumar and Choudhury put it: "Some died ambulating, some died in accidents, some died of hunger, and some even committed suicide. The highways of the country were filled with woebegoneness, screams, and pain of migrant laborers."[22] Can one forget the pictures of persons on the road walking hungry for days, trying to eat the meat of a dead dog run over by passing vehicles, walking under a hot sun with frightening blisters under their feet, or children exhausted from heat and walking or sleeping on a suitcase pulled by their mothers on the road? Human agony rent the air along the highways of the country.

In stark contrast the same government sent special flights to various foreign countries to bring back stranded migrants, especially students and people on short-term work visas. It shows the government's priorities, especially to depict itself as good in the world's eyes. It is not a surprise that while the majority of India's poor struggled to survive during the pandemic with no income, India's top ten billionaires added 60 percent to their total wealth during the first twelve months of the pandemic and the same period gifted forty billionaires to the country.[23] Trampling on the rights of the poor, the marginalized, and minorities, the government also used the lockdown to silence and suppress political dissent, incarcerating social activists, journalists, and so on.[24] The case of Fr. Stan Swamy, a Jesuit priest and human rights activist, who was arrested and died in judicial custody, illustrates how the state suppressed dissent and victimized people.[25]

Only after the initial three-week lockdown was extended repeatedly and stretched on for months did the government finally allow a few special rescue trains. It imposed burdensome conditions for the migrants, however, including registering themselves online, getting COVID-negative certificates from government hospitals, obtaining police permission to cross borders, and more,

---

[21] Shreehari Paliath, "A Year after Exodus, No Reliable Data or Policy on Migrant Workers," *IndiaSpend*, March 24, 2021. See also Kabir Agarwal, "Not Just the Aurangabad Accident, 383 People Have Died due to the Punitive Lockdown," *The Wire*, May 10, 2020.

[22] Kumar and Choudhury, "Migrant Workers and Human Rights."

[23] Adam Tooze, "With the Adani Crisis, Is Narendra Modi's House of Cards at Risk?," *The Wire*, January 30, 2023. See also, Frontline News Desk, "Turmoil at Adani Group a Key Test for India Inc under Narendra Modi," *Frontline*, February 3, 2023.

[24] J. Pickard et al., "In-Focus: COVID-19, Uncertainty, Vulnerability, and Recovery in India," Brighton: Social Science in Humanitarian Action (SSHAP) (2020); Naomi Hossain et al., "The Last Days of Indian Democracy," *Institute of Development Studies*, August 14, 2020.

[25] Anto Akkara, "Indian Catholic Priest's 'Custodial' Death Stirs International Outcry," *National Catholic Register*, July 8, 2021. See also Niha Masih, "Hackers Planted Evidence on Computer of Jailed Indian Priest, Report Says," *Washington Post*, December 13, 2022.

all of which required smart phones and the knowledge to operate them, which the majority of these illiterate laborers did not have. In contrast, wealthier passengers who wanted to travel by upper-class trains simply had to buy the tickets online and get a temperature screening as they got onto the trains.[26] Additionally, many of these special trains got delayed for days, and some reached completely wrong destinations, causing more misery to the hungry passengers. At least eighty people died in these trains.[27]

Toward the end of March 2020, when the government announced a $22.5 billion relief package to support the millions who lost their jobs due to the lockdown, little did the government care that 80 percent of India's migrant workers are in the informal sector and have no real government-approved identification cards or certificates to access these benefits. The majority of these victims belonged to the lower social classes, especially the Dalits and Tribals, who make up the vast majority of the poor in India and about one-third of its population.[28]

Much more could be written on the exploitation of migrant laborers during the time of COVID-19, including the several state governments that increased the legal workday from eight to twelve hours with no extra payment,[29] loss of employment pushing people into further poverty and frustration increasing the suicide rate, and more tragedies. Instead, I concentrate on the cultivation of two virtues—vulnerability and hospitality—well explained by James F. Keenan, which could be a solution to such indifference, rejection, exploitation, suppression, and oppression that cause immense suffering to millions.

Vulnerability

Articulating the theological significance of vulnerability is not an original contribution of Keenan. As Keenan himself says, it had earlier been developed by people like Emmanuel Levinas, Enda McDonagh, Judith Butler, Linda Hogan, Roger Burggraeve, Vincent Leclercq, Erinn C. Gilson, Daniel J. Fleming, and others.[30] However, Keenan has dealt with the subject in much depth and detail. In developing an ethics of vulnerability, he, citing

---

[26] Kumar and Choudhury, "Migrant Workers and Human Rights."

[27] Milan Sharma, "80 Died on Shramik Trains for Migrants: Railway Officials," *India Today*, May 30, 2020.

[28] Govindasamy Agoramoorthy and Minna J. Hsu, "How the Coronavirus Lockdown Impacts the Impoverished in India," *Journal of Racial and Ethnic Health Disparities* 8 (2021): 2–3.

[29] For details, see Kumar and Choudhury, "Migrant Workers and Human Rights."

[30] Keenan, "The World at Risk," 136–40.

the works of Linda Hogan, Enda McDonagh, Margaret Farley, and others, states that vulnerability is a quality of God. Vulnerability characterizes God's ability to enter into the chaos of the world, its sufferings, helplessness, misery, or precarity, and respond to it. This engaging concept can be employed in a context like the dehumanizing situation the migrants faced in India during COVID-19. The ethics of vulnerability, as Keenan proposes, is an important tool to challenge today's world of exploitation, domination, and widespread injustice meted out to large sections of people who are poor and marginalized.

The Ethics of Vulnerability?

Although in general we use the term *vulnerability* to mean the state of being open to harm, here vulnerability means the capacity to enter the chaos of another person's life and respond to that situation positively. Keenan writes, "Comments on vulnerability might surprise the reader who thinks of vulnerability primarily as the condition that raises alarm, concern, or the need to protect."[31] For example, when one reads the parable of the Good Samaritan, it is normal to think of the wounded man as the vulnerable one. However, it is the Good Samaritan who is vulnerable to the condition of the wounded man. Keenan continues:

> This inversion about vulnerability mirrors the inversion in the same parable about the question of the neighbor itself: in answering the question, Who is my neighbor?, we think at the beginning of the parable that the wounded man is the neighbor, but by the end we agree with the scribe that the neighbor is the one who shows mercy. In a similar way the neighbor has gone from being object of concern to being responsive agent.[32]

Citing Enda McDonagh, Keenan asserts that vulnerability begins with God and not with us humans. "God reveals to us God's self as vulnerable by the very act of creation in which God lets the light be, life be, nature be, animal life and human life be. . . . This is a God who lets go and takes risks."[33] Keenan concludes, "Implicit in this then is the assumption that if God is vulnerable, then we in God's image are made vulnerable."[34] It is vulnerability that "defines and establishes us as creatures before God and

---

[31] Keenan, 138.
[32] Keenan, 138.
[33] Keenan, 136–37.
[34] Keenan, 137.

as ethical among one another."[35] This vulnerability makes us respond to the one who is in need of our attention and help, the precarious one. Therefore, "the word *vulnerable* . . . means being able to be wounded, then it means being exposed to the other; in this sense vulnerability is the human condition that allows me to encounter, receive, or respond to the other."[36] He continues: "Vulnerability is our nature; it is the condition for the possibility of our responding, of our being ethical. . . . Our vulnerability is what allows us to love."[37]

Citing Judith Butler, Keenan also distinguishes between the terms *vulnerability* and *precarity*:

> Vulnerability allows oneself to be at risk in response to others; but we should not think that vulnerability is always precarious. My openness to you is not always a fragile one, though I allow myself to be exposed to the other. In instances of responding to the other, I might still take risks, though even those risks themselves are not necessarily precarious.[38]

Explaining the term *precarity,* Keenan turns to the parable of the Prodigal Son, where the one who is actually vulnerable is not the son, but the father. The father in his vulnerability recognizes the precarity of the son from afar, runs to him, embraces him, and restores his sonship in the family. While the younger son suffers from precarity from his loose living, the elder son suffers from the precarity of resentment. The one who is able to enter into the precarity of both sons is the father who is vulnerable to them and who is able to anchor them back into his household.[39] Similarly, in the parable of the Good Samaritan, the Samaritan was the vulnerable one, and the one who lay by the wayside injured and bruised was the precarious one. Keenan writes:

> Being vulnerable, we have the capacity to encounter and respond to another whose vulnerability is precarious, and we can, in our own vulnerability, enter into the precarity of another. But my vulnerability is often present to me and others without any precarity. . . . So though we all are vulnerable, not all experience precarity.[40]

---

[35] Keenan, 139.

[36] Keenan, 138.

[37] Keenan, 139–40.

[38] Keenan, 141.

[39] Keenan, 141.

[40] Keenan, 141.

Vulnerability and the Migrant Crisis

I will attempt to apply vulnerability—understood as the capacity or ability to respond to the other in need—in the precarious context of the millions of migrant laborers who suffered and are suffering unjustly in the hands of an unfeeling government and its enforcers. If the latter ever had developed even a little of this virtue of vulnerability, with interdependency and relationality, thousands of lives could have been saved, thousands of families could still have their father or mother or children with them. The lives of these precarious ones did not matter to the callous ruling establishment.

Keenan points out that the tendency to dominate and exploit and to develop such indifference toward the poor and the marginalized is explained by psychoanalyst and feminist theorist Jessica Benjamin when she says that those who develop this particular tendency to ignore, ill-treat, and exploit others have abandoned their own vulnerability. An obvious example is in the context of men dominating women. Benjamin writes: "The process to develop domination is a twofold alienation. First, the male becomes alienated from his original vulnerable self. Second, he looks to dominate others, often women."[41] Or even more clearly, "Males as children are taught to abandon their own vulnerability and to develop instead a need to dominate."[42] This is perfectly applicable to the situation in India, where members of the upper castes and classes dominate, oppress, and exploit the poor, Dalits, and Tribals on a large scale. The alienation process, I think, is the same, a double alienation: alienation from their own vulnerability and then acquiring the tendency to dominate others. Therefore, if, as Keenan says, "Vulnerability is the capacity to be moral,"[43] India's government and all its administration have completely lost it. The situation is so severe that one can only hope that a mutual recognition and reconciliation can take place and the sense of vulnerability can be recovered so that India's leaders become more relational and moral.

Jesuit Hospitality

Another term that is important in this situation is *Jesuit hospitality*. Drawing on hospitality as understood and practiced in Jesuit spirituality and apostolic life, Keenan makes a clear and original proposal of Jesuit hospitality, which has distinct characteristics. Hospitality is a virtue with strong grounding in

---

[41] Keenan, 140.
[42] Keenan, "Vulnerability and Hierarchicalism," 137.
[43] Keenan, "The World at Risk," 140.

the scriptures. Keenan shows in his article "Jesuit Hospitality?" how God has been hospitable right from the time of creation, and how Jesus and the early church have been extremely hospitable.[44] However, with the distinct spirituality developed by Ignatius and his followers, Christians can appreciate hospitality in yet a new way.

In general, hospitality is the friendliness, welcome, attention, care, and generosity shown to another, a friend or stranger who visits the host. It involves attentiveness to the expressed and unexpressed needs and interests of the one who arrives. As Keenan points out, this is what we see in both the Old and New Testaments.[45] The Creator God, the Father, and the Redeemer God, the Son, are constantly seen as extremely hospitable. Inhospitality is condemnable and leads to damnation, as we see in the case of the people of Sodom. Hospitality was very much practiced in the early church, and the apostles, especially Paul, are seen constantly appreciating the hospitality of the various local churches. The early church also depended much on the hospitality of the elders and special patrons in whose houses the church assembly gathered for prayers and the breaking of the bread. Keenan clarifies that in all these instances hospitality is identified with a receiving church.[46] Also, this is the hospitality that is practiced by many religious congregations, including the Benedictines, Franciscans, Dominicans, and others.

Keenan distinguishes this type of hospitality, a receiving one where the guest, stranger or friend is received well and treated well, from Jesuit hospitality, which is identified with a "sending church." Jesuit identity and spirituality are associated with its mission, which is to go anywhere the greatest service of God and God's people is possible. Quoting St. Ignatius of Loyola and the *Constitutions of the Society of Jesus*, Keenan says that the Jesuit "vocation is to travel through the world and to live in any part of it where there is hope of greater service to God and of help of souls."[47] Again, "the aim and end of this Society is, by traveling through the various parts of the world at the order of the supreme vicar of Christ our Lord or of the superior of the Society itself, to preach, hear confessions, and use all the other means it can with the grace of God to help souls."[48] The fourth Jesuit vow, which authorizes the pope to send a Jesuit on mission to any part of the world, "is guarantor of that mobility 'for the greater good

---

[44] Keenan, "Jesuit Hospitality?"

[45] Keenan, 230–32.

[46] Keenan, 241.

[47] John W. Padberg, SJ, gen. ed., *The Constitutions of the Society of Jesus and Their Complementary Norms* (St. Louis: Institute of Jesuit Sources, 1996), no. 304, p. 128.

[48] Padberg, no. 308, p. 130.

of souls' for which the order was founded."[49] Keenan approvingly quotes Brian Daley's description of a Jesuit as "a kind of apostolic vagabond,"[50] one who goes wherever his mission calls him. "'Wherever there is need or greater utility for our ministries, there is our house.' We live wherever those in need live."[51] According to Keenan, this imitates the church of the apostles, where they traveled led by the Spirit and according to the needs and receptivity of the people. In summary, Jesuit "mission is to go to those most in need; we meet them as apostles of the church; where they are we dwell; and, from that dwelling place, we support those in need."[52]

Jesuit Hospitality and the Migrant Crisis

As mentioned earlier, during the acute migrant crisis, when people were on the road—on foot, on buses, on trains, and on bicycles and tricycles— the best the vast resourceful government machinery could do was remain a mute spectator to the tragedy it itself had sponsored and enforced. The result was the tragic loss of thousands of lives of the poor. The only help for the precarious multitude on the roads and at railway stations, bus stops, and parks came from the good Samaritans—NGOs and volunteers (which, of course, included many Jesuits and Jesuit institutions). Characteristic of Jesuit hospitality, these NGOs and hundreds of volunteers reached out to the needy where they were. Although the contributions of the NGOs and volunteers were like a few drops in the ocean, nonetheless their actions benefited thousands.

This cruel tragedy inspired me to reflect that the government could have done much to relieve the pains and anguish of these migrants if it had even a little bit of that spirit of Jesuit hospitality. While Jesuit hospitality would have been the ideal, any hospitality would have helped. However, that did not happen, and we have already seen the end result. With such a callous atmosphere prevailing in the country, the Jesuits would be well advised to improve their systematic organization of personnel and volunteers who have been beneficiaries of their numerous institutions and ministries, and also to get engaged in conscientization of the huge masses they come in contact with. Not only Jesuits themselves, but all partakers and recipients

---

[49] Originally from John W. O'Malley, "The Fourth Vow in Its Ignatian Context: A Historical Study," *Studies in the Spirituality of Jesuits,* 15, no. 1 (1983): 46–49. Quoted in Keenan, "Jesuit Hospitality?" 236.

[50] Originally from Brian Daley, "'In Ten Thousand Places': Christian Universality and the Jesuit Mission," *Studies in the Spirituality of Jesuits,* 17, no. 2 (1985): 3. See Keenan, "Jesuit Hospitality?" 236.

[51] Keenan, "Jesuit Hospitality?" 237.

[52] Keenan, 237.

of their ministry can practice the virtue of Jesuit hospitality. Although it is a herculean task, it is time that we reinvest in it that the future may be a little better.

Conclusion

In this essay I attempted to communicate the agonies faced by millions of migrant laborers in India during the COVID-19 pandemic. Certainly ordinary humans had little control over the millions of deaths resulting from the pandemic itself. However, in the case of migrant laborers in India's lockdown, the immense suffering endured by the people, and thousands of non-COVID deaths, could have been prevented or reduced if the government had taken steps toward practicing virtue rather than bullying the hapless migrants and trampling upon their basic human rights. I have proposed two virtues—vulnerability and Jesuit hospitality—which I have come to be familiar with through the writings of James F. Keenan, my doctoral guide at Boston College. Without a doubt, an approach of vulnerability and Jesuit hospitality would have assuaged the agony India's poor migrant laborers were forced to undergo during the COVID-19 pandemic.

9.

Virtues for Ordinary Christians . . . Continued

CONOR M. KELLY

Among the many contributions James F. Keenan has made to theological ethics, the one that is most closely associated with his name is the retrieval of virtue for Catholic moral theology. A natural extension of his doctoral research on the distinctions between goodness and rightness, virtue ethics provided the tools to shift the focus of analysis from the licitness of particular acts to the character of the moral agent.[1] This reorientation is recognized as the most consequential feature of the turn to virtue, but the retrieval of virtue ethics also had another profound implication with which the field of moral theology is still coming to terms. Precisely because virtue ethics calls attention to the actor more than the act, it underscores the importance of everyday decisions because every choice, even the most mundane, plays a role in the formation of one's character. As a result, virtue ethics is an excellent resource for a more holistic approach to the moral life, where the emphasis is not on the extraordinary moral quandaries that constitute the typical purview of academic analyses but rather on the ordinary questions regular humans face every day. While the field of virtue ethics is still embracing this potential, Keenan was quick to champion this asset from the start.[2] His 1996 book *Virtues for Ordinary Christians* examined this

---

[1] James F. Keenan, "Proposing Cardinal Virtues," *Theological Studies* 56, no. 4 (December 1995): 709–12.

[2] For an account of how the field grapples with everyday issues, see Daniel J. Daly, "Virtue Ethics and Action Guidance," *Theological Studies* 82, no. 4 (December 2021): 565–69.

question and introduced virtue as a foundational resource for disciples' duty to embody their faith throughout the whole of life.

In honor of Keenan's leadership as an "early adopter" of virtue's prospects for ordinary life, this chapter examines his vision of virtues for ordinary Christians and explores an extension of that vision to the current context. First, the chapter emphasizes Keenan's contributions to the work of everyday ethics. Then it employs the work of one of his students, Yiu Sing Lúcás Chan, to amplify the theological depth of virtue as a tool for ordinary ethics. Finally, it proposes three "primary" virtues for Christians' ongoing efforts to confront the challenges of ordinary life in the twenty-first century. The result is both a deeper appreciation of Keenan's original notion of the everyday potential of virtue ethics and a fuller realization of that potential.

The Dynamic Heart of *Virtues for Ordinary Christians*

As Keenan explains in *Virtues for Ordinary Christians*, the emphasis on virtue in everyday ethics is driven by an interest "not in whatever contemporary topic was dividing the church, but rather in what could be foundational for our family and community lives."[3] While this strategy ultimately generates a list of fifteen virtues that are essential for ordinary life—the three theological virtues of faith, hope, and love; the four traditional cardinal virtues of justice, temperance, prudence, and courage; and an added list of fidelity, self-esteem, hospitality, wisdom, gratitude, sympathy, humor, and physical fitness—Keenan's greatest contributions to the challenge of quotidian morality appear in the book's opening section, where he defends the applicability of virtue ethics for his project. There he notes that virtue is well suited to the ethical questions of ordinary life because it enlivens our consciences and recasts the work of Christian discipleship as a dynamic invitation to further growth. Before considering how we might extend Keenan's list for our new context more than twenty-five years later, I want to focus on these key insights first. They demonstrate what we have to gain by employing virtue as the foundation for everyday ethics, and they also show what we must preserve if we are to remain true to the spirit of Keenan's work while pursuing a faithful expansion that responds to the new questions of everyday ethics we face today.

---

[3] James F. Keenan, *Virtues for Ordinary Christians* (Franklin, WI: Sheed and Ward, 1996), vii.

As Keenan transitions from his introduction to virtue to the examination of specific virtues in *Virtues for Ordinary Christians*, he tellingly includes "A Dozen Questions about Conscience" as his pivot point. The rationale for this inclusion is not hard to discern. "The conscience is important," he clarifies, "because through it we respond to God's call to be a person. We are obliged to become the person God made us to be, and the only way we can understand who we are called to become is through the conscience."[4] As he notes earlier in the text, the conscience's role in helping us appreciate how God continually forms us is crucial, for "the call to be a Christian is the call to grow."[5] Whereas much of the academic framing of theological ethics at the end of the twentieth century, at least in the United States, stressed a view of the moral life oriented to the avoidance of sin, those who appealed to virtue made the choice to "attend, rather, to practices that can better form the pilgrim."[6] In this way virtue promotes a version of morality that is less about the things we must avoid and more about the positive practices that can help us address our deepest desire "to better [our] situation" and realize our full potential.[7]

As Keenan outlines, these distinctive traits make virtue a valuable resource for ordinary morality for two reasons. First, the emphasis on the invitation to growth is better suited to the complexities of everyday moral questions, which are "a lot more complex than the question 'to divorce or not to divorce,' 'to abort or not to abort,'" and similar topics that define quandary cases and presume a "right" answer.[8] Of course, these quandary cases are seldom as straightforward as they appear and, as scholars are keen to note, can even put people in a bind when all the available options for action are imperfect.[9] We cannot presume every quandary is black and white. Nevertheless, Keenan's point about the complexity of ordinary moral choices remains, for these decisions are complicated not only by the tensions of imperfection that constrain quandary cases but also by the challenge of competing goods. By prescinding from the articulation of abstract rules that are meant to apply in all situations, but which cannot anticipate all eventualities, virtue invites agents to confront the deeper question of "who do I want to become through these actions" and

---

[4] Keenan, 28.

[5] Keenan, 20.

[6] Keenan, 24; see also 10–11.

[7] Keenan, 11.

[8] Keenan, 15.

[9] For one discussion of these challenges, see Kate Jackson-Meyer, *Tragic Dilemmas in Christian Ethics* (Washington, DC: Georgetown University Press, 2022).

thereby empowers them to navigate the gray areas of ordinary morality in a way that can lead them to the growth God intends.[10]

Second, the process of relying on virtue in ordinary life is not merely oriented to growth but also facilitates that growth. In the Aristotelian understanding of virtue that has come to inform the Catholic moral tradition through Aquinas, the acquisition of virtue is an ongoing project. Hence, as much as "we acquire [the virtues] by first having actually practiced them," we are also better able to abide by the virtues once we have practiced them.[11] Illustrating this dialectic with respect to temperance, Aristotle explained that "we become temperate by abstaining from pleasures, and at the same time we are best able to abstain from pleasures when we have become temperate."[12] The result is that a virtue-based approach to ordinary life refuses to let agents accept stasis in their moral life and instead equips them to examine their progress in order to see where they can still grow. The more one progresses in virtue, the easier this evaluation will be, for the one who has prudence has an easier time making prudent decisions and the one who has humility is more honest in self-assessment. Just as important, the ongoing acquisition of virtue also makes it easier to take that next step in moral growth once the room for progress has been identified, because the just person has an easier time acting with justice, the compassionate person turns more readily to compassion, and so on. As a result, virtue ethicists talk about virtue perfecting our human nature, either in its capacities or in our relationships.[13]

Given these traits, virtue is ideal for the task of living more ethically in ordinary life, but it is noteworthy that this does not exhaust Keenan's claims about the usefulness of virtue for everyday morality. He does not assert that virtue is the key to a good life in general, but rather that it is the key more specifically to the good life as Christians have come to understand it in light of their faith in God. Keenan's appeal to virtue thus reflects not a philosophical project but a theological one. Therefore, before shifting gears to discuss how the same insights that motivated Keenan to list fifteen virtues can yield additional virtues for our efforts to "better [our] situation" today, I want to give more attention to the theological richness of his project.[14]

---

[10] On the limitations of abstract rules for all situations, see Thomas Aquinas, *Summa Theologiae*, I-II, q. 94, a. 4, c.

[11] Aristotle, *Nicomachean Ethics*, trans. H. Rackman (Cambridge: Harvard University Press, 1968), 1103a 32–33.

[12] Aristotle, 1104a 35–1104b 2.

[13] Keenan explains the distinctions between these two perfections in Keenan, "Proposing Cardinal Virtues."

[14] See again Keenan, *Virtues for Ordinary Christians*, 11.

The Theological Power of Virtue in Ordinary Life

As much as virtue is valuable for ordinary morality because of its emphasis on growth, attentiveness to complexity, and empowerment for progress, it is even more relevant for "ordinary Christians" because it has the potential to yield a theologically robust conception of the good life that supports every Christian's efforts to put his or her faith into practice. Certainly the call to growth provides one dimension of virtue's theological compatibility, for the Christian moral life is ordered to "that perfect holiness whereby the Father himself is perfect" (*Lumen Gentium*, no. 11), a benchmark that cannot tolerate a sense of static accomplishment and instead calls for dynamic maturation. The theological impact of virtue goes beyond this one connection, however, and includes both virtues oriented to theological ends and theological interpretations of what others, including non-Christians, would identify as "ordinary" virtues.

In Keenan's work the theological value of virtue is most evident in his decision to start the list of specific virtues with the theological virtues of faith, hope, and love. These virtues have been extolled by theologians for centuries, with Thomas Aquinas offering the strongest and clearest promotion of a distinct set of theological virtues that orient the human person to the "happiness [that] surpasses the capacity of human nature," which is to say God.[15] In his classic formulation the three theological virtues are specified as the divinely authored dispositions that perfect the intellect (faith) and the will (hope and love) so that humans can understand, pursue, and attain their proper theological end of union with God.[16] While Keenan is informed by this interpretation, he spends less time dwelling on the theoretical descriptions of the theological virtues and, consistent with his assertion that virtues are best understood "as practices," more time focusing on the ways one can embody faith, hope, and love in daily living.[17] Hence, faith is discovered in the invitation to remove our "masks" and confidently come before God as we truly are; hope is incarnated in the "wish to believe" when we are otherwise unconvinced of the persuasiveness of our beliefs; and love is embraced in the prioritization of our internal motivations so that we act on the ones that genuinely constitute our deepest desires.[18] Through these practices the theological virtues do not simply help us lead better lives through our everyday decisions, but they also help us grow in our

---

[15] Aquinas, *Summa Theologiae*, I-II, q. 62, a. 1, c.

[16] Aquinas, I-II, q. 62, a. 3, c.

[17] Keenan, *Virtues for Ordinary Christians*, vii.

[18] Keenan, 37–51.

relationship with God. Notably, this emphasis is a distinguishing feature of Keenan's approach to the theological virtues, for the link to practices treats the theological virtues quite similarly to the way the acquired virtues are understood. Other Thomistic moral theologians are typically more inclined to preserve a strict distinction—if not outright separation—between the acquired virtues and the infused theological virtues.[19] For Keenan, however, the debates about the origin of these virtues is secondary, because he would insist they are theological virtues first and foremost because they serve theological ends.

Virtue likewise supports the theological demands of the Christian moral life even when the virtues in question are not traditionally defined as theological ones. Keenan illustrates this potential in *Virtues for Ordinary Christians*, where, to give just a few examples, the virtue of fidelity is modeled on the way Jesus maintained his commitments to his friends and the virtue of hospitality is justified as crucial for Christians because it is "the virtue that God practices."[20] The fullest illustration of the theological promise of virtue ethics for everyday morality, however, can be seen in Lúcás Chan's integration of scripture and ethics through the lens of virtue. In his reflections on "ethics for real life," Chan builds on the work of his friend and mentor, Keenan, to identify the virtues that will enable Christians to embrace and embody the vision for the moral life found in scripture.[21] By grounding these reflections in the biblical texts of Exodus 20:2–17 (the Ten Commandments) and Matthew 5:3–12 (the Beatitudes), Chan presents even seemingly "non-theological" virtues like integrity as helpful dispositions that are ordered to the theological flourishing of the agent in relationship with God.[22] Chan's methodology is informative, as he exegetes the biblical text and then identifies a corresponding virtue that exemplifies the spirit of the text's moral command. After situating that virtue in the theological tradition, he articulates both practices that promote an agent's growth in that virtue and exemplars whose efforts to incorporate the virtue in their ordinary lives can serve as a model for Christians today.[23] With this strategy Chan supports Keenan's assertions that virtue is crucial for the theological questions of ordinary morality, not just the philosophical ones.

---

[19] For one contrasting approach, see William C. Mattison III, "Can Christians Possess the Acquired Cardinal Virtues," *Theological Studies* 72, no. 3 (September 2011): 558–85.

[20] Keenan, *Virtues for Ordinary Christians*, 61, 107.

[21] Yiu Sing Lúcás Chan, *The Ten Commandments and the Beatitudes: Biblical Studies and Ethics for Real Life* (Lanham, MD: Sheed and Ward, 2012).

[22] Chan, 203–7.

[23] Chan, xxi–xxii.

To give just one example from Chan's use of these categories, Christians can incorporate virtues like reverence and prudence into their relationship with their parents so that they can fulfill the Fourth Commandment's exhortation to "honor your father and your mother" (Ex 20:12). Specifically, they can use these virtues to prioritize their parents' well-being in a way that respects the parents' autonomy (reverence) while also preserving boundaries that might be required to help the adult children address their own limitations (prudence). Chan notes that Christians in particular can put these virtues into practice by incorporating forgiveness and reconciliation into their care for their parents, thereby preserving a relationship through its difficulties and frustrations. When they do persevere in this way, Christians are not simply showing an appropriate level of deference to their parents; they are also honoring their relationship with God insofar as "parents are the visible representatives of God."[24] The virtues thus empower Christians' efforts to fulfill the demands of their faith through ordinary practices, paving the way toward the very growth in holiness that orients the Christian moral life.

What Keenan's and Chan's work highlights, then, is that virtue can illuminate the path through daily life for ordinary Christians not in the abstract realm of ethical theory but in the very practical, messy world. In this concrete realm virtue provides the flexibility necessary to accommodate ambiguity and variation, the ambitious teleological vision needed to inspire growth, and the theological roots required to keep pilgrims on track toward their supernatural end. With these assets in mind, I would like to propose three virtues that deserve special importance in the ordinary life of Christians today.

Additional Primary Virtues for Ordinary Life Now

Virtue ethicists traditionally refer to the cardinal virtues as the ones that have central importance in the moral life, generating the classic list of prudence, temperance, fortitude, and justice. Keenan has reinterpreted this list in light of a relational anthropology and proposed self-care, fidelity, justice, and prudence as the guiding cardinal virtues for Christians.[25] Both lists are helpful for the moral life, but neither is sufficient alone. As Keenan notes, the cardinal virtues "do not purport to offer a picture of the ideal person nor exhaust the entire domain of virtue. Rather than being the last word

[24] Chan, 75, see also 73–79 more broadly.
[25] Keenan, "Proposing Cardinal Virtues," 723–24.

on virtue, they are among the first."[26] Consequently, while I wish to affirm the value of the cardinal virtues for ordinary morality, I also want to add another set of virtues that can be even more responsive to the immediate context in front of us. To give an example from the other side of virtue (that is, vice), Cathy Kaveny has demonstrated that while categories like intrinsic evil can indeed call attention to matters that we would recognize as always wrong, there are still times when we need to be more concerned with specific sins that do grave harm even though they do not show up on the list of expressly prohibited acts.[27] Likewise, the cardinal virtues will always provide clear guides to the practices that will serve our proper end, but there are also "lesser" virtues that will offer even more pertinent guidance in particular contexts, and we can think of these as the primary virtues necessary to do good in a certain time and place. The fact that these virtues have a more narrow, specific applicability does not render them less important for the moral life.

The first of these primary virtues for ordinary life today is humility, which provides a corrective to the vexing problem of polarization in civic life.[28] This polarization depends not merely on people staking out diametrically opposed positions, but also on hewing to those positions with a fierce tenacity. As a result, the "combatants" in a polarized culture war build their armor on an absolutized conviction of self-righteousness, preventing genuine discourse and corroding the common good.[29] The antidote to this posturing is humility, which requires an honest assessment of one's standing in the world. The virtue has deep theological roots, where this honest assessment begins with a recognition and acceptance of one's finitude before God.[30] Further strengthening the relevance for Christians, humility is extolled throughout scripture (for example, Zeph 2:3; Prov 11:2) and explicitly referenced as a defining trait of Christ, who is presented as an exemplar of humility (Phil 2:1–11).[31] Extended to the intellectual realm, epistemic humility allows us to see the actual rather than perceived quality of our arguments, opening the space for us to at least admit the *possibility*

---

[26] Keenan, 714.

[27] M. Cathleen Kaveny, "Intrinsic Evil and Political Responsibility," *America* 199, no. 13 (October 27, 2008): 15–19.

[28] Although polarization garners much attention in the US context, it is a larger global phenomenon. Thomas Carothers and Andrew O'Donohue, *Democracies Divided: The Global Challenge of Political Polarization* (Washington, DC: Brookings Institution Press, 2019).

[29] Richard R. Gaillardetz, "Reflections on Impediments to Synodality: Polarization and the Escalation of Conflict," *Worship* 96 (January 2022): 4–12.

[30] Chan, *Ten Commandments and the Beatitudes*, 164.

[31] Tyler R. Wittman, "Belonging to Another: Christ, Moral Nature, and the Shape of Humility," *Studies in Christian Ethics* 33, no. 3 (August 2020): 392–410.

that we could be wrong.[32] For Christians, this reevaluation can be a natural extension of the desire to subject one's judgments to the final authority of God.[33] In a world riven by polarized options, humility is the salve that can reorient us to the reality that we need one another, especially those whose perspectives are different from ours, if we ever wish to flourish as individual agents and as a community of persons. It must become the virtue par excellence for civic interactions in ordinary life.

Beyond polarization, another moral challenge for contemporary life is the pervasiveness of our entanglements in what theologians describe as structural sin. In an increasingly complex, globalized world, it is impossible for moral agents completely to disentangle themselves from the network of perverse incentives that facilitate, and ultimately encourage, the exploitation of others. The low-wage worker in the United States is required to buy a work uniform manufactured by laborers in sweatshop conditions in the Global South; the well-intentioned European donates old clothes to minimize environmental impact and inadvertently supports the shipment of textiles to African markets where they smother demand for locally made goods; and worse. As theological ethicists like Daniel Finn have argued, these interconnections are intrinsic to the way our world works now, and we have no real way to remove ourselves from the vicious "causal chain" that yields these problematic outcomes.[34] In the face of this reality we are tempted to abandon any effort to improve the world around us because the task seems hopeless. And yet our commitment to charity, which is supposed to motivate the virtuous life for Christians, prevents us from abandoning the work of justice, for to do so would be to abandon our neighbor in need. Perseverance, then, is a primary virtue for ordinary life because it can empower our efforts to reform the structures of sin that haunt our contemporary existence, ensuring both that we will not give up in the face of the intractability of these structural forces and that we will not succumb to the paralysis that can set in when we realize there is no way one person can tackle all the injustices. This is the trait encouraged in the eighth Beatitude ("Blessed are those who are persecuted . . . "), which extols "persisting in righteousness, doing the right thing, even when you are opposed" and frustrated by the seeming inefficacy of those efforts.[35] Perseverance puts these obstacles

---

[32] Lisa Fullam, *The Virtue of Humility: A Thomistic Apologetics* (Lewiston, NY: Edwin Mellen, 2009).

[33] Grant Macaskill, "Christian Scriptures and the Formation of Intellectual Humility," *Journal of Psychology and Theology* 46, no. 4 (Winter 2018): 243–52.

[34] Daniel K. Finn, *Consumer Ethics in a Global Economy: How Buying Here Causes Injustice There* (Washington, DC: Georgetown University Press, 2019), esp. 139–40.

[35] David W. Gill, "Eight Traits of an Ethically Healthy Culture: Insights from the Beatitudes," *Journal of Markets and Morality* 16, no. 2 (Fall 2013): 629.

in perspective and encourages us to redouble our pursuit of righteousness nonetheless, based on the realization that our inability to do everything is simultaneously the freedom "to do something and do it well."[36]

The structures of sin that necessitate perseverance also point toward a third primary virtue for ordinary life today: mercy. This virtue is one that Keenan promotes in his discussions of the moral life, but it did not receive full attention in *Virtues for Ordinary Christians*.[37] In the context of ordinary morality, the description of mercy I have in mind is the theologically robust one advocated by Pope Francis, who insists, "etymologically, 'mercy' derives from *misericordis*, which means opening one's heart to wretchedness."[38] The reason mercy is so valuable for today is due to its roots in the *heart*. Mercy strikes at our affections and invites us to feel the suffering of others as if it were our own. This compassionate disposition is an asset in a world where the technological mediation of the news means that we are at once more aware of the suffering of others across the world and paradoxically more inured to it. Our everyday lives thus lure us into a "globalization of indifference," in which the suffering of our neighbor is a fact we can intellectually acknowledge but a reality we consistently fail to feel.[39] In response to this reflexive distancing we need the virtue of mercy to trigger a genuine preferential option for the poor that is moved at the face of suffering rather than immune to it. With this virtue we can better imitate Christ, who "affirms mercy is not only an action of the Father, it becomes a criterion for ascertaining who his true children are" (*Misericordiae Vultus*, no. 9). For Christians, who are all called to embrace their identity as children of God, mercy truly is a primary virtue for everyday life.

Conclusion

As Keenan's entire corpus has shown (and continues to show), the virtues are apt guides for the day-to-day tasks that constitute the heart of the moral life. The primary virtues proposed here seek to capitalize on this insight, pointing toward practices that will help ordinary Christians live out the

---

[36] Kenneth Untener, "The Romero Prayer" (1979).

[37] James F. Keenan, *The Works of Mercy: The Heart of Catholicism*, 3rd ed. (Lanham, MD: Rowman & Littlefield, 2017).

[38] Pope Francis, *The Name of God Is Mercy: A Conversation with Andrea Tornielli*, trans. Oonagh Stransky (New York: Random House, 2016), 8. This language has notable echoes in Keenan's description of mercy as "the willingness to enter into the chaos of another." Keenan, *The Works of Mercy*, 5.

[39] Pope Francis, "Visit to Lampedusa: Homily of the Holy Father Francis," July 8, 2013.

fullness of their faith in ordinary circumstances. Operating at the service of the cardinal and theological virtues, humility, perseverance, and mercy combine to identify the starting point for the Christian's journey toward the *telos* that those classical virtues help us define. Significantly, each of these primary virtues is targeted at the specific challenges that constitute the most immediate threats to our flourishing now. They thus represent the very best of Keenan's vision for the virtues in ordinary life, as they connect us to our faith and help us better our situation in all its concrete complexity. I can think of no better way to honor his legacy.

10.

Growing in Christ

Liturgy and Virtue on the Road of Discipleship

Xavier M. Montecel

Throughout his career as a theologian, James Keenan has often called for building a bridge between moral theology and liturgical theology. This is but one expression of his essential conviction that the future of the church and of academic theology relies upon the bridges we build and our willingness to cross them. Keenan himself has contributed significantly to the establishment of bridges across cultural, geographic, confessional, ideological, and academic divides. In pursuing this work Keenan embodies the legacy of the teachers who formed him—a generation of moralists that established the foundations of a renewed Christian ethics, focused in part on the reintegration of ethics with other theological subdisciplines.

The relationship between ethics and liturgy is not the most ubiquitous theme of Keenan's work, but it is one of the most consistent and important. Following his early scholarship in bioethics, casuistry, and fundamental moral theology, Keenan's work turns toward emerging conversations in virtue ethics, and it is here that he ultimately articulates the interrelations among prayer, worship, liturgy, and the moral life. As I intend to show, Keenan imagines virtue as the bridge across which liturgical and moral theologians must travel in order to meet and learn from one another. An ethics of virtue provides, in his words, "a very comfortable passageway between ethics and liturgy."[1]

Virtue language provides a set of resources for theorizing the role of liturgy in the life of Christian discipleship. It is an idiom for expressing the relationship between what Christians do in their spiritual and religious practices and what they do in the broader pursuit of their Christian vocation. For Keenan, however, virtue is more than instrumentally useful. If we are to take seriously the application of virtue to Christian morality, we cannot fail to discuss our communities and their practices. We cannot avoid, therefore, a consideration of liturgy. Virtue is not just the glue that binds ethics and liturgy together for the purpose of interesting theoretical discussion. It is a lens that allows us to see that ethics and liturgy, properly considered, belong together in the first place.

In this essay I examine two essential dimensions of Keenan's thought on the relationship between moral theology and liturgical theology. First, I discuss his early insight that the moral life is a response to the spirituality that animates us, or more precisely, a response to the encounter with God that is the heart of prayer. As Keenan's work develops, this integral connection between spirituality and morality provides the foundation for a new bridge between liturgy and ethics. Concerning the human response to the divine encounter, Keenan particularly stresses the role of the virtues. In his view, the revelation of God in prayer is at the same time the revelation of ourselves and a call to embark on the pursuit of virtue. The human choice to accept this call is a choice for growth. This corresponds in Keenan's later work to the role of conscience in discipleship and the notion of sin as failure to bother to love.

Second, I discuss Keenan's vision of the moral life as progressive or developmental in nature. For Keenan, the human response to God has never been all or nothing. It is a process of growth that unfolds gradually. In his later writing on ethics and liturgy, he observes that moral progress is the result of an ongoing dialectic between ascertaining particular virtues that discipleship requires and the articulation of our anthropological vision. Our growth in virtue deepens our understanding of what it means to be human, and that deepened understanding calls us to grow further in virtue. According to Keenan, liturgy is precisely the space in which our understanding of our humanity in Christ is mediated communally, and so it is a touchstone for discipleship that is always on the way. I conclude

---

[1] James Keenan, SJ, "Dialectically Dynamic Teleologies: Ethics and Liturgy in the Key of Virtue," in *"Ahme nach, was du vollziehst": Positionsbestimmungen zum Verhältnis von Liturgie und Ethik*, ed. Martin Stuflesser and Stephan Winter, 23–36 (Regensburg: Verlag Friedrich Pustet, 2009), 24.

my reflection on Keenan's work with some comments on his Christology, his mystical view of discipleship, and possibilities for future work to build on his legacy.

Rooting Morality in Spirituality

It was a cloudy day in Munich when James Keenan decided to take a walk.[2] These were his years of study at the Gregorian University in Rome, and he had traveled to Germany for the summer to study and work in a local parish. On this particular day he was searching for a place to pray. It was a three- or four-mile walk to Dachau, where a fellow Jesuit had assured him there would be a convent chapel and a group of women religious willing to receive him. As he walked, the skies grew darker and so did his spirit. The crisp suburban landscape of Dachau bore no mark of the horror and violence that had happened there. A shining new church, painted entirely white, dared to suggest the presence of God in a town that had seemingly forgotten its own gruesome past and the tremendous guilt of its inhabitants. Keenan arrived, sweaty and angry, at the door of the convent, where one of the sisters rebuffed him. "We're closed; it's Monday." Raging now at the refusal of this place even to allow him to pray, Keenan began to retrace his steps. Walking again past the white church, he thought to himself with disgust, "I did not come to pray in the church where conspirers pray; I came to pray where the persecuted died."[3] Perhaps it was his desire to rest, or some other pragmatic consideration, but in spite of his objection the aspiration to pray won out. Keenan entered the doors of the church, where before him there appeared the figure of Christ crucified: a Jew, hanging not from a wooden cross but from a tangle of barbed wire. He realized that this town knew its guilt deeply, and now Keenan knew his guilt as well. Overwhelmed by shame for his own wickedness and shortsightedness, he began to pray.

What happens when we pray? When Keenan first shared this vignette, in a column for the journal *Church*, he intended it to illustrate the intimate bond between spirituality and morality. In the column Keenan suggests that when we pray we experience a revelation of ourselves as we truly are and at the same a revelation of God's tenderness. On that day Keenan met himself as a man filled with pettiness, selfishness, and judgment.[4] But he also met the presence of a compassionate God, who would not let him be lost.

---

[2] This vignette is taken from James Keenan, SJ, "Rooting Morality in Spirituality," *Church* 12, no. 4 (1996): 38–40.

[3] Keenan, 38.

[4] Keenan, 39.

To pray, Keenan insists, is to know our own badness and yet also to know that we are called and destined for something more. It is to experience the paradoxical blend of vulnerability and confidence that is the beginning of the moral life.[5] Out of spirituality, and the life of prayer in particular, there emerges the first step on the journey of growth into holiness.

Keenan goes on to propose three key notions at the axis of spirituality and morality. First, there is the encounter with God. Above all, prayer is a meeting with God as God, which reveals us to ourselves. It is an uncovering of our identity in its brokenness but also in its promise. For we know ourselves "as we are known" by the God we meet.[6] We walk away from prayer, therefore, with a responsibility to take action, to "see where we have been led and where we have chosen to go."[7] Second, there is movement or feeling. Feeling is constitutive of prayer, and each person feels the presence and action of God in an irreducibly distinctive way. The boundaries and practices that we place around prayer must not constrain the work of God but rather invite and celebrate it. As Keenan writes: "Where we feel the hand of God, we must let it touch, probe, lead. We must let God communicate Godself to us."[8] Third, there is God's providential presence. Prayer reveals God not as a harsh judge but as the cause of our hope, who guides us toward our redemption. However, we cannot be guided if we do not let ourselves be reminded, in prayer, that God is God. When we have learned in our spiritual life that God alone is God, who calls us to ourselves and to our neighbor, then on the basis of this calling the moral life can unfold.

In a follow-up column later that year Keenan provides more depth to the connection he envisions. Theological ethicists have often noted the rift between spirituality and morality that characterizes pre-twentieth-century moral theology.[9] Keenan himself has narrated how the early revisionists endeavored to repair this rift through appeals to historical context, scripture, the life of discipleship, and Christian personalism.[10] Especially worthy of

---

[5] Keenan, 39.

[6] Keenan, 39.

[7] Keenan, 39.

[8] Keenan, 40.

[9] I think especially of Richard Gula, who describes the relegation of interiority to spirituality and the split between moral theology and spirituality during the manualist period. See Richard Gula, *Reason Informed by Faith: Foundations of Catholic Morality* (Mahwah, NJ: Paulist Press, 1989), 7. Keenan himself offers a historical perspective on the relationship between spirituality and morality in James F. Keenan, "Ethics and Spirituality: Historical Distinctions and Contemporary Challenges," *Listening* 34 (1999): 167–79.

[10] James F. Keenan, SJ, *A History of Catholic Moral Theology in the Twentieth Century: From Confessing Sins to Liberating Consciences* (New York: Continuum, 2010). See also James F. Keenan, "Virtue, Grace and the Early Revisionists of the Twentieth Century," *Studies in Christian Ethics* 23, no. 4 (2010): 365–80.

note, for Keenan, is the call of the revisionists to reintegrate the act-analysis of moral theology with the concern for interiority in ascetical theology, particularly visible in figures like Odon Lottin and Gerard Gilleman.[11] However, even among the students of the revisionists, Keenan encountered suspicion toward a spiritualized view of morality. He recounts an exchange with his teacher Klaus Demmer. Rightly concerned with the particularity of moral experience, Demmer insisted that it was not an abstract notion of Christ's presence in our neighbor that should compel a moral response, but rather the need of this person in the concrete. We must love our neighbors as they are. Keenan responds that while we must certainly respond to the other in the concrete, we must also acknowledge the priority of God's initiative. Our response to the other in need is not the result of our own decision prior to the revelation of God that summons and empowers us. In fact, it is only because God has made us capable of compassion that we practice compassion, and it is only because God calls us that we answer.

The priority of divine initiative, then, is what renders the connection between spirituality and morality intelligible, and this yields a response-based model of the moral life. In prayer, God claims us. Having claimed us, God commands us to love God in return. Finding that in order to do this one must love the neighbor as oneself, we embark on the moral life. Keenan summarizes the point succinctly, "The entire business of being moral rests on God's concern for us."[12] We require, therefore, a morality based in spirituality. This will consist in a view of human life not in terms of the sin we should avoid, but rather in terms of what we should pursue in response to God, who has acted first. Of course, what we pursue is the life of discipleship striving toward holiness. Keenan's modeling of this pursuit in terms of a *response* to spirituality is distinctive and indicates the influence of such mentors as Joseph Fuchs and Bernard Häring.[13]

Keenan's response-based model of the moral life was further developed in his later work. For example, he ultimately came to emphasize the conscience as the foundation of moral accountability. Conscience is the place where a moral agent encounters God's personal presence and hears

---

[11] Concerning Lottin, see Keenan, *A History of Catholic Moral Theology in the Twentieth Century*, 41. Concerning Gilleman, see Keenan, 70.

[12] Keenan, "Rooting Morality in Spirituality," 39.

[13] For Häring's view of the moral life as a response to the gracious self-communication of God, see Bernard Häring, *The Law of Christ*, vol. 2, trans. Edwin G. Kaiser (Westminster, MD: Newman Press, 1963), 125–27. See also his concept of "social worship" in Bernard Häring, *The Sacraments in a Secular Age: A Vision in Depth on Sacramentality and its Impact on Moral Life* (Slough: St. Paul Publications, 1976), 106. In Fuchs, I believe human responsivity resides in his treatment of the fundamental option. See, for example, Joseph Fuchs, "Basic Freedom and Morality," in *Human Values and Christian Morality* (Dublin: Gill and Macmillan, 1970), 92–111.

the call to growth. On the basis of conscience the human person responds to the divine initiative and embarks on the adventure of the moral life. It is only through the mediation of the conscience, always in the process of formation, that we can shape a response appropriate to the particulars of our moral situation.[14] Conscience is the territory where spirituality (our experience of the divine initiative) and morality (our response to that summons) converge. Keenan's notion of sin as the failure to bother to love also fits within his response-based paradigm. In Keenan's thought, sin does not reside in wrongful action. It resides, more precisely, in the failure of persons to respond appropriately to the call that claims them. Sin is the failure to strive for the good, the failure to bother to love. It arises from a posture of complacency and self-satisfaction that sees no reason to push forward. For Keenan, we sin not because we were too weak to resist temptation, but because we were strong enough not to answer the voice of God calling us to holiness.[15]

Ultimately, Keenan appeals to virtue ethics in order to articulate the substance of the human response to God. By the late 1990s, he had already made significant contributions to the retrieval of virtue in Catholic theology and ethics.[16] In 1997, Keenan ultimately brought virtue into conversation with his reflections on spirituality and morality in an article entitled "Catholic Moral Theology, Ignatian Spirituality, and Virtue Ethics."[17] Here Keenan takes his cue from Norbert Rigali, one of his favored resources on the connection between spirituality and morality. "In a word," writes Keenan, "the moral life could be a virtuous response to a spirituality that animates us both individually and communally."[18] He examines the work of three English Jesuits—John Mahoney, Thomas Slater, and Robert Persons, the last of whom developed a great spiritual work out of Ignatius's *Exercises*. The genius of Persons was his desire to locate the sickness of sin not in external actions but in "the negligent, unthinking, ungrateful heart."[19] What he offers, for Keenan's purposes, is a bridge between Ignatian spirituality and virtue ethics.

---

[14] See, for example, James F. Keenan, SJ, "Conscience," in *Moral Wisdom: Lessons and Texts from the Catholic Tradition*, 3rd ed. (Lanham, MD: Rowman & Littlefield, 2017).

[15] James F. Keenan, SJ, "Sin," in *Moral Wisdom*.

[16] Space does not permit a complete list of contributions, but one key highlight is the first publication of "Proposing Cardinal Virtues" in the Winter 1995 issue of *Theological Studies* 56, no. 4 (1995): 709–29.

[17] James F. Keenan, SJ, "Catholic Moral Theology, Ignatian Spirituality, and Virtue Ethics: Strange Bedfellows," *Supplement to the Way: Spirituality and Ethics* 88 (1997): 36–45.

[18] Keenan, 36.

[19] Keenan, 40.

Keenan concludes the essay by proposing ten essential points for sealing the connection between the Ignatian spiritual tradition and virtue. These are the priority of the spiritual; morality as a response; deep interiority; the uniqueness of the individual; the need for self-examination; an ongoing task; exercises; a prudent director; an appreciation for human feeling; and a vision of the end.[20] For Keenan, these elements indicate virtue ethics as the idiom in which the moral life is articulated, precisely as a response to the spirituality that animates us. The life of virtue is the human answer, always unfinished, to the encounter with God at the heart of spiritual experience. The virtues enable us, in the space of the particular, to embody a response to that summons experienced in prayer.

It is not long before this implementation of virtue ethics leads Keenan to a consideration of liturgy. This is not simply because liturgy is a kind of prayer, that might give rise to a moral response, but rather because liturgy is a practice belonging to a moral community. Virtue ethics cannot conceive of moral development for the individual apart from the context of community and its practices. As such, Keenan turns to his own community, the church, and its core religious practice, the liturgy. Motivated by the essential insight that "what we do as church shapes us as church," Keenan wonders what it might mean to examine liturgy ethically.[21] He references the driving question behind the book he edited with Joseph Kotva, *Practice What You Preach*.[22] What happens when we ask of our ecclesial practice, "Is it ethical?" According to Keenan, we find the answer by attending to the ways in which liturgy shapes us in virtue. Virtues do not emerge spontaneously; they are formed through practice. Keenan turns to three moments of liturgical practice that shape Catholic moral character: the Entrance Rite, the Liturgy of the Word, and the Eucharist.

Thus, Keenan's analysis focuses specifically on the pedagogical dimension of liturgy. "The eucharistic liturgy," he writes, "is a training ground that helps people enter into union with God."[23] He identifies the various ways that elements of the liturgy lead people into different possible experiences of God. During the Entrance Rite, marking ourselves with the sign of the cross is a profound reminder of our need for God's mercy. God is revealed as the one whose very nature is mercy, and we are revealed as creatures

---

[20] Keenan, 41–43.

[21] James F. Keenan, SJ, "Morality and Liturgy: The Entrance Rite," *Church* 15, no. 3 (1999): 40–41.

[22] James F. Keenan, SJ, and Joseph J. Kotva, Jr., eds., *Practice What You Preach: Virtues, Ethics and Power in the Lives of Pastoral Ministers and Their Congregations* (Franklin, WI: Sheed and Ward, 1999).

[23] James F. Keenan, "Morality and the Liturgy of the Word," *Church* 15, no. 4 (1999): 41.

standing in need of that mercy. We are urged to let God be God.[24] The Proclamation of the Word and preaching immerse us in the story of Jesus and invite us to let it challenge us: to put down our convenient narratives that have domesticated God and to let the vulnerability and costliness of our redemption reach us.[25] During the Eucharist we become participants in the drama of salvation history made present here and now. We are reminded of God's immense mercy and called to practice mercy ourselves.[26]

Keenan's work at this stage parallels the efforts of Protestant thinkers like Stanley Hauerwas and Donald Saliers to explicate the ways communal worship forms Christians ethically.[27] It also anticipates the later scholarship of theologians like M. Therese Lysaught, who examines the embodied dimensions of eucharistic liturgical formation.[28] Like these writers, Keenan offers less attention to any negative dimensions of moral formation in liturgy than to its positive effects. In other words, this body of work tends to presume that liturgy forms us well or at least for the better, opening us to the mystery of our salvation in God. A more critical posture is indicated in his work with Joseph Kotva in *Practice What You Preach*, and it emerges most fully, I believe, in his most recent work on the vice of hierarchicalism.[29] There is much work to be done to build on this legacy and to examine the specter of liturgical vice, leading toward a liturgical ethics and an understanding of the bond between spirituality and morality that is critical, creative, and hopeful.

Discipleship and Development

For Keenan, the foundation of the bridge between ethics and liturgy is the bond between spirituality and morality. The framework of the bridge itself

---

[24] Keenan, "Morality and Liturgy: The Entrance Rite," 41.

[25] Keenan, "Morality and the Liturgy of the Word," 41.

[26] James F. Keenan, "Morality and the Liturgy of the Eucharist," *Church* 16, no. 1 (2000): 38–39. For more on Keenan's understanding of memory in relation to spirituality, see James F. Keenan, "The Powerful Role of Memory in Spirituality and Ethics," *Church* 22, no. 3 (2006): 44–45, 47.

[27] See especially Stanley Hauerwas, *A Community of Character: Toward a Constructive Christian Social Ethic* (Notre Dame, IN: University of Notre Dame Press, 1981); and *Character and Christian Life: A Study in Theological Ethics*, 3rd edition (San Antonio, TX: Trinity University Press, 1985). See also Don E. Saliers, "Liturgy and Ethics: Some New Beginnings," in *Liturgy and the Moral Self: Humanity at Full Stretch Before God: Essays in Honor of Don Saliers* (Collegeville, MN: The Liturgical Press, 1998), 15–35.

[28] M. Therese Lysaught, "The Eucharist as Basic Training: Liturgy, Ethics, and the Body," in *Theology and Lived Christianity*, ed. David M. Hammond (Mystic, CT: Twenty-Third Publications, 2000): 257–86.

[29] James F. Keenan, SJ, "Hierarchicalism," *Theological Studies* 83, no. 1 (2022).

is a progressive or developmental paradigm of the moral life. For Keenan, the human response to God has never been all or nothing. The pilgrimage toward the fullness of our humanity in Christ is always in progress, and our character is always under construction. Sometimes there are clear steps forward, and sometimes clear steps backward. There are detours and surprises in pursuit of the good. From a theological standpoint, one might say that holiness, while certainly realizable here and now, is still always on the way.

What is the role of liturgy or worship in the journey of discipleship? Keenan pursues this question in a 2009 essay entitled "Dialectically Dynamic Teleologies." He begins by pointing out that the virtues are heuristic guides that enable us to make progress toward the right realization of our human identity. They are heuristic because they are teleological; that is, their content is defined by their goal. Inasmuch as the goal itself remains dynamic and outstanding, so too do the virtues. We find ourselves, therefore, in a process of evolution and development. Keenan writes:

> The dynamic interplay between who we are and who we can becomes plays itself out then in this: that as we develop and become more virtuous, our understanding of the virtues, in turn, develops. As we become more realized, we become more aware of the scope of our capabilities. As we attain our horizons, our horizons expand.[30]

The acquisition of the virtues is a historically dynamic process. Moreover, an anthropological vision evolves alongside and together with this process of development. As we grow in virtue, our understanding of human identity—what it is capable of and what it requires—also develops. This widened anthropological vision, in turn, requires the specification of new virtues. A genuine dialectic emerges in which our growth in character and the evolution of our vision of humanity mutually influence each other and draw each other forward.[31]

Of course, Keenan points out, human identity is never solitary. Our personal or individual identity takes its meaning from the larger narrative framework provided by a community and its practices. We determine our anthropological vision and expand, amend, and reformulate our virtues as members of a corporate whole. This brings Keenan into the theological territory of liturgy and the Christian experience of moral development. For Christians, he observes, the point of reference for anthropology is Christ. The revelation of Jesus Christ is the revelation of our humanity in

---

[30] Keenan, "Dialectically Dynamic Teleologies," 24.

[31] Keenan offers further reflections on the hermeneutical structure of this process in conversation with Thomas R. Kopfensteiner, "The Metaphorical Structure of Normativity," *Theological Studies* 58 (1997): 331–46.

its promise and perfection. Christ is our *telos*, our destiny, our standard, our goal. Klaus Demmer insists, however, that our ability to understand this revelation of Christ hinges on our ability to understand moral truth. We cannot apprehend Christ as the embodiment of our anthropological vision unless we are capable of understanding that we are called to this destiny and must follow. To know Christ is to follow Christ, and so we are drawn again into a historically dynamic dialectic:

> As we follow him, we grow concomitantly in our ability to understand him, to hear his call again, to follow him, to understand him yet again as we do, so that we may know what he asks of us.[32]

For Keenan, the role of liturgy in this ongoing process of growth in discipleship is to mediate our understanding of Jesus Christ through the community of faith. It is only in this community and in its celebration that we can adequately appropriate a Christian anthropological vision and grow, little by little, in our ability to see. As we worship together, our understanding of Christ deepens alongside and in partnership with our self-understanding as his disciples.

This entire process is articulated, according to Keenan, in the key of virtue. We grow in Christian virtue and our understanding of Christ, our *telos*, expands. On the basis of that ever-expanding understanding, we revise and reformulate our virtues. All of this is sustained by our liturgical practice as a community of faith. Keenan summarizes the contribution of virtue ethics succinctly and ties together ethics and liturgy definitively:

> Virtue ethics thus provides a bridge for us in this: we can only become ethical if we embody the right virtues. We can only know which virtues are right, if we know who the revealed Christ is. We can only receive that understanding if we are a community of faith which is constituted as such in the liturgy. In short, in the liturgy we effectively mediate our moral becoming as we participate in the self-understanding of Jesus.[33]

To grow in virtue, then, or to progress in discipleship is more than simply to behave well or to act as God desires. It is rather to allow ourselves, in community and nourished by liturgy, to be inducted into Christ's own self-understanding. It is to be conformed to the mind of Christ, to make Christ in a total and all-embracing way the frame of reference for our humanity.

---

[32] Keenan, "Dialectically Dynamic Teleologies," 28.
[33] Keenan, 31.

In his teaching and writing, Keenan frequently credits Fritz Tillmann as the progenitor of the modern emphasis in moral theology on disciple-ship.[34] It seems to me, however, that Keenan, particularly in his work on ethics and liturgy, has progressed beyond Tillmann and beyond the typical model of discipleship, pushing this paradigm into genuinely new territory. By framing discipleship as a process of coming to share in Christ's own self-understanding, Keenan adds to the usual mimetic approach an arguably mystical dimension. Virtue ethics, applied to Christian morality, can easily flatten our Christology. It can render Jesus Christ as our moral exemplar and nothing more. For Keenan, however, Christ is not primarily an ethical ideal to imitate but rather the *telos* itself toward which and into which we are drawn:

> Jesus Christ, however, is not primarily a model. Rather, he makes possible the possibility of our following in his footsteps. He is our end, but by his death and resurrection he has constituted us as his brothers and sisters. He has made us new and it is in understanding him that we become his disciples. He uplifts our understanding of who we can become. He is the possibility of our expectations for ourselves as people.[35]

Not just our teacher, our guide, or our paragon, Jesus Christ in Keenan's thought is our destiny and our true identity. We are not just students of the master but participants in his mystery. The moral life, which begins after all in the terrain of spirituality and prayer, therefore has a fundamentally mystical quality.

Future work to build on Keenan's legacy should take its cue from what I am calling the mystical aspect of his approach to discipleship. Keenan's own analysis of ethics and liturgy from the standpoint of our self-under-standing in Christ remains predominantly noetic. This arguably prevents a deeper examination of the mystical theological meaning of discipleship and its connections to liturgy. Sacramental liturgy is nothing other than the mystery of our incorporation into the person and identity of Christ as we are made living members of his body. In that sense liturgy is an encounter with the mystical goal of discipleship, which is union with Christ and participa-tion through him in the very life of God. The disciple is led into Christ's own body, his own life, which is the life of the Trinity. Such a destiny is the full expression of humanity and the full realization of our virtuous

---

[34] Fritz Tillmann, *Der Meister ruft: Eine Laienmoral für gläubige Christen* (Düs-seldorf: Schwann, 1937); and Fritz Tillmann, *The Master Calls: A Handbook of Morals for the Layman*, trans. Gregory J. Roettger (Baltimore: Helicon, 1960).

[35] Keenan, "Dialectically Dynamic Teleologies," 30.

pursuit. From this perspective liturgy should not be limited to its role as a social practice, which mediates a certain anthropological understanding or habituates certain virtues, but must also be acknowledged as a mystical eschatological event that provides grounding and direction for human identity and hence the moral life. The virtues, in this view, are more than just the good habits we carry from liturgy. Virtues are the means through which we sacramentally embody the presence and action of Christ for the life of the world. Keenan has given us a bridge; it is my hope that ethicists and liturgical theologians alike will cross it.

PART III

BIOETHICS

11.

Ethics of Mercy in a Time of AIDS

A Theology of Vulnerability for Saving Lives

VINCENT LECLERCQ, AA

In the early 2000s, James Keenan was already a recognized moral theologian in France. At that time my main interest was to find in him a genuine historian of Catholic moral theology. Still a graduate student at the Catholic Institute of Paris, I had regularly taken advantage of his erudition. Reading his texts in *Theological Studies* enabled me to understand better what tradition means for Catholic ethics and how it could renew it deeply.[1] For Keenan, there was no moral discernment without referring to its specific historical context. As a historian of moral theology, Keenan was also very attentive to linking Catholic morality to a specific theological context. Later, when I discovered his work on virtue, I realized that such a fundamental perspective is both a resource and a specific goal for ethics. Indeed, theology and virtues can reorient our concrete moral choices and shape our personal and collective conduct.

As a medical doctor by training, I too often complained that bioethics was for many French physicians of my generation only a matter of professional deontology. Interestingly, virtue ethics not only guides us toward the right thing to do but also requires that we do it well and for the right reasons. The aim is to become better moral agents and to perform better as healthcare providers.

---

[1] "[Moral theologians] find the turn to the tradition itself liberating, because inevitably today's scholars use the tradition precisely to move beyond it." James F. Keenan, "Fundamental Moral Theology: Tradition," *Theological Studies* 70 (2009): 142.

Working with James Keenan during my doctoral studies, on bioethics in general and on the issue of HIV/AIDS in particular, his way of teaching and conducting research in this field unveiled to me the best of what fundamental moral theology can bring to medical ethics. Facing the disease, he explored how to provide support and comfort to those who tried to prevent the surge of the disease and dedicated their lives to taking care of patients or their relatives. His attention was centered on persons and their stories. Based on the need to survive the pandemic, his ethics had to be more proactive and founded on real cases rather than on theoretical principles. Allowing the sufferers to give voice to their suffering is a key response to suffering.

Soon the complexity of the narratives showed him that interdisciplinarity was urgently needed. Suddenly there could no longer be "medical ethics" as an isolated discipline with a narrow, professional focus. There had to be a global bioethics whose ethical, medical, anthropological, and social contexts interacted. A health crisis became a *kairos*, a moment of truth guided by God to reflect on our own priorities and the moral norms we teach or follow. If moral theology is truly dedicated to helping our contemporaries lead a better life, it begins in this context by helping them to survive the HIV/AIDS pandemic. As an academic discipline, moral theology had to find the means to reach out and welcome those whose lives were at risk. This essay examines the ways that James Keenan's work played an important role in reshaping global bioethics and in the evolution of Catholic theological ethics more broadly.

Experience, Vocation, and a Theology Centered on Those Most Vulnerable

In my early thirties I realized that the novelty of James Keenan's theological method was consonant with my own clinical and theological perspectives. Given the ways our own narrative shapes the encounters we have, even from a theological point of view, I will briefly share some of my own personal experiences. They set the framework to perceive rightly the challenge of AIDS and the need for new theological thinking.

In 2002, I spent the summer in the north of Benin (West Africa) in a well-equipped but poor and remote medical facility in Tanguieta staffed by a religious order, the Brothers of Saint John of God. There, I found many medical challenges and human miseries, including the ravages of the HIV/AIDS pandemic, and very few healthcare providers to address them. At that time there was no available antiretroviral therapy in West Africa. I was powerless and very upset. Meanwhile, I knew it was the only place to be and very grateful to work there and help the best I could. At the end of my stay, Brother Florent, an Italian surgeon and the medical director of the hospital, with whom I worked for several weeks, asked me: "Vincent, what are your plans now? Come back whenever you want; we need you. Here, we will be waiting for you."

Since that day I have had to regularly ask myself: Why are you *here* instead of being *there* among the sick, the dying, their families, and those who care for them? Two years later my religious order suggested that I extend my theological formation in ethics through a doctorate. Professor Keenan generously agreed to welcome me in Boston and suggested a few months later that I should work on the HIV/AIDS pandemic. I understood immediately that he was inviting me to be part of one of the most exciting challenges of that time. Although such an opportunity was very intimidating for a French-speaking student and an inexperienced scholar, I accepted it. Medicine had taught me the importance of proximity to the most vulnerable. I felt a responsibility to include them more fully in theological research. Christian bioethics offered multiple ways of starting from their situation of personal fragility and their context. What I had learned at the bedside of AIDS patients could be deepened through theological work in which they would be both the first beneficiaries and the main actors.

As a physician, I understood well the moral value of responding to the distress of suffering sisters and brothers, of being called in the middle of the night to the bedside of the sick or the dying, offering medical skills and giving comfort to patients and their relatives. I was already naturally accountable to suffering humanity. Nevertheless, since I was studying theology in the United States instead of taking care of the sick in Tangui-eta, I was looking for solid personal and theological reasons to write on Christian ethics.

Keenan[2] and the French moral theologian Philippe Bordeyne,[3] who was my mentor in Paris, were for me the pioneers who paved my way in moral theology. They showed me why I wanted to become a Catholic ethicist to-day: because theology itself has a special responsibility toward "the least" and the most vulnerable. Earlier and better than I did myself, Keenan un-derstood perfectly well what was at stake in my plan to become a Catholic

---

[2] Jon Fuller, SJ, and James Keenan, SJ, "Educating in a Time of HIV/AIDS," in *Opening Up: Speaking Out in the Church*, ed. Julian Filochowski and Peter Stanford, 95–113 (London: Darton Longman and Todd, 2005).

[3] Philippe Bordeyne, "La référence à la vulnérabilité en éthique de la santé: défis et chances pour la foi chrétienne," *Revue d'éthique et de théologie morale* 239 (2006): 45–75.

ethicist, being a religious brother by vocation, and remaining a physician by profession. Moral theology is not primarily a question of norms, rules, or duties—although it obviously includes them—but fundamentally about living with coherence and integrity. The call is to be faithful to who you are and free enough to act and respond to the challenges of our day. Theology is also about being vulnerable to God's call and transformative action when death seems to dominate the very existence of the least ones.

In the field of medical ethics Keenan opened a new way and a more holistic methodology. Grounded in a vocational theology, his priority was not first to establish moral norms but rather to seek together what we are called to become: as individuals, as societies, as communities facing existential uncertainties and the experience of our own vulnerability. And his objective was to take care of the lives of those suffering most: "Decisions are often found not in the moment, but as Enda McDonagh has taught us, in the narrative. Narratives outline how the vocation to pursue moral truth takes us into the world precisely where there is suffering."[4]

The Importance of Cases, Persons, and Virtue

To honor this vocational morality, Keenan showed us how to mobilize the resources of Catholic tradition. The history of moral theology offers paradigms that allow us to respond to today's challenges. Interpreting them requires integrating history and theology, personal narratives and the full picture of the AIDS crisis, the sacred texts and our social contexts, and taking the risk of the gospel in the service of the most vulnerable.

All of Keenan's students, from his undergraduate Boston College students to his international doctoral students, know how lively his lessons and lectures are. He is keen to illustrate his teaching with stories. In his way of theologizing, stories are not just anecdotes. They open the mind and invite his audience to perceive the moral issue in the dynamics of life. The narratives help each student to better identify what is at stake and avoid theological methods that ignore concrete, lived experience. Each case is aimed to unveil a situation whose moral truth is only perceived in the light of personal and collective experiences, after contextualizing these experiences and crossing disciplines to perceive the "full picture" of them. Through his appreciation for casuistry, rooted in a clear historical vision

---

[4] Jon D. Fuller and James F. Keenan, "Church Politics and HIV Prevention: Why Is the Condom Question So Significant and So Neuralgic?" in *Between Poetry and Politics: Essays in Honor of Enda McDonagh*, ed. Linda Hogan and Barbara Fitzgerald (Dublin: Columba, 2003), 158.

of Catholic moral theology, Keenan contributed to a shift in bioethics from a primarily deontological approach to one that was more attentive to narrative and context. This approach resonated with my medical training, where we frequently engaged case studies. Before Keenan, Catholic bioethics concerning HIV/AIDS focused on prevention and sexual behavior only. The individual sexual act was assumed to be the only responsible factor in transmission, neglecting social factors including poverty, sex work, lack of healthcare access, and men's abuse of women and girls.[5] Meanwhile, Catholic theological ethics banned condoms because they are contraceptive. Very few authors had showed that Christian ethics was also a resource to empower and take care of the most vulnerable. Those who were already affected and infected by the disease were often targeted, considered as chastised by God. Catholic bioethics attacked the lives of those infected rather than providing merciful solutions to the problem as Keenan would later do.

The case of whether to test religious candidates for HIV and whether to admit HIV-positive candidates to religious orders provides a good example of how stories and cases can yield theological and ethical insights. This was a concrete issue that could not be resolved by an overly general analysis. "In order to ascertain what is morally required, we must descend from the general to the specific and consider individual circumstances. . . . A universal policy of exclusion ignores too many circumstances attendant to medical health and moral logic."[6] Keenan pointed out the importance of considering the needs of the people who are ministered to, and he interrogated the consequences of excluding all HIV-positive candidates in highly infected areas. He recalled the Jesuits' tradition of being sent to the margins of society and invited religious orders not to consider their own boundaries as definitively shut. Finally, he underlined the importance of weighing the financial and manpower resources an order would need to use to support candidates with chronic diseases.

Virtue ethics led him to consider three groups of people involved in the moral debate: the actual candidates, the people they serve, and the order itself. Keenan suggested that religious orders contribute to injustice and social stigma related to HIV status when they deny candidates access to realizing their vocation, not because they are ill but because they will be

---

[5] James F. Keenan, "Developments in Bioethics from the Perspective of HIV/ AIDS," *Cambridge Quarterly of Healthcare Ethics* 14, no. 4 (October 2005): 417–18.

[6] James F. Keenan, "Testing Religious Candidates to Religious Orders for HIV," in *Practice What You Preach: Virtues, Ethics, and Power in the Lives of Pastoral Ministers and Their Congregations*, ed. James F. Keenan and Joseph Kotva (Franklin, WI: Sheed and Ward, 1999), 36.

ill. Alongside his focus on persons, Keenan's commitment to casuistry and the detailed circumstances of specific cases helped him articulate the most relevant questions.

Keenan's method also enabled him to enlarge the vision of moral agency, both personal and collective. By considering the tensions between the virtue of justice and concerns about purity, Keenan changed the theological reasoning in bioethics. Relying on Jesus's own virtues, Keenan explained how Jesus's practices reformed purity laws and provided a new hermeneutics for determining membership in the community.

Keenan used this issue of HIV testing to raise additional questions of sexuality, celibacy, or chastity that must be asked before entering the order. He addressed the inhibitions of seminarians, religious, and priests to discuss their own desires or concerns about health or sexuality because they feared rejection or judgment. Consideration of the specific question of testing candidates showed that there are good reasons to reexamine our values and the decisions we made: "Persons who are HIV positive are living with it and they are living better and longer than ten years ago."[7] Many priests have been blessed by encountering people who have tested positive and taught them about life, love, and integrity. Reexamining this question through the lens of virtue showed that religious orders must ask themselves what type of people they want to become through the decision they make. Through a variety of other examples or topics, Keenan demonstrated convincingly that the tradition of the Roman Catholic Church was richer, more humane, and more supple than the way it was usually conveyed by many constituencies in the church.

Broadening Bioethics
through Narrative and Interdisciplinarity

In the case of the AIDS pandemic, what predominated for Keenan in 2005 was the sense of urgency: more than forty million people were living with HIV/AIDS, and an additional twenty-five million had already died. Among the sick, one-third were young people between the ages of fifteen and twenty-four, and almost two-thirds of these were women and girls. Antiretroviral drugs were not yet widely available and were poorly distributed globally. Prevention was insufficient, not to say ineffective, as the number of new infections was still nearly five million per year (thirteen thousand each day). The pandemic was cause for alarm for the welfare of all and an ethical challenge for the whole world. The need was to provide prevention and

---

[7] Keenan, 39.

assistance to all those who were already infected or affected by the disease. The story of the most vulnerable needed to become a more inclusive story.

Many argued for better prevention and broader access. They wanted to motivate others to become more responsive to the pandemic. But few were ready to write about those already infected or affected by the pandemic. Meanwhile stigma, denial, social inequality, and fatalism proved to be as deadly as the HIV virus itself. There was a need to narrate the cases of those who faced the AIDS crisis in order for their stories to draw the world into solidarity.

Keenan's revival of high casuistry in Catholic moral theology in the late twentieth century not only shifted the focus in bioethics to stories and cases, but it also facilitated a broader approach to the AIDS pandemic. His main innovation was to open up to a transdisciplinary discussion that included public-health actors and healthcare providers. As Keenan wrote with medical doctor Jon D. Fuller, SJ:

> While public health officials approach the social with insights about demographic patterns and epidemiological impacts which are fundamental generalizations, the physician can counter with very detailed, experiential narratives for each patient. The former are not simply summaries of those latter narratives, any more than the narratives are only encapsulations of the generalizations. Together, their perspectives, the private and the interpersonal as well as the social and institutional, inform bioethicists—as moral educators—to have a better grasp on human health.[8]

Keenan's edited volume *Catholic Ethicists on HIV/AIDS Prevention*[9] was a first step to provide such an awareness and entails an ethics of mercy at the scale of global urgency. He and other contributors to that book provided theological arguments and rich case studies to promote prophylactics, sustain medical research, enhance healthcare access and treatment distribution, but also to focus more attention on issues of gender, equity, and empowerment for those whose lives were most at risk in this pandemic, those who needed advocates in order to survive. Keenan and his coauthors rooted their argumentation in the social teaching of the church, and the priorities of universal human dignity, justice, the common good, solidarity, and participation. Coming from all over the world, the narratives of the book highlighted what we were learning from the direct witnesses and actors of the pandemic. He deepened and shifted the focus of bioethics and

---

[8] Fuller and Keenan, "Educating in a Time of HIV/AIDS," 97.

[9] James F. Keenan, ed., with Jon D. Fuller, Lisa Sowle Cahill, and Kevin Kelly, *Catholic Ethicists on HIV/AIDS Prevention* (New York: Continuum, 2000).

theological ethics in ways that helped stop the progression of a disaster. As the epidemic unfolded before our eyes, Keenan had the intuition that bioethics was no longer a matter of individual moral standards but rather an ethics based on political and social justice.

For Keenan, the AIDS crisis was an opportunity to denounce the instability and injustices of our world. AIDS was to be understood as a defeat, a failure of medicine to cure what must be treated but also a failure of societies to protect the least and the lowly. This is very much in line with the analysis of the late Paul Farmer, a medical doctor and an anthropologist from Harvard. For Farmer, the inequities of social institutions are manifestations of virulent pathologies of power. Analyzing the spread of HIV in Haiti, Farmer did not hesitate to use the term "structural violence" to demonstrate how "political and economic forces have structured risk for HIV and AIDS, tuberculosis, and indeed, most other infectious and parasitic diseases."[10]

Thus, theological bioethics must be justice oriented and participate in public debate whenever we need to regulate or reorient our practices and empower the most vulnerable. With his colleague Lisa Sowle Cahill at Boston College, Keenan was able to formulate a new proposition for theological bioethics fitting the moral exigencies of the AIDS crisis: AIDS is a social issue, not primarily a sex issue or even a medical issue. Who would live and who would die in the pandemic was more than a clinical question; it was a social and political question. Cahill captures this well:

> I do not see all types of religious advocacy as morally equal or equally representative of the ideals of the Christian biblical and theological traditions. Biblically and theologically grounded norms of justice, as the inclusion of all in the common good with a preferential option for the poor, should energize and renew a theological ethics of inclusion, participation, equality, and empowerment, especially for the least well-off.[11]

For Christians, bioethics became a question of advocacy: providing norms but also formulating a proposal of faith, hope, and charity to save lives in the fragility of our human condition in the following of Christ.

For two-and-a-half decades statistics, forecasts, and plans had been insufficient to curb the epidemic. Regarding the still short history of AIDS, it was already doubtful that medical technology per se would ever be sufficient

---

[10] Paul Farmer, "On Suffering and Structural Violence: A View from Below," *Daedalus* 125, no. 1 (Winter 1996): 262.

[11] Lisa Sowle Cahill, *Theological Bioethics: Participation, Justice, and Change* (Washington, DC: Georgetown University Press, 2005), 16.

to eradicate such a disease. Although medical information, appropriate drugs, and medical follow-up would remain the cornerstone of the fight against HIV/AIDS, we needed also to understand our experience of AIDS from other points of view. Keenan writes, "Unless we reflect on the social, economic, religious, and political infrastructures in which people at risk for HIV/AIDS live, there can be no adequate hermeneutics for the ethics of health in the age of AIDS."[12] The AIDS epidemic needed a broader forum, one that exceeded the boundaries of medicine. Good policy could only be developed if public health and bioethics were both understood to be fundamentally political.

An Everyday Bioethics Grounded in Vulnerability

The rise of biotechnologies and new medical breakthroughs has given us the impression of a growing mastery over genetics, conception, birth, illness, and even death. But paradoxically, the new possibilities of medicine and science have led us also to reexamine our fragilities, whether they are individual or collective. Bioethics forces us to deal with the story of our life in all its complexity and through its vulnerability, especially to infectious or genetic diseases. Such fragility affects us in our personal, familial, and collective stories. It can even cause us to question our faith in the paschal mystery of Jesus Christ. In this sense bioethics reaches out to all of us; it is not the domain of experts or specialists alone, nor is it the business of emergency rooms or extreme dilemmas and extraordinary decision-making alone. Above all, bioethics should be undertaken "from below"[13] as a kind of "everyday bioethics"[14] that calls all of us to reflect and to act.

Consequently, a faith-based view of life and health cannot be reduced to the answers provided by medical technologies alone or the diktat of the so-called Georgetown mantra that emphasized autonomy for decades.[15]

---

[12] Keenan, "Developments in Bioethics from the Perspective of HIV/AIDS," 417.

[13] Maura Ryan, "Beyond a Western Bioethics?" *Theological Studies* (March 2004): 168–74.

[14] Giovanni Berlinguer, "Bioethics, Health, and Inequality," *Lancet* 364 (2004): 1086–91.

[15] In the successive editions of *Principles of Biomedical Ethics*, Tom Beauchamp and James Childress have repeatedly articulated four principles for biomedical ethics: beneficence, non-maleficence, autonomy, and justice. James Keenan diagnosed eloquently that they focused on the professional relationship between patient and physician but failed to explore a conversation between bioethicists and public-health officials and address the AIDS crisis, equity and justice issues that shape the lives of millions among the most vulnerable and impoverished populations.

The ethical or moral stakes in healthcare go far beyond the limits of the Western world and deeper than medical ethics understood as a specialized field of applied or professional ethics. For Keenan, Christian bioethics in a time of AIDS needed an entire refoundation. It had to accompany us with realism in the fragility of our human condition and through the stories that mark the trials of our lives.

By starting from vulnerability—a concept that is both ethical and theological—Keenan has promoted an ethics of life with and for the most fragile. This practice of bioethics starts from lived experience and the incarnation. It requires thinking about the presence of God and salvation not outside or despite vulnerability but at the heart of this vulnerability. Those who are infected and affected by the disease are not only exposed to the consequences of a deadly and devastating virus; rather, "they are people who are vulnerable precisely because their lives and their social settings lack the means and stability needed to live safely in a time of HIV."[16]

Keenan's research would bring the virtues of hospitality and compassion to tackle the pandemic and address vulnerability. Learning from a variety of life stories on the ground—and his own taste for casuistry—Keenan's theological bioethics would seek to promote inclusion and welcome in order to prevent stigma and promote empowerment. The aim was to prevent exclusion wherever more stability was needed. From that perspective those who are affected by AIDS are no longer the problem but part of the solution to a global crisis; any solution to the AIDS pandemic must offer vulnerable people a more stable life. Since shame-related HIV stigma was too often correlated with religious beliefs about punishment from God for not following the word of God, an ethics that begins with vulnerability must overthrow juridical approaches to normative religious ethics. Going forward, theological frameworks that would explain the ongoing AIDS crisis would have to be evaluated on their capacity to reach out to those with AIDS and welcome them instead of dismissing them and assigning blame.

Indeed, vulnerability is a concept that can help us understand the AIDS crisis in both its personal and social dimensions and reach those who are at risk of losing their lives. The first vulnerability is bodily, "but it always occurs in a network of other interactions and vulnerabilities, relational and social, summarized in previous sections under the rubrics of instability and structural violence."[17] In the face of injury and trauma, there is a place for compassion, which is also our personal and collective capacity to be

---

[16] James Keenan and Enda McDonagh, *Instability, Structural Violence and Vulnerability: A Christian Response to the HIV Pandemic* (London: Progressio, 2019), 4.

[17] Keenan and McDonagh, 8.

touched by the suffering of the other. When we understand the social and political dimensions of the pandemic, we also learn to understand more fully that the AIDS crisis is also our own story and not only that of those who contracted the disease. In other words, "HIV and AIDS breed where there is instability; instability arises from structural violence; we can only respond to the virus if we appreciate the value of vulnerability, so as to provide stability and diminish structural violence."[18] As Keenan noted, an ethics of vulnerability also shows the hospitality of theological ethics in a time of AIDS. Indeed, it allows thinking about and bringing about the empowerment of those who were endangered by the epidemic. "Standing with those who are stigmatized, who encounter as the crucified Christ did the harsh reckless judgement of the masses, . . . we need to develop a theology of vulnerability to sustain those at risk, those infected, and their caregivers who live in an unsettling, unstable and isolated world."[19]

Conclusion

James Keenan's academic work and personal commitment to addressing the HIV/AIDS pandemic have changed Christian bioethics and opened new methodological priorities in moral theology. A more global, social, political, and theological bioethics has now emerged from a professionalized, secular ethics. Attentive to circumstances, his bioethics tells the story of the fragility of all life, designated as being the ethical "place" to respond to human suffering and to find the hope of the kingdom. Grounded in virtue ethics and casuistry, his bioethics explores the complexities of our responsibilities and informs an enlarged understanding of our moral agency and how to address medical issues. His bioethics helped build a forum where moral theologians can bring their input and the rich tradition of their discipline. For Keenan, the HIV/ AIDS crisis brought an opportunity to implement a new approach.

AIDS remains a world crisis that needs a global commitment from healthcare clinicians, public-health officials, vulnerable constituencies, and everyday people from all walks of life to prevent transmission and to treat those already affected. Keenan invited us to a transdisciplinary theological bioethics able to integrate the complexity of the pandemic.[20] Attentive

---

[18] Keenan and McDonagh, 3.

[19] James F. Keenan, "Four of the Tasks for Theological Ethics in a Time of HIV/ AIDS," in *AIDS*, ed. Regina Ammicht-Quinn and Hille Haker, 64-74 (*Concilium* 3/2007) (London: SCM Press, 2007), 69.

[20] Keenan, "Developments in Bioethics from the Perspective of HIV/AIDS," 416–23.

to vulnerability, and to the importance of cases and context, his bioethics is person centered rather than principles oriented; it is also focused on empowerment and emphasizes the moral agency of multiple constituencies. His ethics of mercy foregrounds his care for those who are most at risk. In all of these ways, Keenan reshaped Catholic theological bioethics in ways that saves lives.

12.

Medical Education Ethics

Why Medical Schools Need a Culture of Ethics

JOSEPH J. KOTVA, JR.

Few relationships or practices have the morally formative force of an apprentice training under a mentor. Mentors are not mere guides to the acquisition of better technique, they are models displaying the qualities of character and patterns of behavior essential to filling one's role well. Few contemporary roles depend as heavily on apprenticeship as does physician training. Two years of medical school are spent apprenticing with one specialist after another. Residency is also a form of apprenticeship, as are key aspects of medical fellowships. Yet medical education pays little attention to the moral character of those mentors or to what the mentees are learning about who one should be to practice medicine.

Consider the experience of a third-year student during her surgical rotation:

In operating rooms, I did not fare much better. . . . The surg techs would hand me tools with jokes like, "Come on girl, get your hand around that. I think you're going to like it," and "It's a good size, isn't it?" The surgeon, accompanied by the rest . . . would laugh with eyes on me to see if I would signal back. Within 20 minutes, I could not touch a single tool or insert a single item without some phallic rendering or other crass humor. In subsequent surgeries, it did not matter if a patient present[ed] for elective surgery or cancer intervention, no joke was out of bounds in the OR.[1]

---

[1] Email dated November 23, 2022.

Such experiences are not atypical. They are not limited to a few students or physicians or schools or hospital systems.[2]

In confidential conversations with medical students during their clerkships, I've heard countless stories of physicians who feign empathy when the patients are present, only to belittle those patients the instant they are gone. Students routinely hear patients referred to as "dirtbags," "pieces of shit," "worthless," "lazy," "good-for-nothing," "unmotivated," "on the crazy town express," and much worse. Such labels are often used to further diminish homeless populations and others with no economic power. But mentors' bad behavior and morally broken character are hardly limited to surgical suites or making fun of the homeless. Indeed, I heard so many stories of fat-shaming patients at every level of care that demeaning heavy people seems a sport among some physician mentors.[3]

Students absorb worrisome lessons when their mentors make fun of patients behind their backs for being heavy, dismiss entire populations as being "drug seeking," intentionally misgender patients when addressing them, make fun of other physicians for providing appropriate care, blame OB patients' own bodies for pregnancy complications, refuse to apologize for indefensible misdiagnoses, disparage primary care, and discourage

---

[2] Bad role modeling by physicians during medical clerkships is not extensively studied and is hard to quantify. Confidential interviews with students convince me that it is widespread. Joel Gerig, MD, in a 2021 study of third- and fourth-year students at the country's largest medical school, while still himself a medical student, found that the majority of students, during rotations that spanned many hospital systems, reported witnessing and/or participating in morally wrong acts. Joel Gerig, "Moral Injury among IU Medical Students," First Annual Ethics, Equity, and Justice Symposium, Indiana University School of Medicine, South Bend, Indiana, May 5, 2022. Medical student burnout is a longstanding phenomenon. During the third and fourth years burnout is associated with exposure to "cynical" physicians. See Waguih IsHak et al., "Burnout in Medical Students: A Systematic Review," *The Clinical Teacher* 10, no. 4 (2013): 242–45. Wendy Dean and Simon Talbot correctly argue that much of what has been labeled burnout among healthcare workers is actually moral injury. See, for example, Simon G. Talbot and Wendy Dean, "Physicians Aren't 'Burning Out.' They're Suffering from Moral Injury," *Stat,* July 26, 2018. For another student voice, see Anonymous, "Moral Injury in Medical School," in *KevinMD.Com* blog (March 27, 2021).
[3] Student reports on this front match patient experiences. See Marquisele Mercedes, "No Health, No Care: The Big Fat Loophole in the Hippocratic Oath," in *Pipe Wrench,* blog, Spring 2022. https://pipewrenchmag.com/dismantling-medical-fatphobia/; Michael Hobbes, "Everything You Know About Obesity Is Wrong," in *The Huffington Post* (19 September 2018), https://highline.huffingtonpost.com/articles/en/everything-you-know-about-obesity-is-wrong/; Lesley Kinzel, "I Am Fat. I Still Deserve Good Medical Care," in *The Huffington Post* (6 July 2018), blog. https://www.huffpost.com/entry/going-to-doctor-when-youre-fat_n_5b2d421be4b0321a01d0fa25.

female students from pursuing medical specialties because those pursuits will make them "bad parents."

Students also have many stories of wonderful physicians worthy of emulation. Unfortunately, the negative experiences often overwhelm and sometimes outnumber the positive ones. As a third-year student wrote to me: "Emulation is a difficult game, and in a completely new ward-filled world, it's mostly all or nothing. You imitate the great, the good, AND the bad, often blind to which is which."[4] Moreover, legitimate fears of repercussions, including career-ending repercussions, keep students from reporting abhorrent behavior.

Inattention to the moral quality of mentor-apprentice interactions is a sign that medical education is ethically broken. It is hardly the only such sign. Medical education occurs at the intersection of the university, the healthcare system, and medicine as a profession. In *University Ethics: How Colleges Can Build and Benefit from a Culture of Ethics*, James Keenan forges a compelling case that the university system needs to be exposed for its prevalent disinterest in cultivating a culture of ethics.[5] I here want to parallel and complicate Keenan's ethical challenge to the university by calling attention to the lack of ethics in medical school.

Keenan argues that universities teach ethics, but they don't embody ethical behavior, support structures that encourage personal and corporate accountability, or see ethics "as a bedrock for the deliberations of what is best for the University's mission to collectively educate and inform their students for the common good."[6] The highest level of administration rarely has training in ethics or hints that the university should be subject to the same ethical scrutiny as other professions and institutions.

Keenan's argument highlights the unjust pay and treatment of adjunct faculty, the "classism experienced by many students unable to keep up with the cost of education,"[7] the siloed "fiefdoms" of university departments and programs, the ubiquity of cheating and the corresponding lack of practices that encourage integrity, the pervasiveness of hazing, racially themed parties, alcohol abuse, sexual assault, gender and racial bias, and the commodification of education.

By contrast, Keenan foregrounds medicine as displaying the professional ethics to which he is calling the university. I want to complicate the

---

[4] Email dated December 29, 2022.
[5] James F. Keenan, SJ, *University Ethics: How Colleges Can Build and Benefit from a Culture of Ethics* (Lanham, MD: Rowman & Littlefield, 2015).
[6] Keenan, 117.
[7] Keenan, 18.

story that Keenan tells about medicine. Keenan suggests that in response to the moral challenges facing medicine, "physicians intentionally cultivated this culture [of ethics] in their teaching schools, their healthcare centers, and their professional associations."[8] Keenan's passing comment is too generous regarding medical schools; they too lack a culture of ethics.

Protecting the Mental Health and Well-Being
of Medical Students

Another sign that all is not ethically well with medical education concerns mental health. Medical students suffer from rates of depression and anxiety several times higher than the general population. A study of 1,428 medical students from forty US medical schools conducted during the early months of the COVID-19 pandemic found that 24.3 percent of respondents screened positive for depression and 30.6 percent for anxiety.[9] By contrast, the CDC says that the rate of depression in the general population of adults over 18 is 4.7 percent, while the NIH says the rate in 2020 (during the pandemic) was 8.4 percent overall.[10] For anxiety, the NIH indicates that all forms of anxiety disorder combined in the general population is 19.1 percent.[11] Even allowing for the added pressure of the pandemic, medical students had much higher rates of depression and anxiety than the general population.

Troubling levels of depression and anxiety among medical students are not limited to the pandemic years. Just before the pandemic, a US osteopathic medical school found that 56 percent of its students screened positive for anxiety-related symptoms, while 23 percent screened positive for depression-related symptoms.[12] Likewise, a nationwide study begun in 2011 found that nearly one-third (31.2 percent) of the 3,743 medical students who completed both the first- and fourth-year surveys

---

[8] Keenan, 10.

[9] Scott J. Halperin et al., "Prevalence of Anxiety and Depression among Medical Students During the COVID-19 Pandemic: A Cross-Sectional Study," *Journal of Medical Education and Curricular Development* 8 (2021): 1–7.

[10] Center for Disease Control and Prevention (CDC), "FastStats: Depression" (2022); NIH, "Major Depression," National Institute of Mental Health (NIMH), nimh.nih.gov (updated July 2023).

[11] NIH, "Any Anxiety Disorder," National Institute of Mental Health (NIMH), nimh. nih.gov.

[12] Nicole A. Doyle et al., "Associations between Stress, Anxiety, Depression, and Emotional Intelligence among Osteopathic Medical Students," *Journal of Osteopathic Medicine* 121, no. 2 (2021): 125–33.

had signs of depression by the second survey.[13] An Albert Einstein College of Medicine study had similar results. Surveying all students in the classes of 2014 and 2015, in both their first and third years, 28.4 percent of first-year students showed a high risk of depression, while that number jumped to 39 percent by their third year.[14]

Medical education has long known that it is damaging to student mental health. A meta-analysis of data from forty-three countries published between 1982 and 2015 showed a crude prevalence of depression or depressive symptoms of 27.2 percent, with estimates ranging between 2.2 and 5.2 times higher than the general populations in which those studies took place.[15]

Listening to students and looking at the data, it isn't a stretch to view medical education as a form of mental-health abuse. But, instead of fixing the problem, most schools ignore student distress. When it is acknowledged, many schools teach their students resiliency techniques, despite little evidence that these programs improve students' mental health. This typical response adds to their burden by giving them another task: become better at adjusting to a broken system.

An effort at Saint Louis University School of Medicine shows a different way. In addition to a required resilience and mindfulness program, the school made everything pass/fail, cut course content by 10 percent across the board, established thematic learning communities (service and advocacy, research, global health, wellness, and medical education) that drew together students and faculty, and required the course identified by students as creating the greatest stress to have exams "that yielded a higher mean score, to be consistent with other courses in the preclinical curriculum."[16] The result was a 50 percent reduction in depressive symptoms among students and improvement on the Step 1 Licensing Examination. Unlike most schools that continually add content while giving lip service to student well-being, this effort attacked the causes of student distress, including the unrealistic workload and social isolation.

---

[13] Liselotte N. Dyrbye et al., "A Prognostic Index to Identify the Risk of Developing Depression Symptoms among US Medical Students Derived from a National, Four-Year Longitudinal Study," *Academic Medicine: Journal of the Association of American Medical Colleges* 94, no. 2 (2019): 217–26.

[14] Allison B. Ludwig et al., "Depression and Stress amongst Undergraduate Medical Students," *BMC Medical Education* 15 (August 27, 2015): 141.

[15] Lisa S. Rotenstein et al., "Prevalence of Depression, Depressive Symptoms, and Suicidal Ideation among Medical Students: A Systematic Review and Meta-Analysis," *JAMA* 316, no. 21 (December 6, 2016): 2214–36.

[16] Stuart J. Slavin, Debra L. Schindler, and John T. Chibnall, "Medical Student Mental Health 3.0: Improving Student Wellness through Curricular Changes," *Academic Medicine: Journal of the Association of American Medical Colleges* 89, no. 4 (April 2014): 573–77.

Prioritizing Empathy
in Admission and Training

Another sign that medical education is morally broken concerns virtues such as empathy. Although difficult to study, empathy is essential to good medical care, and growth in empathy is a stated goal of both the American Association of Medical Colleges and the Accreditation Council for Graduate Medical Education.[17] Yet most studies show a marked decrease during medical school in student assessments of their ability to empathize with patients.[18] Sometimes this decrease in empathy is evident from the beginning of medical school, but often the dramatic downward slide happens in the third year, as students enter their clinical experience. As Hojat et al. note, this observation means that "the erosion of empathy occurs during a time when the curriculum is shifting toward patient-care activities . . . when empathy is most essential."[19] It is hard to miss the moral irony: the cognitive, emotional, and motivational abilities to identify with patients get worse in medical school. Despite the stated goal of increasing empathy, there is a "hidden curriculum" within medical education that reduces students' ability to identify with patients different from themselves.[20]

Many medical schools try to teach empathy, usually to little effect.[21] Several dynamics are operative. First, the hidden curriculum, including the too-often-present sense that patients are to blame for their own problems, is

---

[17] Sandra H. Sulzer, Noah Weeth Feinstein, and Claire Wendland, "Assessing Empathy Development in Medical Education: A Systematic Review," *Medical Education* 50, no. 3 (March 2016): 300–310.

[18] Daniel C.R. Chen et al., "Characterizing Changes in Student Empathy throughout Medical School," *Medical Teacher* 34, no. 4 (2012): 305–11; Melanie Neumann et al., "Empathy Decline and Its Reasons: A Systematic Review of Studies with Medical Students and Residents," *Academic Medicine: Journal of the Association of American Medical Colleges* 86, no. 8 (August 2011).

[19] Mohammadreza Hojat et al., "The Devil Is in the Third Year: A Longitudinal Study of Erosion of Empathy in Medical School," *Academic Medicine: Journal of the Association of American Medical Colleges* 84, no. 9 (2009): 1182–91.

[20] Reginald F. Baugh, Margaret A. Hoogland, and Aaron D. Baugh, "The Long-Term Effectiveness of Empathic Interventions in Medical Education: A Systematic Review," *Advances in Medical Education and Practice* 11 (2020): 879–90.

[21] While few medical-school efforts to teach empathy show sustained results, it is possible to increase empathy and other virtues in medical students, at least in populations already primed to such growth. See, for example, Zak Kelm et al., "Interventions to Cultivate Physician Empathy: A Systematic Review," *BMC Medical Education* 14 (October 2014); Sari Altschuler, *The Medical Imagination: Literature and Health in the Early United States* (Philadelphia: University of Pennsylvania Press, 2018).

stronger than explicit efforts to cultivate empathy.[22] Second, the curricular structure of medical education is problematic. Most medical students first learn about living patients by cutting into cadavers—lacking pulse, pain, name, or personal story.[23] This inauspicious start is reinforced by a curriculum that prioritizes learning body systems and clinical facts, inculcating the sense among students that empathy is nice but unimportant. The progression and weight of the curriculum implies that medical knowledge is what matters, not the unique person sitting in front of them.[24] Third, medical schools undervalue the importance of empathy in their faculty and student candidates. Evidence indicates that students who enter medical school with high levels of empathy and sustained histories of prosocial activity experience less erosion of empathy during their medical education.[25] There is a need for curriculum reform to address the covert instruction that undermines empathy. There is also a need for institutional change that tilts the selection process toward applicants with more initial capacity for empathy.[26]

While it might seem obvious that medical schools should pick students with virtues such as empathy, it isn't manifest in the medical school selection process. Schools disproportionately value certain cognitive skills over qualities such as empathy and altruism. Indeed, an important study shows that

> medical students are substantially less altruistic than the average American. . . . [And] the social preferences of those attending top-ranked medical schools are statistically indistinguishable from the preferences of a sample of elite law school students.[27]

---

[22] For example, Delese Wear et al., "Making Fun of Patients: Medical Students' Perceptions and Use of Derogatory and Cynical Humor in Clinical Settings," *Academic Medicine: Journal of the Association of American Medical Colleges* 81, no. 5 (May 2006): 454–62.

[23] See Jeffrey P. Bishop, *The Anticipatory Corpse: Medicine, Power, and the Care of the Dying* (Notre Dame, IN: University of Notre Dame Press, 2011).

[24] Emmanuel Costa-Drolon et al., "Medical Students' Perspectives on Empathy: A Systematic Review and Metasynthesis," *Academic Medicine* 96, no. 1 (January 2021): 142–54.

[25] Michelle van Ryn et al., "Psychosocial Predictors of Attitudes toward Physician Empathy in Clinical Encounters among 4732 1st Year Medical Students: A Report from the CHANGES Study," *Patient Education and Counseling* 96, no. 3 (2014): 367–75.

[26] Baugh, Hoogland, and Baugh, "The Long-Term Effectiveness of Empathic Interventions in Medical Education."

[27] Jing Li, William H. Dow, and Shachar Kariv, "Social Preferences of Future Physicians," *Proceedings of the National Academy of Sciences of the United States of America* 114, no. 48 (2017): E10291–E10300.

The study also showed that students choosing high-income specialties (57.1 percent among medical students at top-ranked schools, 47.6 percent at lower-ranked schools) "display a greater level of selfishness relative to those choosing low-income specialties."[28]

Medical education makes future physicians less empathetic, and the selection process itself does not sufficiently prioritize the moral qualities that we rightly presume are essential to good medicine. Of course, many bright students demonstrate high degrees of empathy and altruism, along with a host of other virtues. The problem is that medical education gives insufficient attention to those qualities of character in student admissions—qualities that are then further eroded by hidden dynamics in medical education.

Integrating Consistent Ethics Education and Training

Another sign that medical education lacks a culture of ethics is the lack of consistency in ethics education. In 2004, a survey of medical ethics education in the United States concluded that "despite widespread agreement that ethics should be taught, there is little formal consensus concerning what, when, and how medical ethics is best taught."[29] This conclusion was unchanged by the time that the Project to Rebalance and Integrate Medical Education delivered its "Romanell Report" in 2015:

> There is no consensus about the specific goals of medical ethics education, the essential knowledge and skills expected of learners, the best pedagogical methods and processes for implementation, and optimal strategies for assessment. Moreover, the quality, extent, and focus of medical ethics instruction vary.[30]

Obviously, some variation in delivery approach is appropriate, and most schools either have an ethics course or endeavor to integrate some ethics training into other courses, in part because the major accrediting organizations require schools to gesture toward the importance of ethics and professionalism.

---

[28] Li, Dow, and Kariv.

[29] Lisa Soleymani Lehmann et al., "A Survey of Medical Ethics Education at US and Canadian Medical Schools," *Academic Medicine* 79, no. 7 (July 2004): 682–89.

[30] Joseph A. Carrese et al., "The Essential Role of Medical Ethics Education in Achieving Professionalism: The Romanell Report," *Academic Medicine* 90, no. 6 (2015): 744.

But to say that most schools do something in ethics is superficial because there is no agreement on what that "something" should be. The ethics content at most schools is developed and delivered by people without relevant training. There is little financial or institutional support for a "sufficient number of faculty with appropriate training who are committed to establishing meaningful, ongoing relationships with learners to act as role models, share their own experiences, and teach, observe, give feedback to, and ultimately evaluate learners."[31] Efforts to integrate ethics into other courses often meet resistance from course directors who do not want to give up content hours to ethics. Lack of attention to medicine's "hidden curriculum" means that there are few efforts to "inoculate learners against diminishment of professional behaviors."[32] Even the American Society for Bioethics and Humanities (ASBH), with its nearly two thousand members, has demonstrated little interest in the ethics education of medical students, instead focusing on contentious issues and standardizing the education of clinical ethicists.[33]

Addressing Economic, Racial, and Ethnic Inequalities

Still another sign that medical education lacks ethics is found in the family-income levels of those admitted to medical school. Data from 1987 through 2017 show the remarkably consistent privilege of wealth.[34] Admissions from the top 5 percent of family incomes always constitute 23 percent to 33 percent of all medical students, while students from the bottom 20 percent have never made up more than 5.5 percent of

---

[31] Carrese et al., 750. The report lists these issues as "challenges and opportunities" (pp. 744, 745, 746, 749). If space allowed, I would argue that a careful reading of the literature, including that material cited in the report, indicates deeper, more systematic problems than is suggested by categorizing them as "challenges."

[32] Carrese et al., 748.

[33] Cf. Micah Hester, "What Is the Future of Ethics Education in Medical Schools?" *Reflective MedEd* (blog), June 2, 2016.

[34] Paul Jolly, "Diversity of US Medical Students by Parental Income," *AAMC— Analysis in Brief* 8, no. 1 (2008); Jay Youngclaus and Lindsay Roskovensky, "An Updated Look at the Economic Diversity of US Medical Students," *AAMC—Analysis in Brief* 18, no. 5 (2018). I am indebted to Bethany Lutter for calling my attention to this reality. Bethany Lutter, "Low Socioeconomic Status Students' Performance on the MCAT," First Annual Ethics, Equity, and Justice Symposium, Indiana University School of Medicine, South Bend, Indiana, May 5, 2022.

admissions. The contrast is starker still when we include the next-highest-income group: "Roughly three-quarters of medical school matriculants come from the top two household-income quintiles, and this distribution hasn't changed in three decades."[35]

Medical education's thirty-year failure to improve even marginally its bias in favor of the wealthy is shameful. Classism is baked right into medical education. For all the supposed efforts to improve diversity, the failure to address socioeconomic status and family income in the admission process says a great deal about the actual commitment to diversity. And, at a pragmatic level, since medical students from lower-income families and more challenging socioeconomic situations are more likely than their peers to practice in socioeconomically disadvantaged areas,[36] the admission process contributes to inequities in healthcare access.

Moreover, given the enduring linkage between race/ethnicity and income, itself a function of systematic racism, these unchanging admission numbers suggest that racism is equally baked into medical education. Further inspection of admission numbers confirms medical education's race problem. Over 31 percent of the US population identifies as Black or Hispanic/Latino, but these groups combined make up 11.5 percent of medical students.[37] Medical schools also appear to do a poor job of disabusing students of certain racial stereotypes, such as the notion that Blacks have thicker skin than do whites.[38] Overall, to the detriment of poor and minority communities, medical schools have done little to address diversity within the student body.

---

[35] Youngclaus and Roskovensky, "An Updated Look at the Economic Diversity of US Medical Students." While family income correlates with the likelihood of attending college, the discrepancies between income and matriculation are roughly twice as bad for medical school as for college. For example, students from the lowest 20 percent of family income make up 11 percent of those starting college but only 5 percent of those starting medical school.

[36] For example, Ian B. Puddey, Denese E. Playford, and Annette Mercer, "Impact of Medical Student Origins on the Likelihood of Ultimately Practicing in Areas of Low vs High Socio-Economic Status," *BMC Medical Education* 17, no. 1 (January 2017): 1–13.

[37] USA Facts, "US Population by Year, Race, Age, Ethnicity, and More," usafacts.org (2023); AAMC, "Figure 13. Percentage of US Medical School Graduates by Race/Ethnicity (Alone), Academic Year 2018–2019," aamc.org.

[38] Kelly M. Hoffman et al., "Racial Bias in Pain Assessment and Treatment Recommendations, and False Beliefs about Biological Differences between Blacks and Whites," *Proceedings of the National Academy of Sciences of the United States of America* 113, no. 16 (April 19, 2016): 4296–4301.

Climate Education and Health

The last sign of ethical failure discussed in this chapter is the lack of climate education. A glance at the Planetary Health Report Card shows that most medical schools provide little to no climate-specific education, an unconscionable negligence that leaves students unequipped to understand or address the realities they will face as physicians.[39]

Climate change is already affecting human health, including the direct, dramatic harm from storms and fires, plus the less sensational impacts of degraded air quality and particulate matter, contaminated water, increases in vector-borne diseases, trauma, drought, and forced migration. Moreover, as a major contributor to climate change gases, healthcare compounds this harm, and, due to its lack of climate resiliency, healthcare's infrastructure is sustaining physical damage and suffering logistical challenges.[40]

Every population and every human-organ system is threatened by climate change, and marginalized and vulnerable populations suffer first and worst.[41] The failure to integrate climate into medical education is egregious negligence, not much different from failing to teach any other basic medical skill. Failing to equip students to confront the greatest health crises facing humanity is a monumental failure of ethics.

If we have the ears to hear, the ethical alarm bells about medical school are deafening. Medical training pays scant attention to horrifyingly bad role models. Rates of student depression and anxiety are astonishingly high. Medical education manages to diminish student empathy. The admissions

---

[39] "Planetary Health Report Card," phreportcard.org. Of the nearly two hundred allopathic and osteopathic schools in the United States, eleven received a C+ or better. Nearly three-quarters of schools are not represented in the "Planetary Health Report Card," usually because there isn't enough student climate engagement for those schools to be included. The 2022–2023 report did see twenty-one schools show improvement, including fourteen schools that moved up to a C grade.

[40] For example, Cassandra Thiel and Cristina Richie, "Health Care's Climate Footprint: How the Health Sector Contributes to the Global Climate Crisis and Opportunities for Action," *Hastings Center Report* 52, no. 4 (July-August 2022): 10–16. Also see Practice Greenhealth, practicegreenhealth.org; Health Care Without Harm, noharmglobal.org; and Cristina Richie's essay in this volume on the impact of climate change on healthcare systems.

[41] The best resources on the intersection of healthcare and climate change are Kim Knowlton, Cecilia Sorensen, and Jay Lemery, eds., *Global Climate Change and Human Health: From Science to Practice*, 2nd ed. (San Francisco: Jossey-Bass, 2021); ECHO Institute: US National Hub, "Climate Change and Human Health ECHO Program," iecho.org.

process privileges wealth but undervalues virtues. Explicit ethics training is underfunded and inconsistent. And there is near total inattention to the greatest health crises facing humanity. If space allowed, we could also show that the people running our medical schools rarely have administrative or ethics training, that bullying of women is a protracted problem in academic medicine, that there is a broad failure to provide training in LGBTQ care, and that many students quickly acquire career-shaping debt. We are overdue for an ethical upending of medical education.

13.

Integral Bioethics

Health for the Community of Creation

CRISTINA RICHIE

Let's start from a vision of health for the community of creation, where ecosystems thrive in harmonious balance and even though people get sick, sustainable remedies are available to everyone. Plants are used wisely to cure and treat, and animals enjoy lives of their own in fulfillment of their *telos*. Now, let's turn from this preindustrial image to our current system: industrialized healthcare in the developed Western world, which differs from our vision in ways with tremendous ethical implications. This essay highlights some underconsidered ethical impacts of modern healthcare, offers a contrasting framework of integral bioethics, and applies the framework to human and animal well-being as part of planetary health, thus providing a reordered and just vision of health for all in the community of creation in the spirit of radical inclusivity and honor to the Lord, which James Keenan's work and life embodies.

Ethical Problems in Healthcare

The vision of ideal health, or even sustainable healthcare, is impossible today due, in part, to climate change. The "safe" amount of carbon dioxide in the atmosphere—350 parts per million—has been exceeded.[1] The

---

[1] Christian Azar and Henning Rodhe, "Targets for Stabilization of Atmospheric CO2," *Science* 276, no. 5320 (1997): 1818–19.

World Health Organization estimates that one out of four global deaths are related to environmental factors, with over four million due to air pollution alone.[2] The current course of global climate change puts about half the human population, 3.5 billion people, at increased risk for chronic illnesses including cardiovascular, neurological, and autoimmune diseases and cancer. Climate-change health hazards include death and injury by flooding, famine, vector-borne illness, pollution, and heat.[3] These disproportionally affect disadvantaged populations and increase health inequalities.

The health impacts of environmental degradation are often linked to domestic and international environmental racism. Environmental racism refers to environmental health hazards, such as toxic waste, flooding, and mold affecting residential areas, that cluster in low-income communities with higher proportions of racial and ethnic minorities.[4] While "the economically well-off can choose to live amid acres of green . . . poor people are housed near factories, refineries, or waste-processing plants that heavily pollute the environment."[5]

Environmental racism was highlighted in the United States in 1987 when the United Church of Christ (UCC) Commission on Racial Justice[6] found impoverished locations were deliberately chosen for environmental hazards because, as former World Bank economist Lawrence Summers shamefully stated, the poor "don't live long enough to feel the effects."[7] Linked with a history of colonialism and slavery, environmental racism in the United States is no less than a "contemporary version of lynching a whole people."[8] A follow-up report to the UCC commission twenty years

---

[2] World Health Organization, "Public Health and Environment."

[3] Anthony J. McMichael, Sharon Friel, A. Nyong, and C. Corvalan, "Global Environmental Change and Health: Impacts, Inequalities, and the Health Sector," *British Medical Journal (BMJ)* 336, no. 7637 (2008): 191–94.

[4] Jouni Paavola, "Health Impacts of Climate Change and Health and Social Inequalities in the UK," *Environmental Health* 16, no. 1 (2017): 61–68; Carl A. Zimring, *Clean and White: A History of Environmental Racism in the United States* (New York: New York University Press, 2015).

[5] Elizabeth Johnson, *Quest for the Living God: Mapping Frontiers in the Theology of God* (New York: Continuum, 2007), 187.

[6] United Church of Christ Commission on Racial Justice, *Toxic Wastes and Race in the United States: A National Report on the Racial and Socio-Economic Characteristics of Communities with Hazardous Waste Sites* (United Church of Christ Commission on Racial Justice: Public Data Access, 1987).

[7] Jon Sobrino, *The Principle of Mercy: Taking the Crucified People from the Cross* (Maryknoll, NY: Orbis Books, 1994), 192n7.

[8] Emilie Townes, *In a Blaze of Glory: Womanist Spirituality as Social Witness* (Nashville, TN: Abingdon Press, 1995), 55.

later found that little had changed domestically,[9] while the global environmental crisis widened.

International environmental racism occurs when those in the developing world suffer additional environmental burdens due to the choices of developed-world residents. Carbon-dioxide emissions do not stay within national borders. Pope Francis reminds us that "pollution (is) produced by companies which operate in less developed countries in ways they could never do at home" (*Laudato Si'*, no. 51). Thus, environmental racism is present whenever people are forced to subsist in poverty; when the poor feel the effects, but only infrequently the benefits, of an economic system that emits massive amounts of carbon; and where the health effects of climate change compound other health impacts of racism and poverty.[10]

Moreover, industrialized healthcare presents ethical problems in the ways it tests drugs and procedures on sentient nonhuman animals. Sentience is the ability to experience sensations that may be pleasant or painful, thus the morally relevant sensation is pain.[11] Animals display sentience and pain in relatively obvious ways, such as a dog whimpering or a calf bleating in distress.[12] Many animals that are experimented on for medical research are sentient, and testing and experimentation typically involve some level of pain or discomfort during captivity and experimentation, a process with no benefit to the animals. To be sure, animal testing and research in medicine has, arguably, irreplaceable benefit to humans, and nonhuman animals will continue to be used in medical research for the time being. This does not imply that inaction in reforming animal welfare is acceptable.

These ethical problems flow from another source as well: a disordered attitude toward our expectations of healthcare. This comes in the shape of healthcare overuse which includes excessive carbon-dioxide emissions and rampant use of animals for medical testing and research.[13] The healthcare

---

[9] Robert D. Bullard, Paul Mohai, Robin Saha, and Beverly Wright, *Toxic Wastes and Race at Twenty: Grassroots Struggle to Dismantle Environmental Racism in the United States* (Cleveland: Justice and Witness Ministries, United Church of Christ, 2007).

[10] Paula Braveman and Laura Gottlieb, "The Social Determinants of Health: It's Time to Consider the Causes of the Causes," *Public Health Reports* 129, no. 1, suppl. 2 (2014): 19–31.

[11] Ian Duncan, "The Changing Concept of Animal Sentience," *Applied Animal Behaviour Science* 100, nos. 1–2 (2006): 11–19; Martha C. Nussbaum, "The Moral Status of Animals," *Chronicle of Higher Education* 52, no. 22 (2006): B6–8.

[12] Drew Rendall, Michael J. Owren, and Michael J. Ryan, "What Do Animal Signals Mean?" *Animal Behaviour* 78, no. 2 (2009): 233–40.

[13] Cassandra Thiel and Cristina Richie, "Carbon Emissions from Overuse of US Health Care: Medical and Ethical Problems," *Hastings Center Report* 52, no. 4 (2022): 10–16.

industry is responsible for 4–5 percent of total world carbon emissions,[14] similar to the global food sector.[15] The consequences of these emissions include climate-change health hazards that are disproportionately distributed along the lines of environmental racism and cause damage to animals in a clinical research context, often without proportionate reason. Yet, the health of animals and people, animals and planet, and people and planet are not dichotomous. Another vision of health and flourishing exists, in which all creatures are treated as intrinsically valuable.

Theory of Integral Bioethics

Several modern movements in medicine view all creatures as stakeholders in healthy ecosystems, which summons us back to the ideal vision of health for the community of creation. The One Health movement, promoted by the Centers for Disease Control and Prevention (CDC) and the World Health Organization (WHO), offers a holistic model of animal, plant, human, and planetary health. The CDC describes One Health as "an approach that recognizes that the health of people is closely connected to the health of animals and our shared environment."[16] One Health thus views health care and healthcare delivery as having complementary, and interrelated, interests. Another approach, Green Bioethics, places environmental sustainability into biomedical ethics using interdisciplinary principles.[17] This reduces healthcare's resource burden by prioritizing distributive justice, resource conservation, simplicity, and ethical economics when allocating medical treatments.

Within theological traditions evangelical environmental bioethics integrates environmental ethics and sustainable healthcare using a scriptural method.[18] In Catholicism the concept of integral bioethics has been

---

[14] Josh Karliner et al., *Health Care's Climate Footprint: How the Health Sector Contributes to the Global Climate Crisis and Opportunities for Action* (Healthcare Without Harm ARUP, September 2019).

[15] Peter-Paul Pichler, Ingram S. Jaccard, Ulli Weisz, and Helga Weisz, "International Comparison of Health Care Carbon Footprints," *Environmental Research Letters* 14, no. 6 (2019): 064004.

[16] Centers for Disease Control and Prevention, "One Health Basics," November 29, 2022. See also World Health Organization, "One Health," n.d.

[17] Cristina Richie, *Principles of Green Bioethics: Sustainability in Health Care* (East Lansing: Michigan State University Press, 2019).

[18] Cristina Richie, "Climate Change Related Health Hazards and the Academic Responsibility of Evangelical Bioethicists," *Ethics and Medicine: An International Journal of Bioethics* 36, no. 3 (2020): 175–88; Cristina Richie, "An Evangelical Environmental Bioethics: A Proposal," *Ethics and the Environment* 25, no. 2 (2020): 29–44.

proposed.[19] Though it is still in development, integral bioethics relies on the conceptual work of integral ecology and appropriately expands its sphere of reach into biomedicine and thus biomedical ethics. Here I outline some preliminary aspects of integral bioethics with an eye toward application in the next section.

First, integral bioethics starts from the foundations of integral ecology, a full and expansive vision of harmonious life on earth. *Integral* refers to the interconnectedness of all systems; we are a "network" of creation (*Laudato Si'*, no. 138). Our actions affect one another; that is, just as the body is affected by the environment, so our healthcare use affects the environment, creatures, and other humans. *Ecology* refers to more than the nonhuman environment. Pope Francis notes that "human ecology is inseparable from the notion of the common good" (*Laudato Si'*, no. 156). Attention to the whole person within society is foundational for the common good: all people need access to medicine and healthcare at some point in life. Yet the individual must find a way to thrive without impeding the flourishing of others, remembering that interrelationality is the core of social life. Authentic human ecology is inseparable from ecological protection (*Laudato Si'*, no. 5). Thus, Pope Francis comments, "Since everything is closely interrelated, and today's problems call for a vision capable of taking into account every aspect of the global crisis . . . *integral ecology* . . . respects its human and social dimensions" (*Laudato Si'*, no. 137). These dimensions are set within the parameters of the environment, medicine, healthcare, social life, economics, culture, the common good, and intergenerational justice (*Laudato Si'*, nos. 138–162). When integral ecology is engaged within healthcare and biomedical ethics, it converges into integral bioethics.

Praxis of Integral Bioethics

Humans are tasked with being stewards of earth and keepers of our sisters and brothers. Here I point at two concrete practices to restore the vision of health for the entire community of creation. First, integral bioethics can address human medical suffering when all relevant stakeholders, but particularly policymakers, think globally and act locally by creating lower carbon healthcare systems. Second, integral bioethics can ameliorate the suffering of animals in medical use through the principle of proportionality, by using animals with minimal harm to them and within the legitimate

---

[19] Willis Jenkins, Benjamin de Foy, Simone Kotva, "Integral Bioethics in the Anthropocene," presentation, International Academy for Bioethical Inquiry, co-sponsored by the Albert Gnaegi Center for Health Care Ethics, October 16, 2020.

objectives of medicine. Both applications are set within a fundamental dis-position towards God, which manifests in compassion, justice, and charity for all living beings.

Think Globally, Act Locally: Create Lower Carbon Healthcare Systems

Addressing national and international environmental racism requires an up-stream approach,[20] recognizing that social structures and policies contribute to all forms of systemic racism. Policymakers must be able to recognize ecology and public health, social justice and racism, as a matrix. Two ethi-cal imperatives for healthcare are, first, that the industry not exacerbate climate-change health hazards by expending excess carbon, and second, that healthcare address climate-change health hazards through public health and preventive health measures so that the poor are not disadvantaged by a lack of healthcare and greater exposure to environmental hazards. The aggregate benefits of ecologically conservationist policies will span social justice, healthcare cost containment, and ecosystem health.

Aligned with ecological ethics and values, healthcare systems may implement sustainability initiatives which use *phronesis* (practical wisdom), or numerical carbon-emission reduction, or both. On the former point, the Catholic Health Association (CHA) puts theology into practice by target-ing visible ecological issues like waste prevention and management, green energy procurement and conservation, water conservation, healthy food, environmentally preferable purchasing, green buildings, and transportation in educational resources for its member hospitals.[21] The CHA recognizes that, in the words of Pope Francis, "a true ecological approach always be-comes a social approach; it must integrate questions of justice in debates on the environment, so as to hear both the cry of the earth and the cry of the poor" (*Querida Amazonia*, no. 8). More sustainable healthcare may also occur through legally binding national carbon-reduction strategies, like the United Kingdom National Health Service Carbon Reduction Strategy,[22] which tracks and minimizes healthcare carbon, based on the 2008 Climate Change Act.

The Dutch Green Deal on Sustainable Healthcare encompasses voluntary sustainability initiatives and voluntary carbon reduction. Over two hundred

---

[20] Keith Syrett, "Doing 'Upstream' Priority-Setting for Global Health with Justice: Moving from Vision to Practice?" *Public Health Ethics* 11, no. 3 (2018): 265–74.

[21] Julie Trocchio, "Getting Started," n.d., at https://www.chausa.org/environment_gettingstarted/.

[22] NHS Sustainable Development Unit, *Saving Carbon, Improving Health: NHS Carbon Reduction Strategy For England* (Cambridge: NHS Sustainable Development Unit, 2009).

healthcare entities, like pharmaceutical companies and healthcare facilities, have signed the deal. The Dutch government reports that "signatories to the Green Deal agree to implement measures and pursue objectives under 5 different themes, in addition to their own ambitions and goals . . . promote the health of patients, clients and health workers through better nutrition, and environment and lifestyle interventions . . . increase knowledge and awareness of the sector's environmental and climate-related impact . . . to be carbon-neutral by 2050 . . . reduce use of materials and resources as well as residual waste . . . [and] reduce the environmental burden of pharmaceuticals."[23] This approach provides optimal flexibility and many entry points for sustainable healthcare.

Healthcare policymakers are tasked with overseeing the financial, personal, and carbon resources of the nation and must consider both the responsibility to national residents and the duty not to harm others outside their borders. Nancy Kass notes that while "bioethics emerged out of a need to confront problems close to home, the boundary between local issues and global issues is increasingly blurred in the current environment."[24] In a global world it is shortsighted to see only current residents as stakeholders: "Globalization implies that we think of the common good differently."[25] Emissions from high-polluting countries may affect people in other countries. These people, through geographical mobility, may then become residents in the higher-carbon country and require medical treatments for pre-existing climate conditions. Thus healthcare policymakers can view lower carbon healthcare systems as preventive health on a global scale, or, as Marcel Verweij and Hans Ossebaard suggest, as global "health solidarity." [26]

Reducing healthcare carbon output to decrease climate burden can also be done at the level of individual preventive care, which ultimately benefits the patient through better health; the healthcare system through less carbon; and other people through fewer climate-change health hazards. Reducing the rate of medical problems requiring new or advanced treatment also minimizes the need to experiment on nonhuman animals. Preventive healthcare—like contraception,[27] vaccinations, subsidized nutritious food,

---

[23] Government of the Netherlands, "More Sustainability in the Care Sector," n.d.

[24] Nancy Kass, "Public Health Ethics: From Foundations and Frameworks to Justice and Global Public Health," *Journal of Law, Medicine, and Ethics* 32, no. 2 (2004): 239.

[25] Lisa Sowle Cahill, *Bioethics and the Common Good* (Milwaukee: Marquette University Press, 2004), 19.

[26] Marcel Verweij and Hans Ossebaard, "Sustainability as an Intrinsic Moral Concern for Solidaristic Health Care," Part of a Project Assigned by the Netherlands Health Care Institute (Zorginstituut Nederland), unpublished paper.

[27] Contraception can help to prevent maternal mortality and morbidity, which kills over 300,000 women each year. Andrea Solnes Miltenburg, Birgit Kvernflaten, Tarek Meguid, and Johanne Sundby, "Towards Renewed Commitment to Prevent Maternal

and access to greenspace for exercise—fits within existing healthcare systems. James Childress and Tom Beauchamp have proposed a multi-tiered approach to healthcare, whereby basic standards of care include "public health measures and preventive care, primary care, acute care, and special social services for those with disabilities,"[28] while a second level or third level provides services beyond basic care.

Prevention is not always possible, so healthcare plans ought to form allocation schemes that address clinical necessity, not special interest. In Australia, "elective admissions (mainly elective surgery) rationing is achieved by waiting, at times up to a year for non-urgent surgery, and patients are treated by a hospital-appointed doctor, rather than necessarily the doctor of their choice."[29] This is a start to leveling healthcare access, but eliminating elective treatments could also be considered.

When basic treatments are available to all, "green informed consent" can be used. This includes patient education about sustainability in health practices and respects autonomous decision-making for carbon-intensive treatments or for alternatives.[30] Studies of the carbon footprints of specific procedures already exist in a range of medical fields, from anesthesia to urology.[31] "Green informed consent" may also include discussing climate-change health hazards as a side effect of treatment. Since all treatments have

---

Mortality and Morbidity: Learning from 30 Years of Maternal Health Priorities," *Sexual and Reproductive Health Matters* 31, no. 1 (2023): 2174245. Maternal mortality has decreased in many countries but is increasing in the United States, mostly due to systemic racism and social determinants of health. Regine A. Douthard, Iman K. Martin, Theresa Chapple-McGruder, Ana Langer, and Soju Chang, "US Maternal Mortality within a Global Context: Historical Trends, Current State, and Future Directions," *Journal of Women's Health* 30, no. 2 (2021): 168–77. The United States Affordable Care Act (ACA) in part mandated that employers "offer insurance coverage of certain 'essential' health benefits, including coverage of 'preventative' services." United States Affordable Care Act, "Coverage of Preventive Health Services" (2011), 42 U.S.C. 300gg-13. Included in the preventive services are nineteen forms of contraception that are Food and Drug Administration approved. United States Food and Drug Administration, "Birth Control: Medicines to Help You," fda.gov, updated May 2013.

[28] Tom Beauchamp and James Childress, *Principles of Biomedical Ethics*, 4th ed. (New York: Oxford University Press, 1994), 16.

[29] Ian M. Seppelt, "Australia: Where Have We Been?," in *ICU Resource Allocation in the New Millennium: Will We Say "No"?* ed. David W. Crippen, 3–10 (New York: Springer, 2013), 4.

[30] Cristina Richie, "'Green Informed Consent' in the Classroom, Clinic, and Consultation Room," *Medicine, Health Care and Philosophy: A European Journal* (2023).

[31] Jodi Sherman, Cathy Le, Vanessa Lamers, and Matthew Eckelman, "Life Cycle Greenhouse Gas Emissions of Anesthetic Drugs," *Anesthesia and Analgesia* 114, no. 5 (2012). Seyed Soltani et al., "Hospital Patient-Care and Outside-the-Hospital Energy Profiles for Hemodialysis Services," *Journal of Industrial Ecology* 19, no. 3 (2015): 504–13.

a carbon impact, the effectiveness and necessity of an individual's medical treatments must be weighed with the climate-change health hazards for the patient, their family, and others globally.[32]

Without the option for low-carbon healthcare, absolutely no progress can be made toward more sustainable healthcare systems and their ensuing benefit to public health. All healthcare should be made more sustainable through divestment of fossil fuels. A team of environmental and healthcare ethicists recently concluded that "there is a logical mission inconsistency between advocating for and serving individual and population health while at the same time financially supporting corporations that undermine health,"[33] like fossil-fuel companies. While decarbonization in all sectors is essential, healthcare systems obviously have a vested interest in environmental health.[34]

Address Animal Suffering: The Principle of Proportionality

Animals exist for their own sake; that is, they exist independent of anything else. They are not merely objects or ends for humans, other animals, or any other part of the ecosystem. Thomas Aquinas interprets God's creation of all things "for Himself" to mean that "every creature exists for its own proper act and perfection."[35] In the scriptures Jesus's concern for animals is demonstrated through his allegory of the sparrows (Mt 10:29–31) and his "how much more" teachings in Matthew 12:12. Animals also exist for God's sake. The Hebrew Bible creation story describes God making the animals prior to humankind. They are "good" irrespective of human use. God's speech in Job 38—41 confirms this by emphasizing humans' place within the created order.

Given this respect for animals' creaturely dignity,[36] a morally relevant consideration for the use of nonhuman animals in medical experimentation and testing is the principle of proportionality, which states that "it is unjust

---

[32] Christian Munthe, Davide Fumagalli, and Erik Malmqvist, "Sustainability Principle for the Ethics of Healthcare Resource Allocation," *Journal of Medical Ethics* 47, no. 2 (2021): 90–97.

[33] Erin Lothes Biviano, Daniel DiLeo, Cristina Richie, and Tobias Winright, "Is Fossil Fuel Investment a Sin?" *Health Care Ethics USA* 26, no. 1 (2018): 1–8.

[34] Cristina Richie, "Carbon Reduction as Care for Our Common Home: *Laudato Si'*, Catholic Social Teaching, and the Common Good," *Asian Horizons—Dharmaram Journal of Theology* 9, no. 4 (2015): 695–708; "Catholic Health Care's Responsibility to the Environment," *Health Care Ethics USA* 28, no. 2 (2020): 2–8.

[35] Thomas Aquinas, *Summa Theologica* (Xist Publishing, 2015), first part, q. 65., 2, *sed contra*.

[36] Willis Jenkins, "Biodiversity and Salvation: Thomistic Roots for Environmental Ethics," *The Journal of Religion* 83, no. 3 (2003): 401–20.

to inflict greater harm than that which is unavoidable in order to achieve legitimate . . . objectives."[37] There are two components to the moral equation: the degree of harm and legitimate objectives. Both Europe[38] and the UK[39] have regulated animal testing based on evaluation of harms to the animals. The United States lags behind, but some progress has been made.[40]

One way to justify or evaluate the ethics of harm is through proportionality. Aristotle describes proportionality as a virtue that is destroyed by defect and excess.[41] Given the Aristotelian view of proportionality, integral bioethics might conclude that the higher the order of animals being tested or experimented on, the higher the justification required for the amount of pain being inflicted on the creature. For instance, mammals are a higher order of animal than nonmammals due to their capacity for sentience and suffering.[42] In order to minimize harm, proportionality would ensure that only clinically significant diseases and conditions with few appealing alternatives are tested on sentient nonhuman animals. Proportionality would also propose that interventions that do not require harming animals be attempted first. For example, where appropriate, lifestyle changes could be attempted before drugs or procedures that require animal testing.

Legitimate objective is the most important consideration in experimentation and testing on sentient nonhuman animals. In the case of human research subjects, the Universal Declaration on Bioethics and Human Rights argues that legitimate testing benefits the patient directly, and "research which does not have potential direct health benefit should only be undertaken by way of exception, with the utmost restraint, exposing the person only to a minimal risk and minimal burden and if the research is expected to contribute to the health benefit of other persons in the same category."[43]

---

[37] Lambèr Royakkers and Rinie Van Est, "The Cubicle Warrior: The Marionette of Digitalized Warfare," *Ethics and Information Technology* 12 (2010): 290.

[38] Directive 2010/63/EU of the European Parliament and of the Council, 22 September 2010, on the protection of animals used for scientific purposes, eur-lex.europa.eu.

[39] Animals in Science Committee and The Rt Hon Norman Baker, The Animals (Scientific Procedures) Act 1986 in England, Scotland, and Wales, 6 May 2014, gov. uk/government/publications.

[40] EPA Press Office, "Administrator Wheeler Signs Memo to Reduce Animal Testing, Awards $4.25 Million to Advance Research on Alternative Methods to Animal Testing," September 10, 2019.

[41] Aristotle, *Nicomachean Ethics*, trans. K. Ameriks and D. M. Clarke (Cambridge: Cambridge University Press, 2000), bk. 2, chap. 2.

[42] Jonathan Birch, "Animal Sentience and the Precautionary Principle," *Animal Sentience* 2, no. 16 (2017): 1.

[43] Universal Declaration on Bioethics and Human Rights, Paris, France, October 19, 2005, art. 7.

The majority of testing on nonhuman animals is not for their own benefit, placing this practice under ethical suspicion from the perspective of legitimate objective.[44]

Given, however, the widespread acceptance of animal testing for human benefit, it must proceed based on well-accepted categories like the goals of medicine,[45] the WHO's urgent health challenges,[46] and the British Medical Association's key global health challenges.[47] For example, animal testing for cosmetics has been banned in the UK since 1998.[48] However, vaccines and medications for life-threatening diseases such as cancer and COVID are more significant[49] based on principles of rationing and allocation of scarce medical resources.[50]

Within legitimate medical treatments, protocols surrounding animals kept for experimentation[51] should protect both the animal and the people who work with lab animals, as well as ensuring minimal harm and maximum dignity for the animal during the process of experimentation. Living conditions of laboratory animals should be safe, comfortable, and replicate as much as possible natural living environments, unless the experiment is intentionally designed to avoid these conditions.[52] Henk Jochemsen and Corné J. Rademaker argue that "care should be taken to support . . . the sensitive well-functioning of animals as expressed in behavior natural to

---

[44] Bernard E. Rollin, "The Regulation of Animal Research and the Emergence of Animal Ethics: A Conceptual History," *Theoretical Medicine and Bioethics* 27, no. 4 (2006): 285–304.

[45] Joseph Howell and William Sale, "Specifying the Goals of Medicine," in *Life Choices: A Hastings Center Introduction to Bioethics*, 2nd ed., ed. Joseph Howell and William Sale (Washington, DC: Georgetown University Press, 2000), 62–73.

[46] World Health Organization, "Urgent Health Challenges for the Next Decade," January 13, 2020.

[47] British Medical Association, "Global Health Challenges," December 6, 2022, bma .org.uk.

[48] Helen Prior, Warren Casey, Ian Kimber, Maurice Whelan, and Fiona Sewell, "Reflections on the Progress Towards Non-Animal Methods for Acute Toxicity Testing of Chemicals," *Regulatory Toxicology and Pharmacology* 102 (2019): 30–33.

[49] Yang Ye, Qingpeng Zhang, Xuan Wei, Zhidong Cao, Hsiang-Yu Yuan, and Daniel Dajun Zeng, "Equitable Access to COVID-19 Vaccines Makes a Life-Saving Difference to All Countries," *Nature Human Behaviour* 6, no. 2 (2022): 207–16.

[50] Rosamond Rhodes, "Clinical Justice Guiding Medical Allocations," *The American Journal of Bioethics* 4, no. 3 (2004): 116–19.

[51] Dominik Gross and René H. Tolba, "Ethics in Animal-Based Research," *European Surgical Research* 55, nos. 1–2 (2015): 43–57.

[52] Laura Jane Bishop and Anita L. Nolen, "Animals in Research and Education: Ethical Issues," *Kennedy Institute of Ethics Journal* 11, no. 1 (2001): 91–112.

the species (e.g., pigs wallowing in mud)."[53] In some cases, of course, this would be impossible. Perhaps the experiment calls for confining a gorilla in a lab setting.[54] The reason to justify this must be proportionate. Humans have found that nonhuman animals can be used for medical experimentation, but this does not always mean that they should be used or that they are the most effective means of testing.

Computational models, like the "organ on a chip," are promising alternatives to animal testing for human benefit,[55] although they rely on animal testing to develop prototypes. Due to the differences in biology and physiological structure between humans and nonhumans, some tests are relatively worthless for transferability to human medicine.[56] At the same time, it should be remembered that all clinical trials require human testing before a treatment enters the medical industry, so human testing will always be necessary.[57]

Animal testing and experimentation are not the end of the ethical analysis. That millions of animals are euthanized each year because of human research[58] is problematic in itself,[59] but integral bioethics must also observe that any killing of sentient nonhuman animals, whether in food or medical experimentation, ought to be proportionate to alternatives. This makes the Western approach to consumption of animals for food hard to defend.

---

[53] Henk Jochemsen and Corné J. Rademaker, "Food Systems: How Can the Normative Practice Approach Help toward a Just and Sustainable Food System?" in *Research Anthology on Strategies for Achieving Agricultural Sustainability*, IGI Global (2022), 78–100.

[54] Testing on the "great apes"—chimpanzees, bonobos, gorillas, and orangutans—was banned in the UK by the Animals (Scientific Procedures) Act 1986 and later in the EU, New Zealand, and Austria. The United States and other countries still test and experiment on these hominids.

[55] Christine Horejs, "Organ Chips, Organoids, and the Animal Testing Conundrum," *Nature Reviews Materials* 6, no. 5 (2021): 372–73.

[56] Aysha Akhtar, "The Flaws and Human Harms of Animal Experimentation," *Cambridge Quarterly of Healthcare Ethics* 24, no. 4 (2015): 407–19.

[57] Lassi Liljeroos, Enrico Malito, Ilaria Ferlenghi, and Matthew James Bottomley, "Structural and Computational Biology in the Design of Immunogenic Vaccine Antigens," *Journal of Immunology Research* 2015 (2015): 156241.

[58] Sonali K. Doke and Shashikant C. Dhawale, "Alternatives to Animal Testing: A Review," *Saudi Pharmaceutical Journal* 23, no. 3 (2015): 223–29.

[59] Daniel Cressey, "Best Way to Kill Lab Animals Sought," *Nature* 500, no. 7461 (2013): 130–31.

Animal flesh can be substituted with food from non-sentient sources, which is often healthier,[60] has fewer ethical ramifications,[61] and a lower carbon footprint.[62] According to a 2020 report, the livestock industry contributes between 12 percent and 18 percent to total global greenhouse-gas emissions.[63] All animal use has a carbon footprint. Carbon from animal sources should be used parsimoniously.

At the same time, preserving animals for a more significant purpose—proportionate medical experimentation with minimal harm and legitimate objectives—may be justifiable. Obviously, the use of animals for food is an ethical issue related to healthcare, not only because of animal testing, but also because excessive meat eating is linked to increased disease burdens that contribute to healthcare carbon. This illustrates perfectly the interconnectedness of animal, human, and planetary health; reducing meat consumption reduces global carbon emissions in both agricultural and medical sectors.

Conclusion

Many people live in a society with high-tech healthcare. But all people live in a toxic environment built on the discarded carcasses of animals, where many continue to lack access to the benefits of modern medicine. Humans need healthcare to flourish, but healthcare often expends carbon. Yet we cannot ignore the impact that human activities have on nonhuman flora and fauna. We can no longer maintain a provincial view of community as the village we were raised in. Undoubtedly, total *metanoia* (conversion, reorientation) is necessary to make sustainable ecological decisions and

---

[60] Polly Walker, Pamela Rhubart-Berg, Shawn McKenzie, Kristin Kelling, and Robert S. Lawrence, "Public Health Implications of Meat Production and Consumption," *Public Health Nutrition* 8, no. 4 (2005): 348–56.

[61] Anastasia S. Stathopoulos, "You Are What Your Food Eats: How Regulation of Factory Farm Conditions Could Improve Human Health and Animal Welfare Alike," *New York University Journal of Legislation and Public Policy* 13 no. 2 (2010): 407–44; Alasdair Cochrane, "Labor Rights for Animals," in *The Political Turn in Animal Ethics*, ed. Robert Garner and Siobhan O'Sullivan, 15–31 (Rowman & Littlefield, 2016).

[62] Brian J. Revell, "One Man's Meat . . . 2050? Ruminations on Future Meat Demand in the Context of Global Warming," *Journal of Agricultural Economics* 66, no. 3 (2015): 573–614.

[63] Andrea Gomez-Zavaglia, Juan Carlos Mejuto, and Jesus Simal-Gandara, "Mitigation of Emerging Implications of Climate Change on Food Production Systems," *Food Research International* 134 (2020): 109256.

lifestyle changes. Put another way, if we emphasize only our national health, or human health over animal health, the decisions—the inputs for the moral equation of climate and health—will be fundamentally different than if we regard our decisions as affecting ourselves, animals, and the planet that supports us.

This essay started with a vision. It ends with another: better health outcomes worldwide; respect for all sentient beings and the ecosystem that sustains us; and spiritually reformed and environmentally transformed global citizens. This reordered vision of health for the community of creation must take shape across the imaginative and applied landscape of all sectors. Bioethics, with its special obligation to health, is the natural starting point.

14.

Global Bioethics, the COVID-19 Pandemic, and Theological Bioethics

Cooperation and Solidarity for a Sustainable World

EDWIN VÁSQUEZ GHERSI, SJ

One of the most important contributions James Keenan has made to the field of Catholic moral theology has been to enhance its cross-cultural and global dimensions. Keenan's global vision is reflected in two major works. In the book *Catholic Ethicists on HIV/AIDS Prevention* he brought together a large group of Catholic theologians and ethicists from around the world who addressed this crucial issue and pushed forward Catholic tradition regarding topics in bioethics and sexual ethics. Later, Keenan founded Catholic Theological Ethicists in the World Church (CTEWC), an international group of moral theologians, with the intent of fostering global, interdisciplinary conversations about theological ethics, and making moral theology and Christian ethics more relevant in the life of the church. With Keenan's global concerns in mind, I offer this essay to honor his outstanding work in moral theology.

The damage caused by the COVID-19 pandemic has been immense; it can be measured in millions of deaths, vanished jobs, affected economies, and great suffering. The World Bank estimates that the pandemic has resulted in the loss of three to four years' worth of progress in the eradication of extreme poverty.[1] The pandemic has revealed not only the shortcomings of our healthcare systems, but also the lack of solidarity and cooperation among nations.

In this chapter we see, first, how the pandemic teaches us that we must be prepared to face future pandemics not only with better public health, but above all with the help of multilateralism and cooperation. Second, the COVID-19 emergency allows us to see more clearly that global bioethics is what the current age demands. Global bioethics offers a reflection and a praxis to respond to problems on a global scale such as potential new pandemics and the environmental crisis, among others. Finally, theological bioethics contributes to global bioethics by proposing a way of building a world with greater interdependence and solidarity and by recommending an approach to deliberation and decision-making that is informed by affective wisdom.

The Pandemic and Global Health:
The Need for a World of Cooperation and Solidarity

A lesson from the COVID-19 pandemic is that we should pay more attention to public health. Public health is what society does as a collective to create healthy conditions for the population, seeking equity in health, and consequently, attention for the most vulnerable and excluded.[2] The pandemic has shown that not only were our healthcare systems unprepared to face a challenge of this magnitude, but also that its effects have been felt disproportionally by the most poor and vulnerable populations. It is not true that the pandemic equalizes us; in reality, the effects of this emergency have been worse among the poor and excluded. These inequalities result from inequities that are rooted in our social structures. Therefore it is urgent that we strengthen healthcare systems with a focus on global public health that aims for equity in health and international cooperation.

Another lesson that the pandemic has taught us is that global governance regarding health needs to be reinforced. The World Health Organization (WHO) displayed gaps, errors, and delays in its response to the threat of the new virus, which diminished its leadership and prestige. The nationalism of the United States and other developed countries, manifested in the hoard-

---

[1] Carolina Sánchez-Páramo et al., "La pandemia de COVID-19 (coronavirus) deja como consecuencia un aumento de la pobreza y la desigualdad," Banco Mundial Blogs, October 7, 2021.

[2] Sandro Galea and Roger Vaughan, "Reaffirming the Foundations of Public Health in a Time of Pandemic," *American Journal of Public Health [APH]* 111, no. 12 (December 2021): 2094–95.

ing of vaccines and some medications, has contributed to the weakening of the WHO.[3] These factors have led the commission formed by the medical journal *The Lancet* to propose the creation of a global health board to directly support the WHO in its task of monitoring possible new pandemics and threats to global health.[4]

The third and most important lesson is that no country can face a pandemic like SARS-CoV-2 alone. This is a great opportunity to react against nationalist views that only look out for their own welfare, the lack of cooperation among nations, and the ambition of power. To be prepared for a new global-scale threat, "what's needed is a global coordinated effort, based on the principle of solidarity, to foster equitable health care access."[5] In effect, globalization has created an interdependent world in which there should be no room for narrow-minded nationalism. It is vitally important to champion a more humane world before it is too late: "We call for awareness of the benefits of multilateralism, solidarity, cooperation, and a shared commitment to sustainable development, whether facing pandemics, ending poverty, keeping the peace, or meeting global environmental challenges."[6]

From Global Health to Global Bioethics: Bioethics for a Post-Pandemic World

The pandemic has shattered our certainty and security, and it has reminded us that fragility and vulnerability are part of the human condition. The crisis created by the new virus has shown us that it is vital to invest in primary healthcare infrastructure as well as in the improvement of global health. The context of this worldwide crisis produced by the coronavirus makes it evident that the field of bioethics must adapt its discourse to respond to the new challenges of a globalized world.

Guided by the centrality given to individual liberty and autonomy of moral subjects, American bioethics dedicates great efforts to studying clinical problems and ethical issues derived from the use of biotechnology, but

---

[3] Lawrence O. Gostin et al., "Reimagining Global Health Governance in the Age of Covid-19," *AJPH* 110, no. 11 (November 2020): 1615–19; Camilo Cid et al., *Dos años de pandemia de COVID-19 en América Latina y El Caribe. Reflexiones para avanzar hacia sistemas de salud y de protección social universales, integrales, sostenibles y resilientes* (Santiago de Chile: CEPAL, 2022).

[4] Jeffrey D. Sachs et al., "The Lancet Commission on Lessons for the Future from the Covid-19 Pandemic," *Lancet* 400 (2022): 1265–67.

[5] Anita Ho et al., "Global Disparity and Solidarity in a Pandemic," *Hastings Center Report* 50, no. 3 (2020): 65.

[6] Sachs et al., "The Lancet Commission on Lessons for the Future from Covid-19 Pandemic," 1268.

it does not pay enough attention to topics of health justice. This contrasts with the way in which bioethics manifests in Europe and other regions in the world, where there is greater concern for equity in healthcare.[7]

Without neglecting research in ethics related to the use of biotechnology and problems that affect personal autonomy, post-COVID bioethics should put greater emphasis on topics of health equity. What is needed in this post-pandemic era is bioethics that combines biomedical topics with issues of equity in health and ethical matters related to the environmental crisis. Some years ago Diego Gracia proposed three levels or layers, like evolutionary stages, in the development of bioethics.[8]

The first layer corresponds to the micro level. Micro bioethics deals with clinical bioethics, but also with topics related to control of the body, such as genetics and the use of biotechnology in general. The second layer is the meso level, which involves matters of public health policy, public health ethics, and the ethics of healthcare organizations. The third layer, the macro level, refers to the phenomenon of globalization, the environmental crisis, and responsibility to future generations. Gracia proposes that these three layers (the personal, the institutional, and the global) respond to the same deliberative process. Deliberation, as a method of practical Aristotelian rationality, aims at making prudent and reasonable decisions. Along with deliberation, bioethics has continued to encompass problems that are more and more global, thus redefining its original focus on health and control over the body.

In 1971, V. R. Potter coined the term *bioethics,* which he defined as the dialogue between biology, the humanities, and ethics, in response to the concern that uncontrolled development could put life on the planet at risk.[9] In 1988, in disagreement with the path that bioethics had taken in restricting itself to biomedical bioethics, Potter proposed the concept of global bioethics and stated: "The time has come to recognize that we can no longer examine medical options without considering ecological science and the larger problems of society on a global scale."[10] In these times of globalization and large-scale problems, biomedical bioethics and ecological bioethics

---

[7] R. Fox and J. Swazey, *Observing Bioethics* (New York: Oxford University Press, 2008), 186.

[8] Diego Gracia, "De la bioética clínica a la biótica global: Treinta años de evolución," *Acta Bioética* 8, no. 1 (2002): 27–39; Adela Cortina, "Bioética para el siglo XXI: Construyendo esperanza," *Revista Iberoamericana de Bioética* 1 (2016): 1–12.

[9] Van Rensselaer Potter, *Bioethics: Bridge to the Future* (Englewood Cliffs, NJ: Prentice-Hall, 1971). André Hellegers used the term *bioethics* at Georgetown University at the same time, but in contrast to Potter, he used it in a strictly biomedical sense.

[10] Van Rensselaer Potter, *Global Bioethics: Building on the Leopold Legacy* (East Lansing: Michigan State University, 1988), 2.

should contribute to the search for an ethical framework of planetary reach. This new focus, called global bioethics by Potter, feeds off of the ethics of Fritz Jahr, who defends respect for all forms of life, not just human ones,[11] and off of the ethics of responsibility of Hans Jonas, who incorporates the rights of future generations.[12]

With its effects on the planetary level, the COVID-19 pandemic challenges bioethics to widen its gaze beyond individual ethics to take on social problems and issues of a global nature. Post-pandemic bioethics should aim for consensus in a global society that is currently separated by conflicts and disagreements. The road to achieve this is through global bioethics in the way that Potter sensed, and which today has become evident. Bioethicists such as Henk ten Have have taken up the challenge and begun to give shape to global bioethics for the twenty-first century.[13] This new line of ethics attempts to respond to the sense of urgency and vulnerability in which life on the planet now finds itself. The latent danger of nuclear conflict, climate change, new extreme ideologies, poverty, and the exclusion of millions of human beings, the current pandemic, and possible future pandemics are evidence of the vulnerability and fragility of global society and life in general. Humanity needs wisdom to make life on this planet sustainable.

In the movie *The Day the Earth Stood Still*, an alien named Klaatu, played by Keanu Reeves, is sent by the Counsel of the Galaxy to wipe out the human race because it is endangering Planet Earth. However, the extraterrestrial desists from carrying out his mission when he discovers that humans possess something valuable and unique: love. The wisdom that the world requires is affective knowledge, or knowledge resulting from a close relationship between the rational and the emotional; not the instrumental reasoning that detracts from the progress of science by putting it at the service of the privileged few, but rather, as Adela Cortina proposes, a practical and affective dialogic reasoning that is based on the ethical premise of "wisdom for survival."[14] Deliberation aimed at reasonable and prudent knowledge is inscribed in this dialogic-affective dynamic as a privileged instrument in seeking consensus. This "affective wisdom" contains various elements that express the capacity of the human being to build, in spite of so many indications to the contrary, a global coexistence of peace and

---

[11] Juan Alberto Lecaros, "La bioética global y la ética de la responsabilidad. Una mirada fenomenológica a los orígenes y a los desafíos para el futuro," *Revista Iberoamericana de Bioética*, no. 1 (2016).

[12] Hans Jonas, *The Imperative of Responsibility: In Search of an Ethics for the Technological Age* (Chicago: University of Chicago Press, 1984).

[13] Henk ten Have, *Global Bioethics: An Introduction* (Oxon: Routledge, 2016); and "COVID-19 y bioética global," *Medicina y Ética* 33, no. 1 (2022): 19–52.

[14] Adela Cortina, "Bioética para el siglo XXI," 9.

harmony that includes all peoples and ways of life. We examine this in the following section.

Global Bioethics and Affective Wisdom for Survival

Global bioethics, as has been discussed above, is the appropriate response to the new demands of a globalized post-pandemic world. Bioethics will continue to confront new problems in individual ethics, but it must invariably incorporate the institutional and global levels in its reflection. In these pandemic times Catholic theological bioethics can contribute to bioethics by broadening its gaze beyond individual ethics. As Lisa Cahill observes, "Theological bioethics . . . tends to prioritize distributive justice and social solidarity over individual rights and liberty."[15] This focus comes from a rich Catholic social tradition that includes the common good as one of its fundamental axes. In a recent book edited by M. Therese Lysaught and Michael McCarthy, the authors show how Catholic social teaching illuminates Catholic bioethics by paying attention to social determinants of health and other issues such as immigration and environmental topics.[16] In so doing, Catholic social tradition helps bioethics to overcome its tendency to an individualistic approach. From the perspective of global bioethics and theological bioethics, in the following pages I propose some constitutive traits of affective wisdom, or wisdom for survival, as the path to follow in this period of planetary crisis.

Relationality

Relationality is the anthropological trait that allows us to glimpse the possibility of an ethical framework of global reach. Interdependence, not isolation, is an essential trait of the human condition. The social distancing imposed on us by the health crisis severely affected social life through the absence of physical contact, human warmth, and the sense of mutual belonging. This is a wake-up call to the branch of bioethics that applies the principle of autonomy as if people were isolated individuals. In post-pandemic bioethics the principle of autonomy should be understood as *relational autonomy.*[17]

---

[15] Lisa S. Cahill, *Theological Bioethics: Participation, Justice, and Change* (Washington, DC: Georgetown University Press, 2005), 42.

[16] M. Therese Lysaught and Michael McCarthy, eds., *Catholic Bioethics and Social Justice: The Praxis of US Health Care in a Globalized World* (Collegeville, MN: Liturgical Press, 2018).

[17] Ten Have, "COVID-19 y bioética global," 38–39. See also M. Kottow Lang, "Autonomía relacional en bioética," *Revista Iberoamericana de Bioética* 22 (2023): 1–17.

According to Martin Buber, a Jewish Austrian philosopher who survived the Nazi persecution, relationality is not just sociability but also recognition. "Only when the individual recognizes the other in all of their otherness and thus can recognize himself, as man, and moves from this recognition to penetrate the other, will he have broken his solitude in a rigorous and transformative encounter."[18] This recognition supposes that people establish horizontal relationships in which the other is neither a threat nor an obstacle; on the contrary, through a dialogic relationship individuals lower their defensive shields and learn to see the other as a human being like themselves, with their own demands and proposals, with their own desires and projects for a good life. Thus, dialogic and affective reasoning opens the way for the possibility of authentically human relationships.

In his article "The World at Risk: Vulnerability, Precarity, and Connectedness," James Keenan stresses that vulnerability is a fundamental human trait that helps us to assess the challenge of a world most in need of global cooperation.[19] Vulnerability allows us to understand that human beings need one another to attend to their precariousness. What initially appears to be a fragility, turns out to be a strength: by paying attention to the other in his or her vulnerability, we interconnect and respond as ethical beings. In fact, vulnerability allows us "to be relational and therefore moral." In so doing, we are able to build networks of cooperation, which are fundamental in a time of unprecedented global distress.

Cooperation and Multilateralism

Cooperation and multilateralism are instruments employed in international consensus and must prevail over nationalism, which strives for its own benefit; this has been evident during the pandemic regarding vaccines, with a lack of recognition that the vaccination of one's country alone does not guarantee global safety. As seen in the first section, the report from *The Lancet* emphatically indicates that, in the face of possible new pandemics, the world must take the path of cooperation and multilateralism. Bruce Jennings calls for the establishment of a new social contract with regard to public health, and he notes that "the quality of our collective and individual health depends upon an intricate web of cooperation and interdependence."[20] At the same time, Henk ten Have proposes a roadmap for post-COVID bioethics:

---

[18] Martin Buber, *¿Qué es el hombre?* (México: Fondo de Cultura Económica, 2014), 145.

[19] James F. Keenan, "The World at Risk: Vulnerability, Precarity, and Connectedness," *Theological Studies* 81, no. 1 (2020): 132–49.

[20] Bruce Jennings, "Beyond the Covid Crisis—A New Social Contract with Public Health," *The Hastings Center Report* (May 19, 2020).

In the COVID-19 era, global bioethics must rethink itself to address global phenomena, in which way a new panorama of global health governance will arise, conditions of solidarity and global cooperation will be examined, and the voices of marginalized and disadvantaged populations will be included in the ethical discourse.[21]

A new global health governance is a requirement that has been accentuated by the havoc caused by the pandemic. This endeavor does not require, at least for now, new agencies. Instead, a World Health Organization strengthened in its role of leadership in international health should actively promote cooperation and multilateralism, especially in favor of the marginalized groups and peoples of the Global South.

During the pandemic Pope Francis addressed the United Nations General Assembly to advocate for the strengthening of multilateralism, which he called "the project of God in the world," in opposition to nationalism, protectionism, and individualism, attitudes that exclude the poor and the inhabitants of the peripheries. Toward the end of his virtual message, he affirmed:

We cannot come out the same after a crisis: either we come out better or we come out worse. Thus, at this critical juncture, our duty is to *rethink the future of our common home and common project*. It is a complicated task, which requires honesty and coherence in our dialogue, with the goal of improving multilateralism and cooperation among States.[22]

Francis is conscious of the fact that without cooperation among nations, the world will be incapable of facing the pressing problems of our "common home." We must not lose ourselves in nationalism and protectionism, which stem from selfish forces. We are one human race and should act as such in these ominous times of environmental crisis and the threat of nuclear war.

Social Justice

Buber's call to recognize others in all of their otherness as a way of humanization implies an active quest for social equity that makes it

---

[21] Ten Have, "COVID-19 y bioética global," 22.

[22] Pope Francis, "Video Message of His Holiness Pope Francis to the Seventy-Fifth Meeting of the General Assembly of the United Nations," September 25, 2020. Emphasis in original.

possible to establish horizontal relationships among people. There cannot be authentic recognition if that other lives in a situation of severe social inequalities that affect his or her human dignity. Without social justice it would be a farce to affirm that we are one human race. And this is precisely what wisdom for survival seeks to articulate in global bioethics: we must be capable of recognizing others as human beings, equal in dignity and rights.

Miguel Kottow has proposed a bioethics of protection that entails the defense of victims of social inequality, a reality that is highly present in Latin America. He states that even though all human beings are vulnerable due to their finite and contingent condition, some have already been harmed or made vulnerable by poverty and abandonment. A commitment to protection is due to them while they recover their autonomy and social agency. This line of bioethics reclaims justice for the vulnerable.[23]

In the encyclical *Fratelli Tutti*, written during the pandemic, the pope links justice to fraternity by referring to throwaway culture, which eliminates those that are not useful according to strict criteria of economic productivity. In response to this blatant injustice, the pope proposes fraternity as a "universal love that uplifts people" and integrates them socially through the recognition of their immense value and dignity.[24] In this way justice contributes to taking care of our shared home and all who inhabit it, both human and nonhuman.

Solidarity

Solidarity gives justice a friendly face. While social justice calls attention to those who have been marginalized from the table of life, solidarity makes our commitment to the needs of the other tangible. Its objective is to humanize social life. As we have seen in the first section, social scientists and bioethicists include solidarity as part of the strategy for responding to this and future pandemics. Gostin et al. speak of "global solidarity" in reference to governance of global health.[25] For his part, Henk ten Have criticizes the emphasis given to the principle of autonomy and affirms:

After COVID-19, bioethics cannot keep assuming that autonomy is the dominant ethical principle; it must recognize that taking human

---

[23] Miguel Kottow, "Bioética de protección," in Juan Carlos Tealdi (dir.), *Diccionario Latinoamericano de Bioética* (Bogotá: UNESCO-Red Latinoamericana y del Caribe de Bioética, 2008), 165–67.

[24] Pope Francis, *Fratelli Tutti: Sobre la Fraternidad y la Amistad social*, October 3, 2020, #18–21. 106–111.

[25] Gostin et al., "Reimagining Global Health," 1615–1619.

relationality seriously implies strengthening and embracing social conditions and structures that make solidarity possible.[26]

Global human coexistence is the new awareness resulting from globalization. It implies feeling part of one human race in a dynamic that leads to "recognition of the other in all their otherness." The pandemic offers the opportunity to deepen this new consciousness in the evolution of *sapiens*, in such a way that it is possible to build a world of solidarity and fraternity. There is no other option if we want to save our civilization and Planet Earth from debacle.

In tune with this new planetary conscience, Pope Francis indicates the centrality of solidarity in this path toward humanization: "The Lord questions us and, in the middle of our tempest, invites us to wake up and activate that solidarity and hope capable of giving strength, support, and meaning to those hours" when everything seems to be sinking."[27] And he adds: "As the tragic coronavirus pandemic has demonstrated to us, only together, and taking responsibility for the most fragile, can we defeat global challenges."[28] Practical and affective dialogic reasoning allows us to elucidate that solidarity is a constitutive element of the wisdom for survival proposed by global bioethics.

Responsibility and Care

In the perspective of global bioethics, responsibility and care are fundamental elements. Potter proposes overcoming anthropocentric ethics, which has conferred upon the human being an all-encompassing power over nature. Without wisdom, the use of science and technology has put the planet in grave danger. Global warming is the most severe consequence of imprudent development. In facing this grave danger, it becomes ethically imperative to take into account the interest of not only humans, but also of nonhuman life forms.[29] Hans Jonas's ethics of responsibility has contributed decisively

---

[26] Ten Have, "COVID-19 y bioética global," 46. Several years previously, Juan María de Velasco had shown the need to add the principle of solidarity to the bioethical discourse in response to the insufficiency of the principlist theory of Beauchamp and Childress. See Juan María de Velasco, *La bioética y el principio de solidaridad. Una perspectiva desde la ética teológica* (Bilbao: Universidad de Deusto, 2003).

[27] Pope Francis, *La vida después de la pandemia* (Città del Vaticano: Librería Editrice Vaticana, 2020), 24.

[28] Francis, 59.

[29] Potter developed his ideas without knowing that some forty years earlier Fritz Jahr had sketched out a bioethical framework similar to his. The contributions of this studious German were related only ten years ago by the bioethicists Eve-Marie Engels and Hans-Martin Sass (Lecaros, "La bioética global y la ética de la responsabilidad"). See also Cristina Richie's essay in this volume for more on the theme of green bioethics.

to this change of mentality. According to Jonas, in response to the global problems caused by scientific and technological development, an ethics of global reach, which also includes future generations, is required. Nature ceases to be a mere medium and becomes an end in itself. There is a real responsibility to nature and future generations.[30]

The encyclical *Laudato Si': On Care for Our Common Home* is the proposal of the church's social doctrine to face the grave problems of climate change while also addressing social and economic inequities. It is not possible, states Pope Francis, to seek partial answers to such a complex reality:

> It is fundamental that we seek integral solutions that consider the interactions of natural systems among themselves and with social systems. There are not two separate crises, one environmental and one social, but rather a single complex socio-environmental crisis. The lines for the solution require an integral approach to combat poverty, return dignity to the excluded, and simultaneously care for nature. (no. 139)

Protection of the environment involves addressing the social and economic issues that affect people. In effect, we as humans are facing a very complex socio-environmental crisis. It is not right to show concern for the contamination of the oceans without taking interest in and questioning the social inequalities faced by the poor and excluded. We will not find the integral solutions required by the times we live in that way. We inhabit a "common home." Either we save everyone, or no one is saved. Bioethics must be global and multilateral in order to fulfill its purpose of making a difference in today's complex and interconnected world.

Conclusion

The COVID-19 pandemic is a warning and an opportunity. It revealed the vulnerability of our healthcare systems, as well as the lack of coordinated actions on a global level. But on the other hand, it provides an opportunity to realize, once and for all, that the only way to face global problems, such as a pandemic or climate change, is through cooperation and solidarity among peoples. Global bioethics is a proposal for reflection and action in this time of great transformations. Ten Have writes:

---

[30] Jonas, *The Imperative of Responsibility*; see also Lecaros, "La bioética global y la ética de la responsabilidad."

We now live in a global moral community where fundamental principles are shared by everyone. Global bioethics in this sense is the new language of humanitarianism, emphasizing that we are citizens of the world who have responsibilities to each other. Distance and borders are morally irrelevant.[31]

Cooperation, solidarity, and responsibility are some of these shared fundamental principles. The way to manage them is through global citizenship, or the awareness that as inhabitants of a "common home," we must transform the relationships among ourselves and with the planet to make life sustainable.

Hopefully in the end there will no longer be "the others," but rather only a "we." . . . Hopefully so much pain will not be in vain; we will take a leap forward toward a new way of life and definitively discover that we need each other and are beholden to each other, so that humanity is reborn with every face, every hand, and every voice, beyond the borders that we have created. (*Fratelli Tutti*, no. 35)

As Bishop Pedro Casaldáliga said, our fundamental task is to humanize humanity, to embrace transformative love.

---

[31] Ten Have, *Global Bioethics*, 9.

PART IV

ETHICS OF
SEX AND GENDER

15.

Lifting Up the Voices of Others

James F. Keenan on the Anthropological, Historical, and Practical Conditions for Articulating a Catholic Sexual Ethic

MICHAEL P. JAYCOX

At the annual convention of the Catholic Theological Society of America in 2019, the society bestowed upon James Keenan its highest honor, the John Courtney Murray Award. In his acceptance speech Keenan mentioned that his aim throughout his career has always been to lift up the voices of other people, particularly his doctoral students. Reflecting on my own experience of his mentorship, I recalled with gratitude that he had let me write the dissertation I wanted to write, without imposing any agenda or conceptual framing of his own. When all of his former students who were present in the room stood up, and afterward as we posed for a group photo, I thought to myself that what he did for me, he also did for so many of us. And there we all were, dozens of his former students, from every continent of the world, each with his or her own voice.

As I consider the contributions that Keenan has made to the field of theological ethics, and the applied area of sexual ethics in particular, I continue to think about his habit of lifting up the voices of others. I propose that he has done this in three modes: anthropologically, historically, and practically. While he has not had the opportunity to write at great length in sexual ethics, his work on virtue and moral anthropology offers a reframing of sexual ethics in terms of the moral development of the person. This anthropological shift has set up the theoretical conditions that have enabled

176 Michael P. Jaycox

and inspired other scholars to use their own voices to articulate a more "filled-out" sexual ethic for particular contexts.

Second, I reflect on his ongoing work of historical retrieval and reconstruction. He demonstrates that Catholic traditions regarding sexuality have been defined not only by a preoccupation with sexual sin and the procreative norm but also, and more foundationally, by the pursuit of holiness. In service to this argument he searches Catholic moral traditions for voices that have not received the hearing due to them.

Third and finally, I note his commitment to action in solidarity with others as the appropriate and expected outcome of academic work in ethics. He has acted in tangible ways and in cooperation with others to lift up the voices of women and sexual minorities, both at the global level and at the local level.

Anthropological Mode

Unlike a great deal of Catholic sexual ethics discourse, which uses the language of virtue in service to very dubious ends, an authentic virtue methodology for sexuality considers a person's relational context and asks whether social conditions are contributing to the person's flourishing and fulfillment. Instead of a premature rush to determine which sexual actions are and are not licit, virtue ethics begins with sustained reflection on the *telos* toward which sexual activity (and all activity) ought to be directed: the human person who, in relation to other persons, has become fully mature, integrated, and aligned with respect to his or her agency, and whose actions reflect this maturity, integration, and alignment.[1] The case for any proposed virtues for sexual relationships and activity would have to be made, therefore, on the basis of whether a virtue would, when practiced in specific relational contexts, help agents to become that *telos.* This is what an authentic anthropological method would look like in sexual ethics, and this is precisely what Keenan has articulated.

Keenan offers an approach to virtue ethics that is distinctive in a number of ways. He argues that virtues supply and communicate substantive moral content; they are not merely exhortative in relation to normative ethics.[2] This is so because "any normative ethics finds its origins in a virtue

---

[1] I borrow this language of virtuous "alignment" from Craig Ford, "'Born That Way?' The Challenge of Trans/Gender Identity for Catholic Theology," in *Sex, Love, and Families: Catholic Perspectives,* ed. Jason King and Julie Hanlon Rubio (Collegeville, MN: Liturgical Press, 2020), 85–93.

[2] See James Keenan, "Virtues, Principles, and a Consistent Ethic of Life," in *The Consistent Ethic of Life: Assessing Its Reception and Relevance,* ed. Thomas Nairn, 48–60 (Maryknoll, NY: Orbis Books, 2008), 49.

ethics."[3] Virtues generate norms, not the other way around. Virtue is the more fundamental posture through which every culture and community expresses its moral anthropology. Therefore, norms for sexuality cannot be straightforwardly deduced from the natural law. Rather, when we attempt to rearticulate virtues at a genuinely cross-cultural level, they can supply a modest account of the kind of person who is capable of perceiving the natural law universal to all human cultures and contexts.[4] The work of moral theologians is to reinterpret natural law as progressively unfolding in history and as accessible to virtuous persons in specific contexts.[5] Finally, because this vision of the virtuous person includes several virtues rather than one virtue, and because Keenan has an appreciation for moral complexity and ambiguity, he engages the possibility that there may be tension and even conflict as different virtues make different moral claims upon us in particular contextual situations.[6]

Bringing these anthropological insights to the specific task of articulating a viable sexual ethic, Keenan builds on the feminist scholarship of Margaret Farley and Lisa Cahill, who have reconstructed the meaning of sexuality as a relational capacity.[7] He situates the possibility of conflicting virtue claims in the context of a relational anthropology constituted by relations to self, to particular other, and to general other.[8] Each aspect of our relational identities is governed by an appropriate virtue (self-care, fidelity, and justice, respectively), and we adjudicate conflicting claims among them by the virtue of prudence, which integrates and aligns the other three virtues into a coherent relational identity in pursuit of its *telos*. Prudence offers no pre-determined prioritization or hierarchy of the virtues, for "they have equally urgent claims and they should be pursued as ends in themselves."[9] For example, in the case of a sexual relationship in which one's partner struggles with addiction, it is not possible to know in advance whether to prioritize action guided by fidelity or action guided by self-care. As persons growing in prudence, we are responsible for developing our

---

[3] Keenan, 50. Also see James Keenan, "Proposing Cardinal Virtues," *Theological Studies* 56, no. 4 (1995), 711.

[4] See James Keenan, "Virtue Ethics and Sexual Ethics," *Louvain Studies* 30, no. 3 (2005): 187.

[5] See James Keenan, "Virtue and Identity," in *Creating Identity: Biographical, Moral, Religious*, ed. Hermann Häring et al., 69–77 (London: SCM Press, 2000), 70–71.

[6] See Keenan, 73–74; Keenan, "Proposing Cardinal Virtues," 721; and Keenan, "Virtue Ethics and Sexual Ethics," 189.

[7] See Margaret Farley, "A Feminist Version of Respect for Persons," *Journal of Feminist Studies in Religion* 9, no. 1 (1993): 183–98; and Lisa Sowle Cahill, *Sex, Gender, and Christian Ethics* (New York: Cambridge University Press, 1996).

[8] See Keenan, "Proposing Cardinal Virtues," 723ff.

[9] See Keenan, "Virtue Ethics and Sexual Ethics," 190.

agency and identity with respect to both relationalities, and so we must choose our action as a prudent person would, even (and especially) under adverse circumstances.

Keenan's virtue-based approach to sexual ethics suggests two significant implications. First, sexuality is one relational context among the many contexts in which our habitual actions contribute to the process of becoming a mature, integrated, and aligned person. If every human act is a moral act, as Thomas Aquinas helped us to understand, then this includes sexual activity.[10] Therefore, Keenan's approach brings a high seriousness to conversations about sexual ethics in the academy, the church, and the broader society, a seriousness that secular culture often lacks. A reductively libertarian approach to sexual ethics, in which all is well as long as everyone consents and no one harms another, tends to be the dominant secular approach in US society and popular culture. In a scholarly context this approach tends to be based on a misappropriation of the Foucauldian insight that discursive forces, which are historically contingent, have produced all sexual norms, desires, and identities.[11] Indeed, if all norms for sex merely function to maintain current power relations and do not necessarily promote human flourishing, then the antinomian impulse to reject them is understandable. But Keenan's approach shows us that this libertarian sexual ethic is simply not a morally serious position, despite its appealing simplicity. It lacks critical feminist reflection on the gendered abuse of power in sexual relationships, does not interrogate the white male subject presupposed as the agent seeking to satisfy his sexual desires,[12] neglects the intersection of sexuality with other human goods, and ultimately does not consider the role of sexual relationships and sexual activity in helping us become virtuous persons.

Second, Keenan's approach encourages us to refrain from proposing premature answers to apparently urgent ethical questions about which sexual activities are or are not in accordance with the natural law. Such

---

[10] See Thomas Aquinas, *Summa Theologiae,* trans. Fathers of the English Dominican Province (New York: Benziger Brothers, 1948), I-II.1.3; James Keenan, "Virtue Ethics," in *Christian Ethics: An Introduction,* ed. Bernard Hoose, 84–94 (New York: Continuum, 1998), 89; and Keenan, "Virtue Ethics and Sexual Ethics," 185.

[11] Foucault's anthropology is actually a radical departure from the autonomous, self-transparent, consciously knowing, Enlightenment self presupposed in libertarian thought. See Michel Foucault, *The History of Sexuality, Volume I: An Introduction* (New York: Pantheon Books, 1978).

[12] Catharine MacKinnon's critique of Foucault on these points is especially instructive. See Catharine MacKinnon, *A Feminist Theory of the State* (Cambridge, MA: Harvard University Press, 1989); and Margaret Farley, *Just Love: A Framework for Christian Sexual Ethics* (New York: Continuum, 2006), 18–23.

preoccupation misses the more fundamental question of whether agents are developing into the morally mature persons Christ calls them to become, persons capable of discerning how to act in accordance with the natural law in specific contexts and circumstances that are often uncertain and ambiguous, and that involve potentially conflicting relational claims. In view of Keenan's reminder that virtues always precede norms, prudence and some experience are both necessary in order to navigate the messiness of sexuality, to grow in virtue, and ultimately to know whether particular sexual norms inferred from the natural law actually promote human flourishing in specific contexts.

An appreciation of Keenan's work on virtue and sexuality would not be complete without noting that although he himself has not published extensively in this area of applied ethics, his work nevertheless has exerted a great influence in reframing the conversation about sexuality in the context of Catholic ethics and opened the way for many others, including several of his students, to use their own voices to articulate a more "filled-out" sexual ethic from a variety of critical perspectives. In particular, I highlight the contributions of Lisa Fullam, Todd Salzman, Michael Lawler, Emily Reimer-Barry, Craig Ford, Megan McCabe, and Karen Peterson-Iyer, all of whom have built upon Keenan's approach while also offering their own new insights.[13] Our theological understanding of the relational virtues of human sexuality has been greatly enriched, expanded, and diversified by listening to their voices.

Historical Mode

A large portion of Keenan's scholarship lifts up voices from the past, that is, historical source materials that make reference to what we would today call sexuality. We can characterize the development of his historical work on sexual ethics as a series of expanding circles: He starts with fairly straightforward ethical analysis of the historical development of Catholic

---

[13] See Lisa Fullam, "Sex in 3–D: A Telos for a Virtue Ethics of Sexuality," *Journal of the Society of Christian Ethics* 27, no. 2 (2007): 151–70; Todd Salzman and Michael Lawler, *The Sexual Person: Toward a Renewed Catholic Anthropology* (Washington, DC: Georgetown University Press, 2008); Emily Reimer-Barry, *Catholic Theology of Marriage in the Era of HIV and AIDS: Marriage for Life* (Lanham, MD: Lexington Books, 2015); Ford, "Born This Way?"; Megan McCabe, "Relationships instead of Hooking Up? Justice in Dating," in King and Rubio, *Sex, Love, and Families: Catholic Perspectives,* 27–35; and Karen Peterson-Iyer, *Reenvisioning Sexual Ethics: A Feminist Christian Account* (Washington, DC: Georgetown University Press, 2022).

moral teaching specifically about sexuality.[14] Then he proceeds to situate contemporary debates about sexuality in the context of a more general study of the development of Catholic ethics during the twentieth century.[15] Most recently, he has plumbed the depths of scripture and early Christianity in an effort to recenter all scholarly work in theological ethics, including reflection about the meaning of bodies and sexuality, on fundamental practices and beliefs such as love, mercy, discipleship, holiness, creation, incarnation, and resurrection.[16] In these expanding circles of historical research we can see that Keenan's approach to sexual ethics has become more deeply theological over the course of his scholarly career.

In providing his own historical account of Catholic thought about sexuality, a consistent motivation for Keenan seems to have been the urgency of offering a viable alternative to John Mahoney's influential argument that all Christian moral thought is grounded upon a basic preoccupation with sin. Mahoney's argument obviously holds significant implications for the interpretation of specifically Catholic traditions of moral reasoning about sexuality, such as natural law.[17] By contrast, Keenan lifts up different voices from the past in order to ground his contention that "the tradition was founded on the pursuit of holiness and not, as [Mahoney] believed, on the confession of sin."[18] The theological implications of Keenan's proposed shift in historical perspective are enormous: First, the human body is good because of our creation by God as embodied creatures. It is much easier to regard the body as sinful when it is viewed through a dualistic frame, as a thing possessed by the soul, the passions of which the soul must master. By contrast, the integrated anthropology of early Christianity challenges us to consider that we *are* bodies; we do not *have* bodies. If human persons are good because created by God, then the body is good precisely because it is nothing other than the embodied person. Second, embodied action (whether sexual or nonsexual) is the only way to practice love and resist injustice, activities that are enabled and confirmed by God's decision to become incarnate in the person of Christ. Third, the body is a pathway to holiness, primed to respond to the

---

[14] See James Keenan, "Catholicism, History of," in *Sex from Plato to Paglia: A Philosophical Encyclopedia, vol. 1,* ed. Alan Soble (Westport, CT: Greenwood Press, 2005), 143–53.

[15] See James Keenan, *A History of Catholic Moral Theology in the Twentieth Century: From Confessing Sins to Liberating Consciences* (New York: Continuum, 2010).

[16] See James Keenan, *A History of Catholic Theological Ethics* (New York: Paulist Press, 2022).

[17] See John Mahoney, *The Making of Moral Theology: A Study of the Roman Catholic Tradition* (New York: Oxford University Press, 1989).

[18] Keenan, *A History of Catholic Theological Ethics,* xv.

Spirit, because of the resurrection of Christ's body and of all bodies who are members of Christ.[19]

These foundational theological insights about the meaning of the body were effectively eclipsed by later historical developments in Christian ethical thought that redirected ethical reflection toward the manifestation of sin in the specific context of sexual activity. We could point, for example, to the process by which Augustine's ideas about marriage (that it is defined by fidelity, procreation, and indissolubility) eventually became a hegemonic norm for all sexual activity, or to the social construction of "sodomy" in monastic communities, or to the debate among casuists about whether sexual sins have "parvity of matter." While acknowledging the long reach of these historical traditions, Keenan urges us to consider that the task of reconstructing a robustly theological sexual ethic would require us to return to the earlier Christian sources for discerning the meaning of our embodied, relational selves.

Finally, while Keenan's work in bioethics is not primarily concerned with questions of sexual ethics, his historical work of retrieving, reinterpreting, and reapplying Catholic casuistry traditions in order to address serious issues of injustice in bioethics has contributed to the flourishing of women and LGBTQ people on a global scale. Similar to the moral intuitions of sixteenth-century casuists, Keenan's response to the HIV/AIDS epidemic has been animated by the recognition that we require an ethical methodology attentive to the standpoint of the moral subject who pursues the good, and not reliant upon "ahistorical and acontextual moral principles," because there is a "need many people have to reason rightly in the face of new social problems embedded within a rapidly changing social matrix."[20] Emboldened by this insight, Keenan retrieved the "low" casuistry principles of the seventeenth century (toleration, cooperation, totality, double effect, lesser evil), which had originally been designed to address difficult sixteenth-century cases, and then he reinterpreted these principles by drawing an analogy to a twentieth-century case—using a condom as a prophylactic to prevent HIV transmission.[21] In

---

[19] See Keenan, 36–42.

[20] James Keenan and Thomas Shannon, "Contexts of Casuistry: Historical and Contemporary," in *The Context of Casuistry,* ed. James Keenan and Thomas Shannon, 221–31 (Washington, DC: Georgetown University Press, 1995), 227; also see James Keenan, "Moral Theology," in *From Trent to Vatican II: Historical and Theological Investigations,* ed. Raymond Bulman and Frederick Parrella (New York: Oxford University Press, 2006), 161–78.

[21] See James Keenan, "Prophylactics, Toleration, and Cooperation: Contemporary Problems and Traditional Principles," *International Philosophical Quarterly* 29, no. 2 (1989): 205–20; James Keenan, "Applying the Seventeenth-Century Casuistry of Accommodation to HIV Prevention," *Theological Studies* 60, no. 3 (1999): 492–512; and Jon Fuller and James Keenan, "Condoms, Catholics, and HIV/AIDS Prevention," *The Furrow* 52, no. 9 (2001): 459–67.

effect, he was exercising his own prudence, reviving the older tradition of "high" casuistry in order to save the lives of vulnerable human beings, among whom women and LGBTQ people are disproportionately represented.

Thus, Keenan's historical work on casuistry has taught us not only that moral thought is fundamentally based in prudent reasoning about concrete situations, where case analysis and analogical reasoning are important tools, but also that this methodology holds significant implications for the well-being of vulnerable people struggling to flourish in a context of systemic injustice. His work therefore challenges us to continue employing this methodology in response to current ethical challenges. Consider the rapidly changing cultural constructions of gender and sexuality, which are prompting a reactionary wave of homophobic and transphobic legislation and violence, countered by a human rights movement calling for basic recognition and institutional reform. In this context, what significance might an analogous application of the principle of totality have for the ethical questions being raised about providing gender-affirming care in Catholic hospitals, for example? Here is another instance in which Keenan's work invites others to contribute their voices to the conversation.

Finally, Keenan's historical work demonstrates the importance of framing an ethical challenge with the appropriate language and concepts. While it may be tempting, for example, to frame HIV as a sexual-ethics issue because sexual activity is a vector for its transmission, this framing may predispose us to treat traditional Catholic sexual norms (abstinence outside of marriage, fidelity within marriage, refraining from condom use) as behavior modification strategies, even though these very strategies have historically failed to reduce HIV infections and AIDS deaths from a global-public-health standpoint. The concern to modify individual sexual behavior misses the point. Instead, Keenan shows us that it is important to frame the HIV/AIDS epidemic primarily as a bioethical issue. Engaging the structural turn in public-health discourse from the perspective of moral anthropology, he proposed vulnerability as a central ethical category in the response to HIV/AIDS.[22] Recognizing human vulnerability to structural violence and crafting a merciful policy response to that vulnerability—those are the real ethical challenges.

---

[22] See James Keenan, "Four of the Tasks of Theological Ethics in a Time of HIV/ AIDS," in *Concilium: AIDS*, ed. Regina Ammicht-Quinn and Hille Haker (London: SCM Press, 2007), 64–74; and James Keenan and Enda McDonagh, *Instability, Structural Violence, and Vulnerability: A Christian Response to the HIV Pandemic* (London: Progressio, 2009).

Practical Mode

Over the course of his academic career in theological ethics, Keenan has constantly reminded his colleagues that as "ethical insight, *to be ethical, must end in action,* similarly the task of the ethicist must end in political action."[23] In addition to being teachers and writers, we are also called to be political activists. Keenan practices what he preaches, having engaged in ethical activism in at least three major ways.

First, having learned about the structural and cultural problems in the institutional church that enabled the sexual-abuse crisis and its cover-up, his scholarship has recently turned to the near-complete lack of professional ethics in colleges and universities. This oversight creates in these institutional environments a culture that similarly conceals and normalizes patterns of injustice, including rampant sexual harassment, abuse, and assault.[24] As an appropriate and expected outgrowth of his verbal commitment to professional ethics, Keenan has used his leadership positions at Boston College, in the Society of Christian Ethics, and in the Catholic Theological Society of America to create and cultivate a more ethical culture characterized by systems and policies that ensure accountability.

Second, Keenan has made good on his stated commitments to global solidarity and dialogue across differences through his work as a principal organizer for three international conferences of Catholic ethicists in Padua (2005), Trento (2010), and Sarajevo (2018). In order for the dialogue to be possible, and the solidarity to be demonstrably real, he knew that these conferences would need to be built upon an inclusive culture and an equitable system for fundraising and distributing financial assistance, particularly for interested conference participants traveling to Europe from the Global South. As a result, the presentations and conversations that were able to happen were both unrepeatable and radically transformative. Having attended the Trento conference myself, I recall the extraordinary testimony of Anne Nasimiyu-Wasike, who raised her own voice in protest to the ignoring and silencing of women's voices and elderly voices in the patriarchal context of traditional Kenyan society, as well as in history and

---

[23] Keenan, "Virtue and Identity," 70; also see Keenan, "Four of the Tasks of Theological Ethics in a Time of HIV/AIDS," 67.
[24] See James Keenan, "(The Lack of) Professional Ethics in the Academy," *Louvain Studies* 35, no. 1 (2011): 98–116; and James Keenan, *University Ethics: How Colleges Can Build and Benefit from a Culture of Ethics* (Lanham, MD: Rowman & Littlefield, 2015).

theology.[25] Her voice received an equal hearing alongside more established (white, middle-class, and male) voices from the Global North also writing about sexual ethics, such as Roger Burggraeve.[26] These opportunities for dialogue strengthened cross-cultural knowledge and relationships, which in turn created new cultural expectations and practices of global solidarity among those present. And now, in what is perhaps the most significant expression of Keenan's commitment to lifting up the voices of other people, he and the other organizers have encouraged the members of our guild to stop doing international conferences of Catholic ethicists. Enriched by the opportunities those conferences have provided, the focus is now on turning over those conversations to the regional level while maintaining international relationships through a global network, Catholic Theological Ethics in the World Church.

Third, I offer as a concluding reflection the fact that Keenan translated his ethical scholarship into ethical action in 2003 when, in fidelity to his stated commitment to justice for gay and lesbian couples, he offered his testimony before the Massachusetts legislature against a proposed amendment to the state constitution that would have denied to gay and lesbian couples the full range of civil rights already enjoyed by heterosexual married couples. He made his case not on the basis of arguments about whether gay and lesbian sexual activity should be considered morally permissible, nor on the basis of assertions about the nature of marriage itself and the ideals of love, commitment, and family it represents (as Justice Kennedy would a few years later in the *Obergefell v. Hodges* decision), but rather on the basis of Catholic social thought. It was a matter of social justice, unjust discrimination by the state, and basic social rights. As a result of taking this risk, he lost his appointment on the ecclesiastical faculty at Weston Jesuit School of Theology, and he moved to Boston College.

His decision to take this risk affected my own family life and career in several significant ways: Having access to marriage equality in Massachusetts in 2013, before it was legal elsewhere, has given my family the stability, rights, support, and social recognition we needed to flourish together and in our community and society. It has enabled me to ensure that my spouse has had access to healthcare through my employer when he was not himself employed. It made it much easier for us to adopt our son. And it is one social condition, among others, that has enabled me to write this essay and dedicate it to him. Thank you, Jim, for lifting up my voice.

---

[25] See Anne Nasimiyu-Wasike, "The Missing Voices of Women," in *Catholic Theological Ethics Past, Present, and Future: The Trento Conference*, ed. James Keenan (Maryknoll, NY: Orbis Books, 2011), 107–15.

[26] See Roger Burggraeve, "Historical Building Blocks for a Consistent Relational and Sexual Ethics," in Keenan, *Catholic Theological Ethics Past, Present, and Future*, 86–95.

16.

Conscience and the Continuum of Sexual Violence

MEGAN K. MCCABE

In his writing on conscience James Keenan has traced differences in the theologies of conscience in European and American contexts. As he argues, American theologies of conscience emerged as responses to the Vietnam War and the promulgation of *Humanae Vitae*, and thus emphasize individual freedom. In contrast, European theologians turned to conscience following the horrors of World War II with particular concern for the call to moral maturity and discernment. As Keenan has argued, the United States would benefit from an embrace of the approach to conscience that emerged in Europe in the mid-twentieth century. With its awareness of moral responsibility for human suffering, this approach to conscience offers insight into the moral responses to human suffering and social sin. In particular, I am concerned with the contribution Keenan's theology of conscience can make to discerning moral responsibilities in light of the realities of a continuum of sexual violence. He describes a socially responsible conscience that is attentive to the moral demands posed by suffering, particularly suffering caused by human beings. Such a notion of conscience calls us to responsibility in the face of sexual violence. However, this theological approach is inadequate on its own given the cultural formation that inclines persons to dismiss the far reach of patterns that normalize sexual abuse and prioritize the needs and views of those accused of sexual abuse. Though a socially responsible conscience is essential, it must be shaped by the normative principle of the preferential option for the poor. In so doing, it will be able to respond to the needs of those who are victimized and vulnerable to victimization, not the desires of the powerful, those who are abusers, or those who unconsciously benefit from an unjust status quo.

The Far Reach of Sexual Violence

Sexual violence is a pervasive problem. With one in six women in the United States experiencing rape or attempted rape in their lifetimes, it is a form of violence that disproportionately, though by no means exclusively, shapes the lives of women and girls.[1] Further, feminists' analysis has suggested that rape and sexual assault ought to be understood as part of a continuum of violence that includes coercion and harassment.[2] As Nicola Gavey has argued, this view holds that "while rape is the extreme act, it could be seen as existing on a continuum with more subtle forms of coercion from an unwanted kiss to unwanted sexual intercourse submitted to as a result of verbal pressure."[3] Philosopher Ann Cahill further identifies what she calls the "heteronormative sexual continuum" that names the political underpinnings at work in both sexual assault and "hegemonic, heteronormative sexual interactions."[4] In this context, while rape and sexual assault are criminal acts of violence, there are also ethical questions to consider about forms of sex that may be unwanted but consented to, or in situations in which social scripts constrain women's full freedom and consent.[5]

Such an approach should not be taken to mean that an unwanted kiss and rape are equally violent or to undermine the severity of rape and its effect on those who are victimized. Rather, across the continuum there is a shared logic of gendered norms that maintain male entitlement to women. Gavey maintains that these "taken-for-granted normative forms of heterosexuality work as a cultural scaffolding of rape."[6] For Gavey, this cultural scaffolding includes

---

[1] RAINN (Rape, Abuse & Incest National Network), "Victims of Sexual Violence: Statistics," rainn.org.

[2] Liz Kelly, "The Continuum of Sexual Violence," in *Women, Violence and Social Control*, ed. Jalna Hanmer and Mary Maynard (London: Macmillan, 1987), 46–59.

[3] Nicola Gavey, *Just Sex?: The Cultural Scaffolding of Rape* (New York: Routledge, 2005), 61.

[4] Ann J. Cahill, "Unjust Sex vs. Rape," *Hypatia* 31, no. 4 (2016): 746.

[5] For further ethical and theological implications on social scripts, women's freedom, and women's flourishing, see also Elizabeth Lawrence Antus, "'WAS IT GOOD FOR YOU?': Recasting Catholic Sexual Ethics in Light of Women's Sexual Pain Disorders," *Journal of Religious Ethics* 46, no. 4 (December 2018): 611–34; Karen Peterson-Iyer, *Reenvisioning Sexual Ethics: A Feminist Christian Account* (Washington, DC: Georgetown University Press, 2022).

[6] Gavey, *Just Sex?*, 2.

the legitimized, normalized, and normalizing constructions of aggressive male sexuality and passive female sexuality that provide not only a social pattern for coercive sexuality but also a convenient smoke-screen for rationalizing rape (within heterosexual relationships, in particular) as simply just sex.[7]

Rapists are thus given cultural permission to justify their behavior. And unjust, but not criminal, sexual encounters can inhibit women's well-being and constrain women's sexual agency.[8] Furthermore, Cahill argues, the gendered norms that shape the entire heteronormative sexual continuum that includes both criminal violence and "typical" sex uphold inequality between women and men.[9]

According to this feminist analysis, the problem here is not exclusively one of identifying "bad men" who are perpetrators. Rather, there is an extensive reach of culture that normalizes gendered inequality, sexual coercion, patterns of harassment, and sexual violence. It is the collective participation in these gendered norms, though often unconscious or unaware of the implications, that allows the cultural scaffolding of rape to continue.[10]

Additionally, the shared handing on of rape myths perpetuates conditions that undermine perpetrators' responsibility. Indeed, both women and men who hold rape myths are more likely to maintain narrow definitions of what qualifies as rape, effectively rendering all other forms of rape and sexual abuse as relatively acceptable.[11] One such myth is that the typical rapist is a stranger lurking in the bushes or in a parking garage; this myth is widely circulated in "safety tips" often given to young women. It also shows up in character statements in defense of accused, or even known, perpetrators as good friends or otherwise leaders in communities. As philosopher Kate Manne notes, this approach suggests that only monsters perpetrate sexual abuse. She argues: "Rapists are human, all too human, and they are very much among us. The idea of rapists as monsters exonerates by caricature."[12] It is this myth about who rapists are that overlaps with Manne's diagnosis of what she calls "himpathy." Specifically, "himpathy," in her argument, is

---

[7] Gavey, 72.
[8] Gavey, 70–71.
[9] Ann J. Cahill, "Unjust Sex vs. Rape," *Hypatia* 31, no. 4 (2016): 301–19.
[10] Karen Ross, Megan K. McCabe, and Sara Wilhelm Garbers, "Christian Sexual Ethics and the #MeToo Movement: Three Moments of Reflection on Sexual Violence and Women's Bodies," *Journal of the Society of Christian Ethics* (November 12, 2019); Megan K. McCabe, "A Feminist Catholic Response to the Social Sin of Rape Culture," *Journal of Religious Ethics* 46, no. 4 (2018): 634–57.
[11] Gavey, *Just Sex?* 37.
[12] Kate Manne, *Down Girl: The Logic of Misogyny*, reprint ed. (New York: Oxford University Press, 2019), 199.

"excessive sympathy sometimes shown toward male perpetrators of sexual violence. It is frequently extended in contemporary America to men who are white, nondisabled, and otherwise privileged 'golden boys' such as [Brock] Turner, the recipient of a Stanford swimming scholarship."[13] Within the Catholic Church a similar expression of "himpathy" manifests in cases of community members failing or refusing to believe that the priests they may know in positive contexts can also be perpetrators of horrific violence. Manne argues that generally the values that underly such "himpathy" are considered good, such as loyalty, trusting the evidence that we have of somebody's character, or empathy.[14]

Other rape myths misrepresent victims. One rape myth against victims of abuse or harassment may be the flip side of perpetrator-excusing "himpathy," holding that an, often female, accuser is seeking some kind of revenge or misunderstood her experiences, effectively turning victim into villain.[15] These myths may include that abuse has occurred only if a victim struggled or screamed for help. A rape myth may also hold that only certain people, especially the sexually chaste, make believable victims, drawing on victim-blaming language that women must have been "asking for it" in some way.[16] All of these myths have the power to discourage those who are victimized from reporting or seeking help. This effect is particularly pernicious when used against Black women, who are often stereotyped through racist myths as hypersexual or excessively strong and less likely to experience pain. As a consequence, evidence has shown that Black women are less likely than white women to report sexual abuse.[17]

Feminist theological analysis identifies the cultural conditions that uphold rape and these rape myths as sinful.[18] They undermine the human dignity of persons and serve to normalize acts of sexual violence. This cultural context functions sinfully by shaping what forms of gendered expression, and the correlative association with dominance and submission,

---

[13] Maya Salam, "Brock Turner Is Appealing His Sexual Assault Conviction," *The New York Times*, December 2, 2017; Manne, *Down Girl*, 197.

[14] Manne, *Down Girl*, 200.

[15] Remarks along these lines were used against the testimonies of both Anita Hill and Christine Blasey Ford (Manne, 201).

[16] Diana Scully has shown that some groups of convicted rapists use this same logic to excuse their own acts of violence as somehow "not that bad" or not actually "rape." Diana Scully, *Understanding Sexual Violence: A Study of Convicted Rapists* (Boston: Unwin Hyman, 1990).

[17] Gavey, *Just Sex?*, 27, 51–52; Kelly B. Douglas, *Sexuality and the Black Church: A Womanist Perspective* (Maryknoll, NY: Orbis Books, 1999).

[18] McCabe, "A Feminist Catholic Response to the Social Sin of Rape Culture"; Ross, McCabe, and Garbers, "Christian Sexual Ethics and the #MeToo Movement"; Peterson-Iyer, *Reenvisioning Sexual Ethics*.

are taken for granted as normal and expected. This culture shapes persons. And persons participate in upholding this same sinful culture "through the non-conscious behaviors and citations of gender norms."[19] Though perpetrators alone are responsible for their violent actions, persons within this sinful culture hand on the expectations of gender and sexuality, promote rape myths, and express "himpathy." As Keenan has argued, sin is present in the "failure to bother to love."[20] And, as such, persons sin through a careless failing to respond to those who suffer within this cultural scaffolding of rape. What this cultural context requires is an active response that both prioritizes those who are victimized and takes seriously the responsibility to work toward cultural transformation away from the cultural foundations of rape and the heteronormative sexual continuum. The far reach of this culture requires a moral response grounded in the discernment of responsible moral agents in the particularity of their own lives and situations in which they find themselves.

Conscience and the Call to Love of Neighbor

James Keenan has argued in favor of a recovery and embrace of an understanding of conscience as a call to love God, neighbor, and self. Such an approach is deeply rooted in his assessment of the recovery of conscience in Europe following the Second World War. In what he calls a reaction to the "widespread participation of Catholics in unimaginably heinous conduct during the war,"[21] moral theologians developed a theology of conscience as a call to develop a robust moral agency. As he argues, these European theologians believed that the approach to conscience that had existed in the moral manuals in the eighteenth to twentieth centuries not only failed to foster a moral response but "helped lead the way to an obediential passivity in the laity that left them unprepared for the dictatorial rule of the Nazis and their Fascist allies."[22] The theology of conscience that emerged from this context was deeply relational while also "always mindful of the responsibility to hear the call of Christ."[23]

---

[19] Ross, McCabe, and Garbers, "Christian Sexual Ethics and the #MeToo Movement," 350.

[20] James F. Keenan, "Raising Expectations on Sin," *Theological Studies* 77, no. 1 (March 2016): 165–80.

[21] James F. Keenan, "Redeeming Conscience," *Theological Studies* 76, no. 1 (March 2015): 133.

[22] James F. Keenan, "Called to Conscience: Americans Must Recognize Their Own Capacity for Evil," *America* 216, no. 1 (January 2, 2017): 14.

[23] Keenan, 14.

This theology of conscience was ultimately embraced by Vatican II's *Gaudium et Spes*:

Deep within their consciences men and women discover a law which they have not laid upon themselves and which they must obey. Its voice, ever calling them to love and to do what is good and to avoid evil, tells them inwardly at the right moment: do this, shun that. For they have in their hearts a law inscribed by God. Their dignity rests in observing this law, and by it they will be judged. Conscience is the most secret core and the sanctuary of the human person. There they are alone with God whose voice echoes in their depths. By conscience, in a wonderful way, that law is made known which is fulfilled in the love of God and of one's neighbor. Through loyalty to conscience, Christians are joined to others in the search for truth and for the right solution to so many moral problems which arise both in the life of individuals and from social relations. (Flannery, no. 16)

Here we see that conscience makes demands to discern how to make real the love of neighbor. These demands are not merely to obey but to discern and search for moral truth in light of the pressing problems of their communities.

For this reason Keenan argues that the US context would benefit from a retrieval of the insights of the European theologians. He notes that the awareness and reckoning with collective guilt was a key feature of the European approach to conscience that emerged in the postwar period. In this work, "Europeans began a process of understanding their capacity for evil."[24] In contrast, American approaches tend to emphasize not responsibility and obligation to God's will, but instead individual freedom. American theologies of conscience were shaped by a different context: resistance to the Vietnam War, and the reaction to *Humanae Vitae*. As Keenan incisively argues, "These moments of conscience were not begun, as they were in Europe, with the collective social acknowledgment of the profound human violations of moral law."[25] These approaches instead thought of conscience in relation to what is commanded or required. Specifically, American moral theologians continued to look to Rome for answers to moral questions, ultimately emphasizing an understanding of the moral life in relation to commands or laws.[26] And, as a result,

---

[24] Keenan, 14. For how Keenan's analysis of European context shaped a specific moral theologian, see James F. Keenan, "Bernard Häring's Influence on American Catholic Moral Theology," *Journal of Moral Theology* 1, no. 1 (January 1, 2012): 23–42.

[25] Keenan, "Called to Conscience," 15.

[26] Keenan, "Redeeming Conscience," 133.

American theologies of conscience never made the shift to moral agency, but instead understood conscience as the free choice to opt in or opt out of particular external commands. American approaches to conscience, thus, fail adequately to account for the demands of conscience to make real the love of God and neighbor. They do not reflect a responsible moral agency but merely one's relationship to set rules.

In the context of attention to sexual and gendered violence, understanding conscience in relation to laws or commands has potential negative consequences for the well-being of those who are victimized or who are threatened by victimization in a rape-prone and sexist culture. If conscience is understood as looking to formal guidance or law for answers, it is easy to conflate the standards of criminal law with ethical standards regarding realities of sexual and gendered violence. Specifically, when potential perpetrators are legally presumed innocent or may not be convicted or prosecuted, an accused person is often believed to have been wronged or even harmed by the accusation. It is true that all persons are owed due process, both legally and in the policies of various social institutions. Due process is particularly critical in the face of racist stereotypes of Black men as dangerously hypersexual.[27] However, in practice, calls for due process may be conflated with the excessive sympathy for the accused, which turns the accuser into a perpetrator. Moreover, considerations of moral responsibilities in response to realities of sexual violence cannot all be answered by a conscience that is primarily concerned with duties or freedom to a command or law. Such an approach fails to center the needs or well-being of survivors. It also fails to consider the responsibilities persons have to work to counter and transform the cultural scaffolding of rape.

In contrast, the call to moral responsibility of the postwar European theologies of conscience offers a way forward through a vision of the moral responsibilities persons have to one another. As Keenan argues, this approach to conscience is not merely about the individual's moral standing but is necessarily relational and social. He explains, "Though deeply interior, the conscience is the key to our relationships with others, our world, ourselves, and our God."[28] This social dimension is evident in the concerns of the European moral theologians who, along with their communities, were struggling to respond to the realities of fascism and the Holocaust. Conscience, properly understood, grounds each decision. But the failures of the theologians and their communities are not about the individual's avoidance of sin, as previously understood by the moral manuals. It is instead "the way the disciple hears and responds to the triple command to love through

---

[27] Douglas, *Sexuality and the Black Church.*
[28] Keenan, "Called to Conscience," 17.

virtue."[29] It is conscience that allows persons not only to discern their general responsibility to others and their communities, but also to discern the specific actions that must be taken to make real this responsibility and call to love in the concrete.

However, despite this hope that conscience can call persons and societies to moral responsibility for social ills, these same realities of social injustice have the potential to limit conscience. As Bryan Massingale has argued, realities of oppression, specifically cultural racism, trouble confidence in the capacity of conscience, even when understood through the lens of postwar European theologies. In the personalist perspective of *Gaudium et Spes* and the European theological approach advocated by Keenan, conscience formation is linked to character development and moral maturity rather than with a particular judgment and decision. For Massingale, this model of conscience formation offered by European moral theologians will fail to foster moral agents' response to social injustice because the culture in which the moral agents live is itself malformed and inclined toward sin. Thus, he is concerned not merely with realities of social injustice, but how "cultural formation facilitates blindness and/or indifference to social injustice" even as people seek to form socially responsible consciences.[30] That is, it is the formation of conscience itself that makes persons, and communities, unable to respond meaningfully to systems of injustice and domination. Here Massingale offers a constructive intervention to Keenan's theology of conscience when he argues that theories of conscience formation rely on "the conscious awareness and intentions of the moral agent."[31] But this conscious awareness is undermined by the formative nature of cultural racism.

In this way Keenan's important but perhaps overly optimistic call for a robust recovery of conscience as hearing God's call to love in a socially responsible manner is unable to meet the challenge of entrenched systems of injustice that shape one's ways of perceiving and being in the world. Consciences are not merely the capacity to hear God's call to respond to social ills but are shaped and formed by social context. Above, I point to a cultural scaffolding of rape, including various rape myths, that is more than unjust systems in which persons participate. It disposes moral agents to accept as "normal" gendered inequality and patterns of abuse. In such a situation shaped by this manifestation of cultural sin, a person's values

---

[29] James F. Keenan, "To Follow and to Form over Time: A Phenomenology of Conscience," in *Conscience and Catholicism: Rights, Responsibilities, and Institutional Responses*, ed. David E. DeCosse and Kristin E. Heyer (Maryknoll, NY: Orbis Books, 2015), 13.

[30] Bryan N. Massingale, "Conscience Formation and the Challenge of Unconscious Racial Bias," in DeCosse and Heyer, *Conscience and Catholicism*, 56.

[31] Massingale, 62.

and understandings of expected gender roles are formed sinfully according to patterns of dominance and violence. One result is that the violence that shapes sexuality and gender roles may not be seen for what it is. In such a case consciences are not formed in a way that allows for the possibility of choosing behaviors and ways of being in the world that work to transform culture. Even more, a conscience formed in this culture has been shown to promote "himpathy" and a correlative suspicion of those who name their experiences of abuse.

Keenan calls for a retrieval of a robust concept of conscience in order to respond to social problems. He argues that we need an "examination of conscience to awaken us from our complacency and to an awareness of a collective accountability."[32] Such an examination of conscience is a key component of conversion, both individual and collective.[33] In the face of extensive realities of sexual abuse and gendered violence, conversion of both persons and society is necessary. However, a malformed conscience cannot be appropriately examined. A conscience formed by rape myths or the values of loyalty and empathy that can be distorted into "himpathy" will be a conscience that is incapable of truly hearing the call to love the neighbor who has suffered, or is vulnerable to, sexual or gendered victimization. In order to build on the important interventions of both Keenan and Massingale, a normative principle to guide the formation of a socially responsible conscience in the midst of sinful cultural contexts is needed.

Consequently, consciences must be formed through an intentional cultivation of the preferential option for the poor.[34] Theological and doctrinal insights into the preferential option for the poor emerged later and in a different context than the theologies of conscience of postwar European moral theologians. The preferential option for the poor, though consistent and rooted in the entire biblical witness, emerged formally in the Latin American context. Yet both theological approaches offer ways of wrestling with the realities of human suffering and human responsibilities for suffering. Though the preferential option for the poor emerged in response to economic inequality and poverty, the phrase has expanded to include other forms of victimization and oppression. It includes those who suffer the negative effects of sexism, including the injustice and violence made possible by the cultural scaffolding of rape.

---

[32] Keenan, "Redeeming Conscience," 138.

[33] Keenan, 138.

[34] For other approaches to the formation of conscience in the context of social sins, see Lisa Fullam, "Joan of Arc, Holy Resistance, and Conscience Formation in the Face of Social Sin," in DeCosse and Heyer, *Conscience and Catholicism*, 69–82; Massingale, "Conscience Formation and the Challenge of Unconscious Racial Bias."

The preferential option for the poor is, first and foremost, a claim about God. It maintains that God's love is preferential precisely because it is universally and gratuitously offered. As Roberto Goizueta argues, a neutral God would not be a universally loving God because "a neutral God would be one whose very refusal to 'take sides' would, de facto, serve the interests of the powerful minority."[35] The claim of the preferential option for the poor is not rooted in the moral superiority of the poor or oppressed compared to the powerful, but is about God's commitment to the well-being and flourishing of all. Because of God's own choice to opt for the poor, we too are called to opt for the poor. This call applies to the poor themselves as well, who are "not to abandon their own communities by 'opting' for the values of power, wealth, and violence."[36]

In the context of high rates of gendered and sexual violence and the cultural scaffolding of rape, to opt for the poor is to opt for those who are and have been victimized. It can also include opting for those who are particularly vulnerable to victimization. When the preferential option for the poor forms consciences, it serves as an epistemological orientation to love the neighbor, and not merely in theory. Rather, truly to love one's neighbors equally, the love itself must be preferential to those who suffer victimization. To fail to do so would not achieve an idealized neutrality or objectivity but would privilege the well-being of perpetrators or would-be perpetrators.[37] As Keenan has argued, the model of conscience that is a call to moral responsibility must be social. Thus, it is not enough to limit the conscience formed by the preferential option to adjudication of particular cases. In fact, doing so would fail truly to respond to the complex problems posed by "himpathy" and the cultural scaffolding of rape. What is needed is a robust moral agency that takes seriously the responsibility to hear the call of Christ and enact it within the particularity of a person's and a community's contexts.

A socially responsible conscience formed by the preferential option is one that is able to wrestle with complicity in upholding the cultural scaffolding of rape in a wide variety of ways, including subtle and unconscious actions. It is also able to discern the specific actions one must take to sup-

---

[35] Roberto S. Goizueta, "Liberation Theology I: Gustavo Gutiérrez," in *The Wiley Blackwell Companion to Political Theology*, ed. William T. Cavanaugh and Peter Manley Scott, 2nd ed. (New York: John Wiley and Sons, 2019), 282.

[36] Goizueta, 283.

[37] Brock Turner is one such perpetrator; he was found assaulting a passed-out woman behind a dumpster. Despite the severity of his actions, his defenders presented him as the victim of unfortunate circumstances, and he received sympathy from the judge in his criminal case despite being found guilty. Liam Stack, "Light Sentence for Brock Turner in Stanford Rape Case Draws Outrage," *The New York Times*, June 6, 2016.

port victim-survivors and work to undo the cultural sin that undergirds and manifests in gendered inequality, coercion, harassment, and material violence. All the possibilities of such a responsible conscience cannot be offered here, outside of the particularity in which persons find themselves. Still, this approach would guide persons to consider the social implications of "himpathy." Excessive sympathy and loyalty to the accused certainly has the potential to fail to hold a specific perpetrator accountable and to undermine the full humanity and well-being of one who has been victimized. But there are further social ramifications; for example, in communities in which such "himpathy" is voiced, the survivors, perhaps unknown, within the community may be further harmed by the communication that sexual and gendered violence is not that serious or worthy of being condemned. It will further excuse the ability to recognize and hold other perpetrators within the community accountable. A socially responsible conscience will consider the wide variety of ways of being that can either resist or uphold the gendered norms that are part of the heteronormative sexual continuum. It will recognize that perpetuating rape myths and violent gender standards normalizes sexual violence. Most important, such a socially responsible conscience formed by the preferential option will center the perspectives and needs of those who are harmed by gendered and sexual violence rather than those of the powerful. In so doing, it will allow persons to discern how they, in the specific circumstances in which they find themselves, must work to transform their culture to one that resists sexual violence and promotes gender equality.

17.

Virtue Ethics and Moral Knowledge in a Racist and Hetero/Sexist World

CRAIG A. FORD, JR.

When I first met Jim Keenan and started working with him in the fall of 2013 at Boston College, I wasn't sure I wanted to become a virtue ethicist. The traditional account of virtue ethics struck me as naively optimistic, inadequate to confronting moral evils like racism and hetero/sexism.[1] Jim Keenan turned me into a virtue ethicist with his insight that the virtues are fundamentally relational, perfecting our dispositions to interact with others in justice and love. Building on this relational understanding, Catholic virtue ethics can learn from the insights of queer thinkers and scholars of color that *eros* is one epistemological key to overcoming these moral evils that divide us. These insights offer a way to compensate for the sinfulness of morally formative communities when we further incorporate the eschatological insight that we may be formed by exemplars from the future.

---

[1] I use the catachresis *hetero/sexism* or *hetero/sexist* to denote three different discriminatory realities. The first one refers to discriminatory stances taken against those who do not identify as *straight* or *heterosexual,* and thus identifies *hetero/sexism* in the typical sense. The other two discriminatory realities are based on gender. On the one hand, the word *sexism* draws attention to the oppressive realities of patriarchy and misogyny that have oppressed women throughout history. On the other hand, *hetero* draws attention to the dimension of *hetero/sexism* that presumes a binary account of gender difference, and thus draws attention to accounts of gender that are transphobic or, more broadly construed, antiqueer.

Limitations of Traditional Virtue Ethics

For virtue ethicists, the person who possesses moral excellence has the virtues. They are the person, to borrow some phrasing from Nicholas Austin, who possesses the means "to know what is to be done (prudence), act from choice and not mere passion (temperance), do so for a due end (justice), and act firmly and immovably (fortitude)."[2] As appealing as this sounds, this is where my objections began. After all, how exactly does one learn how to make these shiny, excellent decisions? Exemplary figures in the tradition from Aristotle to Alasdair MacIntyre answer that we learn to make virtuous decisions by living in virtuous political communities (or, per MacIntyre, within "traditions of inquiry") with virtuous people from whom we can learn to be virtuous. As straightforward as this sounded, it also seemed decidedly naive. Just in my lifetime I had witnessed the vehement resurgence of white supremacy in the events associated with Ferguson, Missouri, and Charlottesville, Virginia, along with the ascendancy of figures like Donald Trump. The last several years have produced anti-trans bills across the United States. Today, I continue to witness efforts to prohibit the telling of our nation's racist history via laws that ban so-called "critical race theory," as well as efforts to dismantle affirmative action, a major means by which the United States has attempted to atone for its racist history. To put it mildly, I am quite skeptical that, writ large, any virtuous political community exists in the United States, and I am equally skeptical that the Western tradition of thinking, which bequeathed to the world colonialism and its associated traumas, is any better on this score.

My objection to virtue ethics boiled down to this: it is not at all clear how moral goodness can be guaranteed if morality is dependent on the judgment of communities that are already themselves embedded in morally compromised social contexts and are themselves the recipients of self-interested and otherwise flawed styles of moral reasoning. This is no less the case if one turns from an idealized political community to another community such as the church—even as Stanley Hauerwas, one of the strongest proponents for the latter view, has. Hauerwas argues that the church's fundamental identity is to form virtuous character among Christian disciples by being faithful to the "story of God" in a hostile world.[3] But it's not clear how this gets out of the problem either: Europe's colonial destruction and decimation of other cultural worlds was underwritten by racist and hetero/sexist European

---

[2] Nicholas Austin, SJ, *Aquinas on Virtue: A Causal Reading* (Washington, DC: Georgetown University Press, 2017), 116.

[3] E.g., Stanley Hauerwas, *A Community of Character: Toward a Constructive Social Ethic* (Notre Dame, IN: University of Notre Dame Press, 1981), 91.

Christian *theology* throughout the modern period, and it was carried out by members of the *church* under the banner, among other titles, of the doctrine of discovery.[4] And to the extent that the church remains complicit in racism and hetero/sexism in the present, this heritage continues to the present day.[5]

Nevertheless, virtue ethicists in Hauerwas's mold deal with this problem with a twofold move: first, they emphasize the extra-institutional identity of the church—perhaps using a metaphor like "community of disciples" or "people of God"—and second, they hold out Jesus as the virtuous exemplar after whom virtuous people model their lives.[6] Now, far be it from me to deny that Jesus is the example whom Christians should imitate. My point, following on the brilliant work of the late New Testament scholar Dale Martin, is that the Jesus that Christians imitate in virtue is constructed by Christian communities, and that, more often than not, the Jesus remembered by Christians often significantly resembles the biases and proclivities of the Christians doing the remembering. This is a simple recognition of an epistemological limitation: any and all of the Jesuses we can imagine for imitation live in our memories as inflected by our present concerns and intellectual inheritances.[7] The Jesus that is real to us is the Jesus we carry

---

[4] Especially exemplary in this regard is Pope Nicholas V's 1452 letter *Dum Diversas,* which authorized violence and enslavement at the service of what was later called the doctrine of discovery. In response to this and similar papal letters, two Vatican dicasteries repudiated the doctrine of discovery in 2023. However, their statement still sought to obscure the relationship between church teaching and colonialist violence when it misleadingly insisted that the doctrine of discovery "is not part of the teaching of the Catholic Church." See the Dicastery for Culture and Education and the Dicastery for Promoting Human Development, "Joint Statement on the 'Doctrine of Discovery,' 30.03.2023," press.vatican.va.

[5] See Bryan Massingale's famous *Racial Justice and the Catholic Church* (Maryknoll, NY: Orbis Books, 2010); and Jemar Tisby, *The Color of Compromise: The Truth about the American Church's Complicity in Racism* (Grand Rapids, MI: Zondervan, 2019). The best example of hetero/sexist teachings remains the current positions of the Roman Catholic Church on sexual orientation and gender identity; see, for example, Dicastery for the Doctrine of the Faith, *On the Pastoral Care of Homosexual Persons* (1986), and Dicastery for Catholic Education, *Male and Female He Created Them: Towards a Path of Dialogue on the Question of Gender Theory in Education* (2019). I critique these teachings in Craig A. Ford, Jr., "Transgender Bodies, Catholic Schools, and a Queer Natural Law Theology of Exploration," *Journal of Moral Theology* 7, no. 1 (2018): 70–98.

[6] This is exactly what Hauerwas does in *Community of Character* (92, 36–52).

[7] See Dale B. Martin, "Sex and the Single Savior," and "Familiar Idolatry and the Christian Case against Marriage," in *Sex and the Single Savior: Gender and Sexuality in Biblical Interpretation* (Louisville, KY: Westminster John Knox Press, 2006), 91–102 and 103–24, respectively. More recently, see his *Biblical Truths: The Meaning of Scripture in the 21st Century* (New Haven, CT: Yale University Press, 2017), esp. 71–110 and 169–220.

forward in our traditions—those same flawed traditions with their flawed patterns of moral reasoning producing flawed individuals from whom we are apparently supposed to learn moral excellence. Whence the optimistic judgment that virtue ethics will get things right?

On the one hand, the postmodern milieu that had seemed to provide so much clarity—clarity about why white supremacy persisted and changed; clarity about why cis-heteronormativity is so hard to break—seems to cast into doubt the possibility of learning the sort of excellence that a virtue theory would appear to offer. There seemed to be no foundation upon which a virtue theory could systematize its account of moral goodness that could illuminate some individuals and communities as virtuous and others as vicious. But on the other hand, I felt I had been nourished by communities, by social movements, and by role models—by individuals and collectives, in other words—who I thought were virtuous. My own experience urged me to accept virtue theory's fundamental insight: good people make good decisions and make other people good decision-makers by passing along what they know to others.

Jim Keenan's virtue ethics gave me an ethical language adequate to describing my own experience of moral formation in communities confronting the evils of racism and hetero/sexism. The key was that the locus of moral goodness—a moral goodness that strives for right action—lies in conceiving the human person as a fundamentally *relational* reality. As relational, each person achieves moral excellence to the extent that the person exhibits justice (right relationship with others), fidelity (right relationship with emotional intimates), self-care (right relationship with ourselves), and prudence (the virtue that helps integrate all of the other virtues within the individual's life).[8] Keenan's relational virtue theory resonated with my own moral intuitions: the building blocks of morality seem to be less about observing duties (as in deontology) or maximizing outcomes (as in consequentialism) and more about obtaining the practical wisdom that negotiates between and beyond these ethical goals.

More important, relational virtue ethics resonated with what I continue to learn from scholars of color and queer thinkers. At their roots, evils like racism and hetero/sexism stem from a failure to achieve ethical relationality across lines of difference. In response, the ethical imaginations of many queer scholars and scholars of color have offered ways to restore

---

[8] As found in James Keenan, "Proposing Cardinal Virtues," *Theological Studies* 56 (1995): esp. 723–29.

this ethical relationality.[9] In the space remaining, I want to provide a sketch of how queer scholars and other scholars of color deepen Keenan's insight into relationality as the scaffold upon which to conceive of the virtues. They do so by conceiving virtuous relationality specifically as a desire for an ethical co-presence with one another—a co-presence that is as erotic as it is embedded within an imaginative horizon that tethers aspects of the reign of God to our present. And in doing so, these thinkers, I believe, shed light on what it may mean to think about moral knowledge within a virtue theory that wants to take the forces of racism and hetero/sexism head on.

Ethical Relationality among Queer Scholars and Scholars of Color

In Keenan's enumeration of the cardinal virtues based on relationality, one of the two that he retains from the traditional list is the virtue of justice. Unlike in Thomas's theory, where justice and the common good are compatible with certain forms of inequality depending on one's station in life,[10] Keenan imports a modern sensibility about justice into his definition. "First," Keenan writes, "our relationality generally is always to be directed by an ordered appreciation for the common good in which *we treat all people as equal*. Apart from all specific relations, *we belong to humanity and are expected to respond to all its members in general, equally and impartially*" (emphases added).[11] *Common good. Justice. Equality.* These are all words that have been used historically as putatively universal concepts, but yet they all have been, in the white Christian imagination, compatible with atrocities and indignities aimed at persons who have been identified as not white enough. In a postmodern imagination these words, however

---

[9] Importantly, many is not all. Some thinkers see an ontological antagonism at the root of our social existence that renders genuine progress or reconciliation impossible. One of the best representatives of this sort of thinking—called queer negativity—is Lee Edelman, *No Future: Queer Theory and the Death Drive* (Durham, NC: Duke University Press, 2004). Among black thinkers, see "Afropessimist" thinkers like Frank B. Wilderson III, *Afro-Pessimism* (New York: Liveright Publishing, 2020). Though I do not have the space to respond to these perspectives in this essay, I believe these thinkers mistake an ideological distortion of reality for reality itself. The only antidote for the devastating critiques these thinkers make is hope, regarded within the Thomistic tradition as a virtue that comes from God alone.

[10] Thomas Aquinas, *Summa Theologiae* II-II 61.2, resp.

[11] Keenan, "Proposing Cardinal Virtues," 724.

beautiful they sound, ring hollow. Many scholars of color have revealed how, despite the ostensible progress of history, patterns of white domination continue to recur; despite transitions from slavery, to legal segregation, to mass incarceration, the racial story in the afterlife of colonization remains marked by white dominance and black subjugation.[12]

Within Christian history one contemporary scholar whose work in this regard stands as exemplary is black scholar Willie James Jennings. In his studies of whiteness, Jennings highlights the specific *theological* distortions that occurred in the European Christian imagination that, in turn, funded the colonial project. Chief among these distortions was the identification of the progress of the reign of God with the progress of the European colonial project, along with its concomitant establishment of white racial identity as the standard for the display of God's saving power.[13]

A similar hollowing out of words like *common good, justice,* and *equality* has taken place with respect to hetero/sexism. Galatians 3:28, where one reads that there is "neither male and female" in Christ Jesus, is read today as a bastion of gender equality. Yet for the majority of Christian history up to about the twentieth century, this equality in Christ was nevertheless compatible with gender inequality on earth.[14] Indeed, the "separate but equal" ideology that proved so treacherous in the US racial context can also be detected in conversations about gender. This ideology stood at the root of the "separate spheres" philosophy that confined women to the home and regarded men as the public representatives of the household starting in the nineteenth-century United States,[15] and it now has hardened (in no small part due to John Paul II's *Theology of the Body*) into the theological notion of gender essentialism, the idea that each person is born only and

---

[12] See Michelle Alexander, *The New Jim Crow: Mass Incarceration in the Age of Colorblindness* (New York: New City Press, 2012); Douglas A. Blackmon, *Slavery by Another Name: The Re-Enslavement of Black People in America from the Civil War to World War II* (New York: Doubleday, 2008); Lisa Lowe, *The Intimacies of Four Continents* (Durham, NC: Duke University Press, 2015); and Alexis Shotwell, "Remembering for the Future: Reckoning with an Unjust Past," in *Against Purity: Living Ethically in Compromised Times* (Minneapolis: University of Minnesota Press, 2016), 23–54.

[13] Willie James Jennings, *The Christian Imagination: Theology and the Origins of Race* (New Haven, CT: Yale University Press, 2010). Another important contribution is Kelly Brown Douglas, *Stand Your Ground: Black Bodies and the Justice of God* (Maryknoll, NY: Orbis Books, 2015).

[14] Dale B. Martin, "The Queer History of Galatians 3:28: 'No Male and Female,'" in Martin, *Sex and the Single Savior*, 77–90.

[15] Kathy Rudy, "'Haven in a Heartless World': The Historical Roots of Gendered Theology," in *Sex and the Church: Gender, Homosexuality, and the Transformation of Christian Ethics* (Boston: Beacon Press, 1997), 15–44. See also, more recently, Elisabeth Schüssler Fiorenza, *Congress of Wo/men: Religion, Gender, and Kyriarchal Power* (Eugene, OR: Wipf and Stock, 2016), esp. 31–64.

either a male or a female, destined to be socialized as a man or as a woman, respectively. Gender essentialism stands at the root of the Roman Catholic Church's official opposition to transgender identity and gender-affirming care, and it also sits at the root of its various teachings that prescribe gender-specific roles for men and for women, notably the restriction of sacramental priesthood to men alone.[16]

Also notably—and once again through crucial connections made in John Paul II's theology of the body—gender essentialism rests at the root of gender complementarity, which undergirds the theological legitimacy of heterosexual desire while pathologizing homosexual desire. Summarizing the effects of this hollowing out in a devastating analysis, Latinx theologian Melissa Pagán argues that this official heteronormative Catholic anthropology perpetuates a colonial relationship that has historically dehumanized and destroyed non-European cultures that had earlier been hospitable to diverse sexual and gender expressions. "The Roman Catholic anthropology of complementarity only allows space for heteronormative subjects," Pagán writes. "All others are labeled 'It' and left undocumented in their being in the name of the divinely created order."[17]

When one reckons with the reality of racism and hetero/sexism, it seems that talk of justice and equality is quite compatible with an unjust, unequal reality. And yet the fight for a truly just world continues to distinguish the work of both scholars of color and scholars working with queer thought. To illustrate this, let's return to the work of Willie James Jennings. In his monograph *After Whiteness: An Education in Belonging,* Jennings finds that the fundamental moral problem we face is one of malformation into whiteness—a malformation that dominates and destroys under the masculinist and colonialist pretense of obtaining self-sufficiency.[18] Jennings means to show that the world that perdures in the aftermath of colonialism features new maps by which we chart our desire for the future, penetrating even our idea of the good life. In this aftermath whiteness's desires are not restricted to those who would identify as colonists. They affect all of us to the extent that we wish to make ourselves in the image of the self-sufficient person, white or not. Whiteness, which Jennings defines as "a way of being in the

---

[16] I have explained the connections between John Paul II's theology and contemporary theologies that resist transgender identity and gender-affirming care in Ford, "Transgender Bodies, Catholic Schools, and a Queer Natural Law Theology of Exploration."

[17] Melissa Pagán, "*Les Indocumentadxs*: The Coloniality of Gender, Complementarity, and Rethinking Border Being/s," *Journal of Feminist Studies in Religion* 38, no. 1 (2022): 180–81.

[18] Willie James Jennings, *After Whiteness: An Education in Belonging* (Grand Rapids, MI: Eerdmans, 2020).

world and seeing the world that forms cognitive and affective structures able to seduce people into its habitation and meaning making," now is available to anyone.[19]

A more crucial point for our purposes is the way whiteness distorts our desires by sundering both our recognition of and desire for a life together. "White self-sufficient masculinity," Jennings writes, "is not first a person or a people; it is a way of organizing life with ideas and forming a persona that distorts identity and strangles the possibilities of dense life together."[20] Whiteness entrances our moral vision with a self-sufficient individualism, and it accomplishes this feat through the creation of moral and emotional distance from others that is the necessary condition for apathy and, worse, exploitation. Not only may white people become morally malformed through whiteness in ways that correspond to the privileges they receive in white supremacist societies, but Jennings *also* observes that persons of color may be malformed by whiteness to the extent that they, too, mobilize a concept of the good life marked by a rejection of a "dense" life together.[21]

From the vantage point of virtue ethics, Jennings helps us see that whiteness is a vice that distorts both how we think and how we desire. This is important because, in virtue ethics, the locus of moral attention is not so much action (though this obviously matters) as it is the *person*. Jennings's analysis thus throws into relief the ways whiteness has the potential to turn us into vicious persons when we pursue it by seeking to arrogate to ourselves a way of living marked by self-sufficiency that is willing to take advantage of others while simultaneously sequestering ourselves from the empathy that would refuse such an immoral relation. According to Jennings, whiteness inculcates in us a refusal of communion with each other, a refusal to be present to one another beyond the narrow perspective of networking for something that we want, a refusal

> to envision shared facilitation, a refusal to place oneself in the journey of others, a refusal of the vulnerability of a centeredness from below (rather than from the towering heights of whiteness), where the sense of my own formation is not only still open, but where I am willingly being changed not by a nondescript other but by nonwhite peoples historically imagined at the sharp point of instruction.[22]

---

[19] Jennings, 9.

[20] Jennings, 8–9.

[21] Jennings, 6–7.

[22] Jennings, 141. By "sharp point of instruction" Jennings draws attention to instructor-learner relationship in the colonialist racist imagination: white people teach; black people (and other nonwhite people) learn.

For Jennings, if the modus operandi of the vice of whiteness is emotional and moral distance, then the antidote to this vice is *eros*, the desire for one another beyond capitalist and utilitarian logics "woven first and foremost in utility and aiming at profit."[23]

Of course, Jennings's notion of communion is theologically rich. In *After Whiteness*, communion is always paired with the gospel image of the "crowd," the people in the Gospels who encountered God in the person of Jesus. The crowd could present a potentially dangerous gathering. "Fear is a crowd failing, violence is a crowd addiction, and ignorance is a crowd's stubborn habit of collective mind,"[24] Jennings writes. But the goal of this gathering in God is communion, "that sense of God-drenched life attuned to life together,"[25] or, phrased differently, "a matter of lure and longing deeply embedded in a desire to see God change the lives of those around us, healing the sick, delivering the captives, overturning the powers that be, and raising the dead to new life."[26] The antidote to whiteness—and here I use my own wording—is a desire for co-presence animated by nothing other than love, love that is not only desirous of the other (*eros*), but also a love desirous of being carried outward and upward back into the heart of God (*caritas*).

This leads us back to Keenan's definition of the virtue of justice that perfects us with respect to other persons. Alongside Jennings, Keenan recognizes that the nature of the malady in our world is fundamentally relational. Any solution must be based in justice, understood as the desire to value and treat everyone equally in order to achieve the common good. In other words, the solution is relational too. Scholars like Jennings remind us that we can traverse the path towards justice only if we face whiteness head-on with its legacy of historical and moral traumas. The communion that justice requires rests on the other side of cultivating *eros* for one another, of gathering in the precariousness of the crowd that awaits God's healing, God's antidote. In Thomistic virtue theory, that antidote to whiteness is *caritas,* the virtue that builds friendship both with God, and through God, with others, even one's enemies.[27] *Eros,* that desire for intimate co-presence, has the power to heal. It provides a pathway beyond the hollowed-out words that have been distorted by white supremacy and racism. It is God's return to us of a "new heart" of flesh in exchange for our "heart of stone" (Ezek 36:26).

As queer people have come to know, *eros* also provides a way out of the distortions of hetero/sexism as well. One of its most important

---

[23] Jennings, 144.
[24] Jennings, 143.
[25] Jennings, 13–14.
[26] Jennings, 20.
[27] *ST* II-II 23.1, 27.7, 27.8.

cartographers is queer black thinker Audre Lorde. Lorde speaks of the erotic, *eros*, in epistemic terms, not only as knowledge that "is the nurturer or nursemaid of all our deepest knowledge,"[28] but also as knowledge that "becomes a lens through which we scrutinize all aspects of our existence."[29] This knowledge is an embodied knowledge, an experiential knowledge,

> a measure of the joy which I know myself to be capable of feeling. And that deep and irreplaceable knowledge of my capacity for joy comes to demand from all of my life that it be lived within the knowledge that such satisfaction is possible, and does not have to be called *marriage*, nor *god*, nor *an afterlife*.[30]

The knowledge conferred by the erotic is also sexually mediated, giving one the capacity to step outside of discourses of shame. "In touch with the erotic, I become less willing to accept powerlessness, or those other supplied states of being which are not native to me, such as resignation, despair, self-effacement, depression, self-denial." It is knowledge that shares spaces with pleasure—in Lorde's words, knowledge that results in her "moving into sunlight against the body of the woman I love."[31] And it is, finally, liberative: "We have been raised to fear the *yes* within ourselves, our deepest cravings. The fear that we cannot grow beyond whatever distortions we may find within ourselves keeps us docile and loyal and obedient, externally defined, and leads us to accept many facets of our oppression as women."[32] And yet, "recognizing the power of the erotic within ourselves can give us the energy to pursue genuine change within our world."[33] *Eros*, then, not only leads us toward a political co-presence marked by justice, as Jennings argues, but it also leads us toward those sensuous, even (homo) sexual co-presences, closing the moral, emotional, and yes, even physical, distances that oppressive forces have erected.

Other queer scholars have also shown how love, erotic or not, has the potential to transform the church. Marcella Althaus-Reid notes that there is a theology within our sexual stories, a theology that is "tentative, unfinished,

---

[28] Audre Lorde, "The Uses of the Erotic: The Erotic as Power," in *Sister Outsider: Essays and Speeches by Audre Lorde*, 53–59 (Berkeley, CA: Crossing Press, 2007 [1984]), 56.
[29] Lorde, 57.
[30] Lorde, 57.
[31] Both quotations in this paragraph are from Lorde, 58.
[32] Lorde, 58.
[33] Lorde, 59. For another important account that reflects on *eros* in a specifically theological key (though to similar ends), see Carter Heyward, *Touching Our Strength: The Erotic as Power and the Love of God* (San Francisco: Harper San Francisco, 1989).

as is a sexual Jesus. The stories open our eyes to different networking strategies and also to sources of empowerment."[34] They lead to new ways to understand doctrines and, indeed, even the Bible itself. Appropriating the see-judge-act method widely known in Catholic social teaching, Althaus-Reid writes, "The key to working in this popular style, is to let life circulate and only hang on to the radical principles in the Bible which subsume the rest: justice, peace, and love/solidarity."[35] Love, in the end, must guide all, even if the path laid out by love is not immediately clear. Dale Martin adds:

> Admittedly, love as a mere principle or "abstract concept" is not "sufficient" as a foundation for reliable knowledge about ethics. But nothing is. . . . Whether an interpretation is finally Christian will not be predictable ahead of time, but one central test by which we attempt to make that determination, a test for the Christian ethical value of an interpretation, will be more than anything whether it promotes love of the other.[36]

As a heuristic for Christian ethics, love of other must be joined by love of self, which Keenan thematizes as the virtue of self-care. The virtue of self-care honors the "unique responsibility to care for ourselves, affectively, mentally, physically, and spiritually."[37] In his essay "Virtue Ethics and Sexual Ethics" Keenan remarks that self-care "does not let oneself be taken advantage [of] in any relationships, sexual or otherwise," and that it encourages one to undertake sexual activity only on comfortable terms, whether that results in delaying or seeking sexual activity. But most important for our consideration here, self-care in a sexual key recognizes that we are "embodied and alive with passion," and that the desires associated with those passions can be good.[38] Self-care is the virtue that listens to one's own embodied self as the locus of moral insight, where honoring erotic passion may be a path toward relating rightly to ourselves. Thinkers like Lorde, Althaus-Reid, and Martin, then, deepen and provide greater texture to Keenan's insight that the moral life cannot be complete unless we relate rightly to ourselves, letting a critically informed and deeply intentional account of (self-)love lead the way.

---

[34] Marcella Althaus-Reid, *Indecent Theology: Theological Perversion in Sex, Gender, and Politics* (Philadelphia: Routledge, 2000), 130.

[35] Althaus-Reid, 130 (for context, see 125–32).

[36] Dale B. Martin, "Conclusion: The Space of Scripture, the Risk of Faith," in Martin, *Sex and the Single Savior*, 169.

[37] Keenan, "Proposing Cardinal Virtues," 727.

[38] All of the above quotations are from James F. Keenan, "Virtue Ethics and Sexual Ethics," *Louvain Studies* 30, no. 3 (2005): 195–96.

Eros, Eschatology, and Liberation

Eros as the antidote to white supremacy, racism; *eros* as the pathway to-ward other-directed and self-directed love as the antidote to hetero/sexism: *Eros* is the path to deeply needed forms of liberative political and sexual co-presence. And, because these proposals are primarily about relational dispositions we must cultivate as persons in order to bring about this lib-erative co-presence, the insights surveyed above from thinkers black and white, queer and not, can easily find a home in the virtue tradition of think-ing, especially one where the cardinal virtues—those virtues upon which the rest of the moral life hinge—are primarily relational, as in the virtue theory of Jim Keenan.

But one thing remains. Even with this account of virtue ethics informed by queer scholars and scholars of color, how does one learn it, given the flaws of our moral exemplars in community? This was, after all, my chief complaint. Here also my thought has been sharpened by queer scholars and scholars of color. The emerging answer has been not necessarily to think about those in the past, or perhaps about even those in the present, but in-stead to turn toward a future yet to arrive, yet nevertheless already in our grasp, and to take notice of who and what shines in that light as exemplary.

For queer-of-color scholar José Muñoz, what queer communities do to survive in a world of oppression—including everything from producing art to making ends meet—is ultimately linked to knowledge of a better world, utopia. Such knowledge is mediated by hope, and it motivates queer persons and those who act in solidarity with them to draw this utopia closer to the present.[39] Specifically naming queer desire as "a deviation, a reorientation, signaling that we want a world that doesn't yet exist, we desire it, and we practice the world we don't have yet in the present," Alexis Shotwell calls us to act within the horizon of a "prefigurative politics," that organizes our world through "open normativities." What makes these normativities "open" is that they privilege cultivating widespread diversity among ways of life—sexual or otherwise—foreclosing only those practices that, based on past experiences of harm, we know we do not want to perpetuate.[40]

Among black scholars thinking also along the horizon of a prefigura-tive politics, Robin Kelley believes that the black radical tradition itself is a movement animated by "freedom dreams," that is, "a common desire to

---

[39] See José Muñoz, *Disidentifications: Queers of Color and the Performance of Politics* (Minneapolis: University of Minnesota Press, 1999), and his *Cruising Utopia: The There and Then of Queer Futurity* (New York: New York University Press, 2009); see also Craig A. Ford, Jr., "Black Queer Natural Law: On Brownness and Disidentifica-tion," Political Theology Network, November 11, 2022.

[40] Shotwell, *Against Purity*, 179, 184, 155, respectively.

find better ways of being together without hierarchy and exclusion, without violence and domination, but *with* love, compassion, care, and friendship."[41] Along similar lines Vincent Lloyd argues that the black experience in the United States is imbued with a sense of the "Black Fantastic," which "destabilizes, at least momentarily . . . by bringing into the field of play those potentials we have forgotten or did not believe accessible or feasible." The Black Fantastic can be found in black comedy, black press, and most especially, black music.[42] Lloyd also sees it in contemporary black social movements aiming at Black Futures, "a label that joins a sense of the anti-Black world's demise and the imperative to imagine radically new ways of living together" beyond the forces of domination that oppress.[43] "The content of the [Black] tradition allows us to realize our most deeply human desire, to attend to who we are beyond what the world says we are, beyond the objects that domination would make us into."[44]

This attention to a world that is not yet, but affects the world that is—and, in just that instant, renders the future, however momentary, the present—is the business of eschatology. Queer scholars and scholars of color have turned toward the already-but-not-yet future in order to anchor their vision of a just world. This future discloses various social movements and individuals who point to it, and, as such, become the exemplars upon which a virtue theory depends for guidance in right action. They are exemplars because they model right relationality. On the one hand, they model right relations to ourselves and to every other person. This insight is connected to Jim Keenan's work. And, on the other, they model right relations by giving us a path for our own erotic moral formation, not only toward others in a political co-presence but in a sensuous, sexual co-presence that points beyond a world of racism and hetero/sexism. These are the insights connected to the work of queer scholars and scholars of color.

Animating this entire process at a formal level is *caritas*, a virtue that transcends a mere political register and beckons to a genuinely theological one, for God is love (1 Jn 4:8). *Eros* and *caritas* thus converge in this relational virtue theory, suggesting that the work of building right relationship with one another is constitutive of building right relationship with God. This insight, of course, is not the sole insight of Keenan or the scholars

---

[41] Robin D. G. Kelley, *Freedom Dreams: The Black Radical Tradition*, rev. ed. (Boston: Beacon Press, 2022 [2002]), xxxix.

[42] Vincent W. Lloyd, "What Is Black Tradition?" in *Religion of the Field Negro: On Black Secularism and Black Theology*, 97–112 (New York: Fordham University Press, 2018), 106–7.

[43] Vincent W. Lloyd, *Black Dignity: The Struggle against Domination* (New Haven, CT: Yale University Press, 2022), 96.

[44] Lloyd, 151.

whose work I've engaged here. It was also Jesus's central insight. As we read in Matthew's Gospel:

"Teacher, which commandment in the law is the greatest?" [Jesus] said to him, "'You shall love the Lord your God with all your heart, and with all your soul, and with all your mind.' This is the greatest and first commandment. And a second is like it, 'You shall love your neighbor as yourself.' On these two commandments hang all the law and the prophets." (Mt 22:36–40)

From one angle, this essay can be seen as a meditation upon these very words of Jesus. These words from the Word Made Flesh that, in turn, invite further enfleshing by the church spread out across time and space, rest as the central font from which Jim Keenan's relational virtue theory, based in justice, fidelity, and self-care, draws. For my part, I've sought to show how the work of queer scholars and scholars of color allow this relational theory to resonate with theological projects that explicitly seek to dismantle the forces of racism, white supremacy, and hetero/sexism—in a phrase, those projects that seek to dismantle systems of domination—by offering new ways to envision *eros* as an epistemological key. "Systems of domination mute or mask our access to our loves, or they separate intellectual, emotional, and bodily loves," writes Vincent Lloyd. If this essay has been successful, it has been because it has tried to point us toward an eschatological horizon laid out by love. "The more we attend to our own loves," Lloyd writes in a felicitous series of last and hopefully lasting words, "the more we repair the psychic harm—the wounds to the soul—inflicted on us . . . at the end of days, when the world is free from domination, all will love."[45]

---

[45] Lloyd, 72.

18.

The Integration of Being and Acting in One's Sexual Life

Articulating a Viable Sexual Ethic for Homosexual Persons

RONALDO ZACHARIAS

Sexual identity[1] is a constitutive dimension of human personality and, therefore, a crucial element for achieving personal fulfillment and experiencing happiness. Because, as a community of faith, we are called to accompany people in the process of integrating sexuality into their project of life through our educative and pastoral ministry, we cannot continue having one ethic for heterosexual persons and another one for homosexuals. The first affirms unity between being and acting, and the second, dichotomy.

This essay illustrates the problematic dichotomy that homosexual persons face between being and acting in their lives. This dichotomy results from ecclesial teaching that, while instructing us to welcome homosexuals as they are, does not allow them to live according to their sexual identity. Additionally, I propose some elements of a viable sexual ethic for homosexual persons, that, favoring the integration between being and acting, will help them reach personal fulfillment, happiness, and the realization of God's will for them.

---

[1] By *sexual identity* I mean sexuality as a constitutive dimension of identity that includes also *sexual orientation*—a person's physical, romantic and/or emotional attraction toward other people—and *gender identity*—a deeply felt and experienced sense of one's own gender.

It is my firm conviction that using a virtue-ethics lens when articulating sexual ethics is essential in resolving the present dichotomy in the treatment of heterosexual and homosexual persons in sexual ethics. This approach gives priority to the kind of faithful person one is becoming in and through the choices and decisions one makes. Virtue ethics can be a method that integrates being and acting.[2] Because of this, I base my reflection on the wonderful inspiration that James Keenan proposed to me when he guided me through the field of virtue ethics during my doctoral studies. He encouraged me to look at sexuality through the lens of virtues and "to put some flesh"—and I would dare to say, some "sexual flesh"—on the skeleton of the cardinal virtues he proposes: justice, self-care, fidelity, and prudence.[3] In so doing, I show that we need to replace act-oriented ethics with virtue ethics. This will help homosexual persons give priority to how they can best express their sexual identity and realize themselves as sexual beings.

The "Be But Don't Do" Theory

Twenty-five years ago, Edward Vacek already had articulated the tension in calling people to treat homosexual persons with respect and dignity while also asking homosexuals to deny their sexual identity. He writes:

> It seems a violation of humanness automatically to deprive homosexuals of the values that Christians have found in sexuality. Such values include pleasure, romantic feelings, companionship, mutual support, sexual outlet, ecstasy, intimacy, and interpersonal communication. It seems to compound "unnaturalness" to insist that persons not heterosexually inclined must simply, without further considerations, be sexually inactive.[4]

---

[2] James F. Keenan, "Virtue Ethics and Sexual Ethics," *Louvain Studies* 30, no. 3 (2005): 182.

[3] I refer here to one of the best experiences of my life as a doctoral student, guided and supervised by Keenan. The result of such an experience is partially and poignantly expressed in my dissertation: *Virtue Ethics as the Framework for Catholic Sexual Education: Towards the Integration between Being and Acting in Sexual Education.* STD diss. (Cambridge, MA: Weston Jesuit School of Theology, 2002). Keenan also refers to such an experience in "Virtue Ethics and Sexual Ethics," 193.

[4] Edward C. Vacek, "A Christian Homosexuality?" in *The Philosophy of Sex: Contemporary Readings*, 3rd ed., ed. Alan Soble (Lanham, MD: Rowman & Littlefield Publishers, 1997), 135.

I agree with Vacek, and I believe it is necessary to question whether sexual continence alone can serve personal fulfillment, especially when not embraced as a personal calling. In other words, we cannot expect everyone to learn to love by controlling their passions and restricting their sexual lives to heterosexual marital acts. This for two reasons: first, controlling one's passions does not automatically teach one how to love; second, marriage is not a possibility for homosexual persons in the Catholic Church. It seems to me that, as a community of faith, we are responsible for helping people—including homosexuals—to commit themselves to those with whom they are in a relationship of just, faithful, and caring love. To deeply understand what is at stake here we need to turn our attention to the church's teaching on the subject.

According to the church's teaching, homosexual persons can never acquire sexual maturity from the individual or interpersonal point of view.[5] Although pastoral care of homosexual persons "should be considerate and kind," and although "their culpability will be judged prudently," for the church, no one can provide "moral justification for their actions." According to the objective moral order, "sexual relations between persons of the same sex are necessarily and essentially disordered" and homosexual acts "may never be approved in any way whatever."[6] Nor can the homosexual condition itself be viewed as benign: "Although the particular inclination of the homosexual person is not a sin, it is a more or less strong tendency ordered towards an intrinsic moral evil and thus *the inclination itself* must be seen as an *objective disorder*" (emphasis added).[7]

The church imposes a duty to oppose even civil, legal recognition for homosexual unions[8] and forbids them from church blessing because "there are absolutely no grounds for considering homosexual unions to be in any way similar or even remotely analogous to God's plan for marriage and

---

[5] Congregation for Catholic Education, *Educational Guidance in Human Love: Outlines for Sex Education* (November 1, 1983), no. 101. Hereafter EGHL. Although all post–Vatican II documents on sexuality explicitly refer to homosexuality, only the 1992 *Catechism of the Catholic Church* defines it: "Homosexuality refers to relations between men or between women who experience an exclusive or predominant sexual attraction toward persons of the same sex." *Catechism of the Catholic Church* (October 11, 1992), no. 2357). Hereafter CCC.

[6] Congregation for the Doctrine of the Faith (hereafter CDF), *Persona Humana: Declaration on Certain Questions Concerning Sexual Ethics* (December 29, 1975), no. 8. See also EGHL, no. 101.

[7] CDF, "Letter to Bishops of the Catholic Church on the Pastoral Care of Homosexual Persons" (October 1, 1986), no. 3. Hereafter PCHP.

[8] CDF, "Considerations Regarding Proposals to Give Legal Recognition to Unions between Homosexual Persons" (June 3, 2003), no. 5.

family."[9] Consequently, homosexual persons cannot suppose that living out their homosexual orientation is a morally acceptable option because it is not.[10] It does not matter whether the relationship between them is lived within the context of a loving and life-giving union. Such a union, according to the divine plan, can be celebrated only between a man and a woman in the sacrament of marriage. Those who engage in homosexual activity act immorally, because it is "only in the marital relationship that the use of the sexual faculty can be morally good."[11]

Because "homosexual activity prevents one's own fulfillment and happiness by acting contrary to the creative wisdom of God,"[12] homosexual persons who seek to follow the Lord "are called to enact the will of God in their life by joining whatever sufferings and difficulties they experience in virtue of their condition to the sacrifice of the Lord's Cross. . . . To refuse to sacrifice one's own will in obedience to the will of the Lord is effectively to prevent salvation."[13]

The only way homosexual persons can follow the will of the Lord is by embracing "a chaste life,"[14] avoiding homosexual activity. This is the concrete content of the cross that they are called to embrace, a cross that, if united to the sacrifice of the Lord, "will constitute for them a source of self-giving which will save them from a way of life which constantly threatens to destroy them."[15]

Despite the fact that "homosexual acts are intrinsically disordered," that they are "contrary to the natural law," that they "close the sexual act to the gift of life," that they "do not proceed from a genuine affective and sexual complementarity," and "under no circumstances can they be approved,"[16] homosexual persons "must be accepted with respect, compassion and sensitivity" and not be subjected to any kind of "unjust discrimination."[17]

Whether we are heterosexual or homosexual, it is not easy to accept this teaching, especially as the language of the documents hardly expresses

---

[9] CDF, "*Responsum* of the Congregation for the Doctrine of the Faith to a *Dubium* regarding the Blessing of the Unions of Persons of the Same Sex" (February 22, 2021), no. 7. The explanatory note quotes here: FRANCIS, Apostolic Exhortation *Amoris Laetitia*, no. 251.

[10] PCHP, no. 3.

[11] PCHP, no. 7.

[12] PCHP, no. 7.

[13] PCHP, no. 12.

[14] PCHP, no. 12.

[15] PCHP, no. 12. This same content is affirmed in the Pontifical Council for the Family, "The Truth and Meaning of Human Sexuality: Guidelines for Education within the Family" (December 8, 1995), no. 104.

[16] CCC, no. 2357.

[17] CCC, no. 2358.

respect, compassion, and sensitivity.[18] It is even more difficult to convince homosexual persons that their way of life threatens to destroy them or that their sexual intimacy prevents their own fulfillment and happiness—claims supported by no scientific or experiential evidence—or that their sexual attraction is an evil that can compromise their salvation—a claim opposed by the living faith of homosexual Christians.

I deeply believe that if the church were willing to listen to the experiences of homosexual persons, as Keenan has called it to do, it would find its theories called into question.[19] The ecclesial teaching on homosexuality cannot ignore the fact that ethical questions surrounding it "are questions about real persons—questions about identity, place in community, relationships, and callings."[20] Questions about *John and John,* and *Mary and Mary*, are not about mere theories or problems.[21]

How can we interpret the spiritual motivation—sharing the sacrifice of the Lord's cross—given to a theory—"be but don't do"—that practically signifies the imposition of a way of life—celibacy? How can we reconcile a pastoral position that, while stressing the importance of caring for homosexual persons, denies them the values found in sexual expression? Doesn't the "be but don't do" theory suggest there is something wrong with *being* homosexual?

If we consider, as Marciano Vidal suggests, that homosexuality is the human condition characterized by feeling constitutively attracted toward persons of the same sex, we will realize that such a condition is much more than a genital phenomenon. It is "the anthropological condition" of a man or a woman who seeks personal fulfillment and happiness. It is a way of existing and living that cannot be reduced to sexual expressions.[22] It is part of one's sexual identity and, because of that, needs to be integrated into

---

[18] Todd A. Salzman and Michael G. Lawler, "Human Dignity and Homosexuality in Catholic Teaching: An Anthropological Disconnect between Truth and Love?" *Interdisciplinary Journal for Religion and Transformation in Contemporary Society* 6 (2020): 123.

[19] James F. Keenan, "The Open Debate: Moral Theology and the Lives of Gay and Lesbian Persons," *Theological Studies* 64 (2003): 150.

[20] Margaret Farley, *Just Love: A Framework for Christian Sexual Ethics* (New York: Continuum, 2006), 271–72.

[21] Aristide Fumagalli, "Le interviste—12. Aristide Fumagalli," in Luciano Moia, *Chiesa e omosessualità. Un'inchiesta alla luce del magistero di papa Francesco* (Milan: San Paolo, Cinisello Balsamo, 2020), 176.

[22] Marciano Vidal, *Ética da Sexualidade* (São Paulo: Loyola, 2017), 119. See also Beatrice Brogliato and Damiano Migliorini, *L'amore omosessuale. Saggi di Psicoanalisi, Teologia e Pastorale in dialogo per una nuova sintesi* (Assisi: Cittadella, 2014), 131–42.

one's personality and project of life.[23] Consequently, "the anthropological claim of homosexual orientation as a deep-seated dimension and objective disorder in homosexual persons is in serious tension with the claim that homosexual persons have human dignity."[24]

For virtue ethics, the question of any objective disorder in homosexual people cannot have priority over the moral task of helping them realize themselves as sexual beings by developing dispositions that enable them to initiate, maintain, and nurture virtuous relationships of intimacy.[25] If we look through the lens of virtues like justice, fidelity, self-care, and prudence—all informed by mercy—it is easy to see how we must proceed.

Justice calls for recognizing in others what we want to be recognized in us. Considering that we all want to promote our moral right to love, be loved, and express love in the positive mode of an intimate relationship and commitment, it is unjust to deny the same rights to homosexual persons. Fidelity calls for integrity of conduct. Denying homosexual persons the right to express who they are through what they do would be requiring disloyalty of them. Self-care calls for acceptance and positive appreciation of the self. It disrespects homosexual persons to require that they live as if they were not homosexuals. Prudence requires that priority should always be given to the kind of person one is becoming in establishing just, faithful, and caring relationships. We cannot forget—as David Matzko McCarthy reminds us—that "gay men and lesbians are persons who encounter the other (and thus discover themselves) in relation to persons of the same sex. This same-sex orientation is a given of their coming to be, that is, the nuptial meaning of human life emerges for a gay man in relation to other men and for a woman when face to face with other women."[26] What should have priority in the moral assessment is the role of any relationship in enhancing the sense of self-worth, in affirming the good of the persons, in appreciating the value of the other, in promoting personal and mutual well-being and in strengthening the love that unites, heals, and sanctifies the persons involved.[27]

---

[23] Aristide Fumagalli, *L'amore possibile. Persone omosessuali e morale cristiana* (Assisi: Cittadella, 2020), 165–66.

[24] Salzman and Lawler, "Human Dignity and Homosexuality in Catholic Teaching," 123–24.

[25] Michael J. Hartwig, *The Poetics of Intimacy and the Problem of Sexual Abstinence* (New York: Peter Lang, 2000), 74.

[26] David Matzko McCarthy, "The Relationship of Bodies: A Nuptial Hermeneutics of Same-Sex Unions," in *Theology and Sexuality: Classic and Contemporary Readings,* ed. Eugene F. Rogers, Jr. (Oxford: Blackwell Publishing, 2002), 212–13.

[27] See Fumagalli's good synthesis of theologians who condemn, tolerate, or affirm the goodness of homosexual acts: *L'amore possibile,* 88–107.

Considering that sexual attraction—as Daniel Maguire rightly says—"is deeply interwoven into the human desire and need for closeness and for trusting relationships,"[28] we cannot suppose that such a desire is proper only to heterosexual persons. Those attracted to persons of the same sex also desire a significant other in their lives and—as Vacek reminds us—should not be deprived of the values that Christians have found in sexuality.[29] It could be argued that sexual attraction does not necessarily lead to sexual intimacy. This is fine. But when it does, we cannot automatically infer that it cannot open the way to a closer union and a trusting relationship.

Virtue ethics cannot consider sexual desire in isolation from the whole life of the person. Drawing us out of ourselves to reach the other in his or her most profound intimacy, sexual desire is called to serve mutuality. If we are all equally human, sharing the same basic needs, desires, and hopes, then it is more than unjust to impose upon homosexual persons a theory that asserts that who they are is all right as long as they *do not act on it.* Daniel Maguire rightly calls the "be but don't do" theory a "twisted logic."[30] While stating that love between heterosexuals is "uniquely expressed and perfected" through sexual language, it requires that love between homosexuals, to be judged as moral, must be sexually mute. If justice calls for impartiality and equality, if fidelity calls for particularity and singularity, if care calls for wholeness and uniqueness—as James Keenan asserts[31]—a twisted logic like this compromises not only the integration of the virtues into someone's life, but also the role of prudence in realizing the claims that derive from these virtues in a concrete situation.

The "be but don't do" theory—in stressing that who I am is all right as long as I *do not act on it*—leaves no room for any option besides continence. But the church's association of *not acting on it* with chastity is very problematic. Chastity consists in the capacity to guide sexual desire to serve love and integrate it in the development of the person.[32] This implies personal effort and self-control but not necessarily continence. Recognizing that chastity can be practiced in continence does not mean that one is synonymous with the other. From the perspective of virtue ethics, we need to ask if continence for homosexual persons is always a path to the virtue

---

[28] Daniel C. Maguire, "The Morality of Homosexual Marriage," in *A Challenge To Love: Gay and Lesbian Catholics in the Church*, ed. Robert Nugent (New York: Crossroad, 1987), 120.

[29] Vacek, "A Christian Homosexuality?" 133.

[30] Maguire, "The Morality of Homosexual Marriage," 126.

[31] James F. Keenan, "Proposing Cardinal Virtues," *Theological Studies* 56 (1995): 708–29.

[32] Keenan, "Virtue Ethics and Sexual Ethics," 181.

of chastity. The "be but don't do" theory seems to suggest that homosexuals are "condemned" to be celibate.

The lives of vowed religious who embrace celibacy as "an exceptional gift of grace"[33] help us understand the tensions underlying the "be but don't do" theory. The church recognizes that even those who embrace celibacy as a state of life require a degree of psychological and affective maturity because the total continence celibacy requires is not easily practiced even when freely embraced.[34] No doubt continence is required in many situations, but it is problematic to impose it as the singular path to chastity for homosexual persons. Total continence is extremely difficult for those who voluntarily embrace it.[35] Homosexual persons should not be held to what seems to be impossible, even for heterosexuals, simply because they are homosexuals.[36] The idea is so self-contradictory that it challenges the church's own prohibition on admitting to seminary and holy orders "those who practice homosexuality, present deep-seated homosexual tendencies or support the so-called 'gay culture.'"[37]

From the perspective of the virtue of justice, celibacy cannot be a gift from God for some simply because they are heterosexual persons and choose to live a certain way of life, while being a requirement for others simply because they are homosexual persons.[38] The virtue of fidelity calls us primarily to transform life into a reciprocal gift, not to embrace

---

[33] Vatican Council II, *Perfectae caritatis: Decree on the Adaptation and Renewal of Religious Life* (October 28, 1965), no. 12. Hereafter PC. See also Sacred Congregation for Religious and Secular Institutes, *Evangelica testificatio: Apostolic Exhortation on the Renewal of Religious Life* (June 29, 1971), no. 15: Celibacy is "a precious *gift* of divine grace which the Father imparts to *certain* people" (emphasis added).

[34] PC, no. 12. See also Vatican Council II, *Optatam totius: Decree on Priestly Training* (October 28, 1965), no. 10.

[35] See, for example, PC, no. 12: "Religious, therefore, at pains to be faithful to what they have professed, should believe our Lord's words and, relying in God's help, they should not presume on their own strength."

[36] I am joining Maguire and Anthony Kosnik in their criticism. See Maguire, "The Morality of Homosexual Marriage," 122–23; and Anthony Kosnik et al., *Human Sexuality: New Directions in American Catholic Thought*, a study commissioned by the Catholic Theological Society of America (New York: Paulist Press, 1977), 214.

[37] Congregation for Catholic Education, "Instruction Concerning the Criteria for the Discernment of Vocations with regard to Persons with Homosexual Tendencies in view of their Admission to the Seminary and to Holy Orders" (August 31, 2005), no. 2,§4. For a critical analysis of such an instruction, see Ronaldo Zacharias, "Orientação afetivo-sexual: para além da cultura do 'não pergunte, não diga'," in *Formação: desafios morais*, ed. José Antonio Trasferetti, Maria Inês de Castro Millen and Ronaldo Zacharias (São Paulo: Paulus, 2018), 201–33.

[38] See Maguire, "The Morality of Homosexual Marriage," 123.

the sufferings "associated" with a cross that was not chosen. The virtue of self-care, urging respect for the dignity of the person, reminds us that while certainly a homosexual person can find fulfillment in embracing celibacy for reasons of faith, not all homosexuals find fulfillment in the same way. From the perspective of the virtue of prudence, in order to live a good life, we all—homosexuals as well as heterosexuals—have the unique responsibility of finding the best way of realizing ourselves.

Lifelong sexual abstinence, if not embraced as a gift of the Lord, can be very harmful for homosexual persons because it denies them the chance to cope constructively with their personal condition. If imposed as a cross, it also precludes them from the possibility of learning how to be a steward of the values found in sexual intimacy. It is hard to accept that sexual abstinence is *the best* that can be proposed or even that it is *all* that needs to be required from those who want to learn how to love and discern the demands of love. We need to refuse a notion that "love among equals cannot be of radical donation, care for the life of each other, structural fidelity, stable reference and safe trust."[39]

Toward the Integration of Being and Acting in the Lives of Homosexual Persons

It becomes clearer why the "be but don't do" theory conveys an ambiguous message. While the distinction between orientation and behavior is helpful in order to justify that behavior can be chosen, and therefore, controlled— an insight heterosexual persons also need—the theory wrongly suggests that it is possible to judge actions independently of their relationship with the person who acts. Andrea Grillo correctly stresses that "a double scission continuously threatens the ecclesial argumentation: the first one between the person and their actions and relationships; the second one between the formal welcoming of the person and the substantial exclusion of the same person based on the inadequate consideration of their tendencies and actions."[40] Any judgment of an action must include evaluation of its relationship with the person performing the action.

Virtue ethics calls us to prioritize the kind of person one is becoming through one's actions, and to focus on the quality of the relationships within which sexual intimacy takes place. In doing so, the main question is not whether one is homosexual or heterosexual, but *how best* one can

---

[39] Andrea Grillo, *Cattolicesimo e (omo)sessualità. Sapienza teologica e benedizione rituale* (Brescia: Morcelliana, 2022), 21. See also Fumagalli, *L'amore possibile,* 175.
[40] Grillo, *Cattolicesimo e (omo)sessualità,* 9.

express—even under less than ideal or optimal circumstances—the values found in sexuality and in loving and committed relationships.

Considering that the virtues of justice, fidelity, self-care, and prudence perfect who we are and the ways we relate to one another, any definition of chastity must incorporate elements that best honor the needs of the persons and the integrity of the relationships. Practically speaking, this means the requirements of chastity cannot be prescribed independently of the persons and relationships in question.

A richer notion of chastity can help articulate a viable Christian ethic of homosexuality. Such an articulation needs to consider at least three elements. First, like heterosexuals, homosexual persons are asked to strive for the values the Christian community has found in sexuality. There are no special or distinct norms that govern the morality of homosexual activity. Most important is the quality of the relationship, which must always be based upon respect and anchored in the virtues of justice, fidelity, and care. It is important to remember that—as Anthony Kosnik says— "the norms governing the morality of homosexual activity are those that govern all sexual activity, and the norms governing sexual activity are those that govern all human ethical activity."[41] We should require from homosexual relationships what we would require from any heterosexual couple. For Maurizio Faggioni, if on the one hand, "it would be difficult to sustain the consistency of a same-sex practice with the paradigm of a Catholic sexual anthropology and ethics," on the other hand, "it would be unfair not to appreciate how much goodness could be expressed by a relationship sustained by same-sex love." Depending on the significance of the human values present in a homosexual relationship, it remains difficult to deny that such a relationship "can produce, by the grace of God, the good."[42]

Second, we are used to thinking of complementarity in terms of gender: sexual differentiation is assumed as a sine qua non to authentic human mutuality. From this perspective, homosexuality will always lack complementarity and, thus, authentic mutuality. We need to consider whether gender complementarity is the only complementarity possible. Experience shows that genuine relationships of mutuality require more than simply a different-sex partner. The same is true for partners of the same sex. A viable ethic for homosexual persons needs to overcome notions of complementarity built upon sexual differentiation. As Michael Hartwig writes, "Mutuality

---

[41] Kosnik, *Human Sexuality*, 214.

[42] Maurizio Faggioni, "Le interviste—1. Maurizio Faggioni," in Moia, *Chiesa e omosessualità. Um'inchiesta ala luce del magistero di papa Francesco*, 49–50.

is built upon 'personal' complementariness,"[43] and personal complementariness supposes but also transcends gender differentiation. We need more than a genital sexual relationship in order to achieve mutuality. Moreover, a genital sexual relationship alone does not guarantee complementarity, as many heterosexuals' history confirms.[44]

Third, a viable ethic for homosexual persons must start from the fact that homosexuality is not merely a "lifestyle." As Patricia Jung and Ralph Smith assert, homosexuality "is, like heterosexuality, one expression of the human sexual vocation."[45] Our sexuality opens us to reach out to others, and we express our sexual identity in such a reaching out. Because of this, it is not possible to ignore our sexual orientation as an important component of our sexual identity. *How* we ought to live sexually, then, is a question of response to the gift God gave us. I am not suggesting that there are no limits for sexual expression, only that no limit can be exclusively defined by sexual orientation. As Jung and Smith rightly state, "The task of ethical reflection is to articulate the appropriate and, for Christians, theologically responsible and faithful boundaries that create constructive, genuinely mutual sexual behavior."[46] Only an inclusive sexual ethic can embrace such a task.

An inclusive sexual ethic must begin with a definition of sexuality that, according to Salzman and Lawler, "finds love and truth in all just and loving heterosexual, homosexual, and bisexual potentially-reproductive and non-reproductive acts," recognizing "both homosexual and heterosexual orientations as objectively ordered and that potentially reproductive heterosexual and non-reproductive heterosexual and homosexual acts may be moral sexual acts."[47]

We must never forget the fact that men and women and their relationships—whether heterosexual or homosexual—are much more than mere objects of doctrine. They were created by God and entrusted also to themselves. An inclusive sexual ethic cannot make normative claims while disregarding that we all were created to be free in corresponding to God's love and in finding ways that allow us to integrate being and acting in just, faithful, and caring relationships.

---

[43] Hartwig, *The Poetics of Intimacy and the Problem of Sexual Abstinence*, 231.

[44] For an important reflection on the holistic understanding of complementarity, see Todd A. Salzman and Michael G. Lawler, *The Sexual Person: Toward a Renewed Catholic Anthropology* (Washington, DC: Georgetown University Press, 2008), 138–61.

[45] Patricia Beattie Jung and Ralph F. Smith, *Heterosexism: An Ethical Challenge* (Albany: State University of New York Press, 1993), 105.

[46] Jung and Smith, 143.

[47] Salzman and Lawler, "Human Dignity and Homosexuality in Catholic Teaching," 119, 123.

Conclusion

Joseph Selling reminds us that "what is first and foremost is persons and relationships."[48] On this basis an inclusive sexual ethic assumes relationship quality as the primary point of departure for any moral evaluation of human sexual intimacy. When we look at homosexual relationships, we are called to focus on their substance rather than on their institutionalized form.

It is a matter of justice to promote the moral right of all to love and be loved and to express love in positive modes of intimate relationships and commitments; to affirm a diversity of responsible sexuality and to celebrate responsible and meaningful sexual relationships; to promote equality and impartiality and to empower people to build inclusive communities. In short, we must embrace and celebrate sexuality for the gift that it is to everybody of any gender identity or sexual orientation.

Homosexual persons also need and want to integrate their physical desires with emotional attachment. Unfolding their identity free from discrimination, they can share their aspirations without being afraid of rejection. Paying attention to the other and to the other's project of life, they can be entirely present in their mutual donation. Experiencing reciprocal care, they realize that they themselves can be a reciprocal gift in each other's lives. Integrating being and acting in their lives, their level of intimacy and commitment can assume different meanings and greater depth. Fidelity, even in homosexual relationships, is called to serve love, to preserve the values that people consider worthy to be preserved and be part of their story.

Grillo sums it up best: "[We must] formulate a series of conditions, horizons, possibilities within which a word of good, an appreciation of life, a gaze of understanding and esteem may descend upon every single existence that chooses the stable communion and the fidelity and solemnity of the interpersonal relationship."[49] Human persons cannot be separated from their sexual identity, and human actions cannot be morally evaluated without including personal conscience and history. Moreover, virtue ethics is the best way toward a new paradigm in sexual ethics beyond what Grillo rightly describes as a doctrinal "short circuit" between absolute respect for homosexual persons and absolute condemnation of any act of homosexual love.[50]

For me, such a "new paradigm" is very far from being "new"; it is the fact that God is love, mercy, and tenderness. By being love, "then God

---

[48] Joseph A. Selling, "The Development of Catholic Tradition and Sexual Morality," in *Embracing Sexuality: Authority and Experience in the Catholic Church,* ed. Joseph A. Selling (Aldershot: Ashgate, 2001), 157.

[49] Grillo, *Cattolicesimo e (omo)sessualità,* 20.

[50] Grillo, 136.

inevitably dwells in the love of homosexual partners . . . [and] the mutual love of the partners images God's love for humankind and impels them mutually toward God."[51] By being merciful, God does not hesitate to enter the lives of homosexual persons to respond to their needs, especially when they are pushed to the margins of society because of their sexual identity.[52] By being tenderness, God is willing to transform the lives of all those homosexual persons who also were saved by love and mercy.[53] Love and mercy constitute an ethical response to homosexual persons, and tenderness makes a community of faith bend lovingly and mercifully in front of them, especially when they suffer because of their sexual identity. Tenderness evinces love and mercy as firm affective dispositions to create an interior space of hospitality to the other.[54] In such a "space," the other can reveal his or her vulnerability and fragility without fear of being judged for who he or she is and for what he or she does or has done. Dwelling in the intimacy of the other implies dwelling in his or her vulnerability and fragility, helping the person to be reborn to a new life, a life where the integration between being and acting is a must. In short, a new paradigm in sexual ethics should be authentically evangelical. It must be based on an evangelical spiritual- ity, animated by a deep conviction that "the Holy Spirit sows in the midst of human weakness."[55] No one should presume to limit the "space" where the Spirit can act.

---

[51] Salzman and Lawler, "Human Dignity and Homosexuality in Catholic Teaching," 131.

[52] Keenan, "Virtue Ethics and Sexual Ethics," 192.

[53] Carlo Rocchetta, "La teologia della tenerezza: dagli ultimi decenni a Papa Fran- cesco," in *La virtù della tenerezza. Il "vangelo" di Papa Francesco,* ed. Mariangela Musolino (Assisi: Porziuncola, 2019), 20.

[54] Pierangelo Sequeri, "La tenerezza: etica ed estetica dell'amore," in Musolino, *La virtù della tenerezza,* 45.

[55] Francis, *Amoris laetitia,* no. 308.

PART V

SPIRITUALITY AND MORALITY

19.

Religious Life in a Synodal Key

A Virtuous Beginning

Maria Cimperman, RSCJ

This essay was written shortly after the conclusion of the global Synod on Synodality (2021–24), through which Pope Francis invited the entire global church to reflect on how the Church can journey together. As a synod participant, a scholar and practitioner of consecrated life, and a student of the gifted virtue ethicist James Keenan, my aim in this essay is to create a dialogue among synodality, insights and practices of religious life, and virtue ethics. Placing these three strands of the church's tradition and practice in dialogue allows us to understand how to live into each more fully. I highlight three necessary dimensions of synodality—listening, sacred conversation, and co-creative collaboration—in order to articulate synodality as a virtue. The practices of sacred conversation used in religious life yield rich insights for growth in the virtue of synodality, whether we are or are not members of a consecrated community.

Synodality and Virtue in This Ecclesial Moment

Pope Francis is calling the entire church to synodality, a continuation of the renewal ushered in by the Spirit in Vatican II. Cardinal Joseph Tobin describes this time as a "new phase in the reception of the Second Vatican Council that recovered the Church as the People of God as the central hermeneutical criterion of the Council's ecclesiology."[1] As a particular way of walking together

---

[1] Joseph Tobin, "Pope Francis and the Journey of Synodality," Sacred Heart University, April 19, 2023.

as the people of God, Francis asserts strongly, "It is precisely this path of synodality which God expects of the Church of the third millennium."[2] As Chapter 2 of *Lumen Gentium* reminds us, the church is the people of God. Francis is not only reminding us that all the baptized are the church; he is also trying to enlarge a sense among the baptized that the baptismal call is to participation in the church through the gifts each has received from the Spirit. The equal dignity, participation, and co-responsibility of all the baptized is necessary for the church. Grounded in scripture and tradition, the call to synodality today is essential to the life and mission of the church.[3]

To this end Francis convened a synodal process for the entire church to discern how the Spirit is moving and how we are called to walk together as the people of God on mission.[4] Francis is trying to help the church experience a way of walking together in which people listen and are heard, difficult conversations can be engaged in respectfully, and communal discernment becomes our way for the sake of the gospel mission. Francis is trying to help us see synodality as the church's ordinary way of proceeding rather than as something reserved only for large decisions in the church body. In its 2018 seminal document, "Synodality in the Life and Mission of the Church," the International Theological Commission (ITC) states:

> First and foremost, synodality denotes the particular style that qualifies the life and mission of the Church, expressing her nature as the people of God journeying together and gathering in assembly, summoned by the Lord Jesus in the power of the Holy Spirit to proclaim the Gospel. Synodality ought to be expressed in the Church's ordinary way of living and working. In this sense, synodality enables the entire people of God to walk forward together, listening to the Holy Spirit and the Word of God, to participate in the mission of the church in the communion that Christ establishes between us. Ultimately, this path of walking together is the most effective way of manifesting and putting into practice the nature of the Church as the pilgrim and missionary People of God.[5]

---

[2] Pope Francis, "Address for the Ceremony Commemorating the 50th Anniversary of the Institution of the Synod of Bishops," October 17, 2015.

[3] E.g., Rafael Luciani, *Synodality: A New Way of Proceeding in the Church* (Mahwah, NJ: Paulist Press, 2022), and *The Synodal Pathway: When Rhetoric Meets Reality*, ed. Eamonn Conway, Eugene Duffy, and Mary McDaid (Dublin: Columba Books, 2022).

[4] The Synod on Synodality officially opened on October 10, 2021.

[5] International Theological Commission, *Synodality in the Life and Mission of the Church*, March 2, 2018, no. 70a. Two other dimensions of synodality mentioned are (1) official structures and ecclesial processes that assist the church with discernment (no. 70b) and (2) occasional synodal events that can include the whole people of God at various levels on topics for discernment (no. 70c). While I mention these two at various places, the focus of this essay is on no. 70a.

Synodality is to be the "specific *modus vivendi et operandi* of the Church, the People of God."[6] For this to be, "the involvement and participation of the whole People of God in the life and mission of the Church"[7] is necessary. This would require changes of mentality, practice, and structures. To live synodality as it is described above would mean a change from a hierarchical way of leadership to a more inclusive, egalitarian, and horizontal style of leadership and membership.[8]

Synodality will require the grace of conversion. Both the ITC and the Preparatory Document for the Synod, citing *Evangelium Gaudium,* recognize this: "In carrying out her mission, the Church is called to constant conversion, which is a . . . pastoral and missionary conversion, too; this involves renewing mentalities, attitudes, practices and structures, in order to be ever more faithful to her vocation."[9] Although we need grace, the fact that our conversion must be constant points to the need to practice synodality in both dispositions and actions.

As synodality is thus a way of being and acting as church, virtue ethics can deepen our understanding and living of synodality. Here I am indebted to Keenan's work on virtue,[10] which has inspired more than one generation of scholars to bring virtue ethics to contemporary realities in the moral and social life of church and society. Virtues are dispositions (habits of character), acquired and demonstrated through practices, that are essential for becoming a particular kind of moral person, community, church, or society. Both dispositions and practices are necessary for growth in virtue. Keenan's definition of mercy as "a willingness to enter into the chaos of another,"[11] is an example of this. One needs a disposition of willingness and repeated, conscious action or practice in order to become merciful. This both/and quality is equally present in synodality. Understanding synodality as a virtue of persons or communities invites both personal, communal, and ecclesial dispositions and practices toward becoming a particular way of being church, the people of God.

---

[6] International Theological Commission, no. 6.

[7] International Theological Commission, no. 7.

[8] As Keenan argues, achieving this will require not only reforming the structures of clerical governance but addressing the endemic cultural problem of hierarchalism in the church. See James Keenan, "Hierarchicalism," *Theological Studies* 83, no. 1 (March 1, 2022): 84–108.

[9] Francis, Apostolic Exhortation *Evangelii Gaudium,* nos. 25–33, *AAS* 105 (2013) 1030–1034; Fifth General Conference of the Episcopate of Latin America and the Caribbean, *Final Document of Aparecida,* 365–72.

[10] See, for example, Daniel Harrington and James Keenan, *Jesus and Virtue Ethics: Building Bridges between New Testament Studies and Moral Theology* (New York: Sheed and Ward, 2005).

[11] See James F. Keenan, *The Works of Mercy: The Heart of Catholicism,* 3rd ed. (Lanham, MD: Rowman & Littlefield, 2017).

In this essay I begin some explorations of imagining synodality as a virtue and consider three necessary dimensions of synodality: listening, sacred conversation, and co-creative collaboration. To open and make concrete these dimensions of synodality, I engage consecrated life as a conversation partner.[12] The ITC specifically mentioned that religious congregations, "many of which have come into being spurred on by charisms given by the Holy Spirit for the renewal of the Church's life and mission, can offer significant experiences of synodal approaches in the life of communion and of the dynamics of communal discernment at the center of their lives, as well as stimuli to discovering new methods of evangelization."[13] This is true. It is also true that consecrated life needs ongoing renewal and revitalization. I propose a new virtue of synodality as a disposition communities and individuals can strive for in the church. The virtue of synodality, in its threefold dimensions of listening, sacred conversation, and co-creative collaboration, calls for a deepening in the key components of consecrated life: prayer, community, and ministry. In bringing synodality and consecrated life into conversation, I hope to begin to articulate what the virtue of synodality entails, explain how consecrated life can enrich our understanding of synodality, and begin to name what consecrated life is being called toward in living synodality more fully.

Listening

Synodality requires a great deal of listening at levels we do not regularly engage. Listening requires both openness and practice. It is a mutually receptive and responsive listening.[14] During retreat one year the director who accompanied me listened at a level I had not before experienced. As I ordinarily do on retreat, I came each day to share my prayer, reflections and connections to my life. Ordinarily the director would pick up on something I said. However, this Benedictine began with, "I heard your tone of voice shift when you mentioned this. I could hear the awe . . . or disappointment . . . in your voice," or "you leaned forward when you spoke about this," or "your entire being [words, emotions, body] proclaimed your experience of the gospel passage." His observations were accurate. He listened deeply, beyond words. The experience of being listened to opened and deepened my prayer. I listened to times in my life that knew pain and woundedness.

---

[12] In this essay I use *consecrated life* and *religious life* interchangeably.

[13] International Theological Commission, *Synodality in the Life and Mission of the Church,* no. 74.

[14] Thanks to Rafael Luciani for this powerful description.

Some of the wounds had healed, and I felt gratitude for God's healing. Those unhealed came forth to be heard. The listening spaces—of God encountering me, and me encountering God, and the shared encounter with a retreat director as it was in process—formed part of the healing process, as did the occasions when my director shared narratives that shed a helpful light on my own.

My retreat director is a Benedictine, and the Rule of St. Benedict begins with the word "Listen." One of the gifts a religious institute or order brings to the church is its charism, a particular gift of the Spirit given to serve the church and world.[15] What can we learn about listening from the Benedictine charism or spirituality, and how can we practice what we learn? For Cistercian Agnes Day, OSCO, love and listening are keys to her life. She writes: "Listening implies an attentive waiting, a ready openness full of hope. We want to listen to God, and this listening is our prayer, our inner space, our very emptiness, which God fills. . . . We do not listen for what we might have expected or imagined, but for the God of surprises."[16] The listening synodality asks for is attentive, steeped in a hope beyond what is seen because the source of that hope is God.

Listening requires silence to hear the other and to allow encounter with what has been offered. Listening silently asks for the layers underneath to be heard. A mark of Benedictine life is hospitality, a helpful image for listening. Hospitality offers welcome to the other person. The Prologue of the Rule of St. Benedict asks one to "incline the ear of your heart," a wonderful image for hospitable listening. In such listening, one can be moved in new and not expected ways.[17] I learned this completing a dissertation with Jim Keenan, for when nothing was moving in my writing and I wanted to cancel our scheduled meeting, he declined my request, remarking this is when we most need to meet. He listened, I listened, and inevitably something moved during the meeting, even to unanticipated directions in a chapter.

Francis reminds us that synodality "is a mutual listening in which everyone has something to learn. The faithful people, the college of bishops, the Bishop of Rome: all listening together, all listening to the Holy Spirit, the 'Spirit of truth' [Jn 14:17], in order to know what he 'says to the Churches' [Rev 2:7]."[18] This attitude of listening is one in which we are open to learn-

---

[15] Charism does not belong to religious life but to all to whom the Spirit bestows the gift that is also found in the congregation.

[16] Agnes Day, "'With Widened Hearts': A Commentary on the Prologue of the Rule of Saint Benedict," *Cistercian Studies Quarterly* 51, no. 3 (2016): 275.

[17] Filip Veber, "Abbot Primate Gregory Polan Speaks about 'Listening' in Benedictine Spirituality," April 12, 2023.

[18] Francis, "Address of His Holiness Pope Francis: Ceremony Commemorating the 50th Anniversary of the Institution of the Synod of Bishops."

ing from one another, including to learn what we had not expected. We are called, as church and in religious life, to listen to God and to listen together, to what the Spirit is asking of us.

Such listening can change us, bring us to conversion, if we listen beyond our own horizons. Reflecting on the Latin American synodal processes, Daniel De Ycaza, SJ, and Mauricio López Oropeza shared that "the Holy Spirit works through the voice of the people. Only by listening to the people will we be able to discern in them the will of God."[19] When he listened to the Syrophoenician woman seeking healing for her daughter, Jesus went beyond his own cultural boundaries and prejudgments to see her dignity and the truth in her words. In religious life we must also open ourselves to the encounters that challenge and call us forth, the cries of creation and humanity, including those in our own communities. We must listen together to the Spirit calling. Synodal listening must permeate all our encounters, for as De Ycaza and Oropeza remind us, "If the synod does not transform us through the encounter with 'the most unlikely,' not even the most persuasive of documents will produce the desired fruit of making us a Church that walks more synodically and allows itself to be challenged . . . in order to move toward a true culture of synodality in the Church."[20] Sacred conversation helps build such a culture.

Sacred Conversation

In addition to listening, the virtue of synodality is marked by sacred or spiritual conversation.[21] Sacred conversation is the way we build community on the journey together as the people of God. *Sacred* acknowledges the dignity and importance of the other and the conversation (topic) at hand. Sacred conversation asks for respectful engagement with one another, with respect rooted in our human dignity as *imago Dei*. We belong to God and to one another as God's creation. All of God's creation, of which humans are a

---

[19] Daniel De Ycaza, SJ, and Mauricio López Oropeza, "Synodal Conversion: Walking Together from Blindness to Light," *La Civiltà Cattolica*, March 24, 2023.

[20] De Ycaza and López Oropeza.

[21] For a good description of the process of spiritual conversation, see "Spiritual Conversation," synod.va. While spiritual conversation is a good method and used frequently in the synodal process, religious congregations practice distinct methods that can also be helpful. Various groups of Sisters of St. Joseph, for example, use a method of "Sharing from the Heart." I use the term *sacred conversation* to denote the broad variety of practices of spiritual listening, including but not limited to the one the synod calls spiritual conversation.

part, is sacred. Sacred conversation is the way in which we come together to listen, share with one another, and seek to hear God's movements in the gathering.

Conversation requires participation. It is an expectation of membership in most religious orders that willingness and openness must accompany one's participation. Participation is part of our call as baptized members of a faith community of believers and as disciples of Jesus. Sacred conversation also requires willingness. Sometimes trust has to be built or rebuilt in the relationship for depth of sharing. We need time and space for this.

Sacred conversation brings us to vulnerable spaces. Keenan stretches us and brings together a variety of voices into the definition of vulnerability: "The word vulnerable does not mean being or having been wounded, but rather means being able to be wounded. . . . It means being exposed to the other. . . . Vulnerability is the human condition that allows me to encounter, receive, or respond to the other, it allows us to be aware of others and their dignity, to take risks in meeting and recognizing others."[22] Vulnerable conversation draws us interiorly and exteriorly. It implies we are listening closely enough to be affected and changed by the other, enough to be transformed interiorly in a way that changes what I do.

We need to find ways to share our narratives, speak our truths, in spaces worthy of our vulnerability and trust. In the sharing during a sacred conversation, persons are vulnerable whether they are speaking or listening, capable of being hurt as well as opened up to new possibilities from the encounter. For some, healing is possible in sacred conversation, in the experience of listening deeply to another and in the experience of being listened to.[23] Certainly, the need is great in our church and religious life for healing of all kinds. In religious life I regularly encounter men and women who still remember, with pain, experiences of hurt from formation, leadership, ministry, or community. The pain they still hold and carry impacts them, their community, and their ministry. Healing is God's to do, but there is much the community can also do. When we practice such sacred conversation, bringing our full selves, with our gifts, capacities, hurts, and willingness to grow, religious community can offer opportunities for vulnerability and

---

[22] James F. Keenan, "Linking Human Dignity, Vulnerability and Virtue Ethics," *Interdisciplinary Journal of Religion and Transformation in Contemporary Society* 6 (2020): 59; see also "Restoring Social Trust: From Populism to Synodality," *Theological Studies*, 84, no. 1 (2023): 110–33.

[23] Certainly not all healing can happen in sacred conversation contexts. There are many paths, including therapy, that serve healing. However, for some, healing does happen in the context of safe, sacred conversations.

healing.[24] Pope Francis acknowledges this as he describes the synod as a "grace-filled event, a process of healing guided by the Spirit."[25]

It is in the vulnerability they demand that sacred conversations offer ways to dialogue through difficult topics. *Fratelli Tutti* offers the image of the polyhedron (a three-dimensional shape that has many faces) to "represent a society where differences coexist, complementing, enriching and reciprocally illuminating one another, even amid disagreements and reservations" (*Fratelli Tutti*, no. 215). Listening allows us to hold the creative tension necessary to engage differences, understand, and together, with interior freedom, seek to hear the Spirit's call (*Fratelli Tutti*, no. 190). Francis reminds us that "authentic social dialogue involves the ability to respect the other's point of view and to admit that it may include legitimate convictions and concerns," that others have something to offer. "Differences are creative," says Francis, "they create tension and in the resolution of tension lies humanity's progress" (*Fratelli Tutti*, no. 203).

> In a true spirit of dialogue we grow in our ability to grasp the significance of what others say and do, even if we cannot accept it as our own conviction. In this way, it becomes possible to be frank and open about our beliefs, while continuing to discuss, to seek points of contact and above all, to work and struggle together. (*Querida Amazonia*, no. 108; see also *Fratelli Tutti*, no. 203)

Sacred conversation offers space for dialogue in which we are heard, hear the other, and together work to find a way forward. Newer members in religious life regularly ask how we deal with disagreements in community. I find myself sharing stories, both of how we struggle and how we work through struggle, admitting that sometimes there can be a long wait to work through conflicts. The key is to stay open, even for a seemingly unlikely result—the Spirit dwells in openness and gifts us with surprises. There are few public examples of overcoming conflict in our polarized US church. Witnessing to their sacred, vulnerable efforts to dialogue and inviting others to share their experiences are important ways for those in consecrated life to serve the church. We must create more spaces for sacred conversation and learn again skills for dialogue.

---

[24] In many constitutions of religious institutes, life in community is described with language that invites this.

[25] Francis, "Homily for the Holy Mass Opening of the Synodal Path," October 10, 2021.

The sexual-abuse crisis reminds us that even as sacred conversation can build unity in the church, the desire for unity must never override listening to those on the peripheries of power. Catholics must be free to voice healthy cautions and disagreements in a synodal church. Here again Keenan makes a significant contribution, bringing theologians and experts together in a volume he coedited to respond to the great wound of the abuse crisis in the church.[26] Daniel Bogner's essay in that volume questions "whether synodality sufficiently addresses the 'systemic' causes that have led to instances of sexual abuse within the Catholic Church" and argues that "strong forces within the Church prioritize a 'soft' understanding of synodality as 'inclusion of different voices' over substantive changes in canon law and ecclesiology. Such changes, however, would be necessary to make the desired improvements binding and effective."[27] These questions must be raised and addressed. A synodal church must be open to such questions and critiques, willing to learn and be transformed by learning, capable of discerning and acting on decisions.

Let me conclude this section with a few words on communal discernment as one process that utilizes sacred conversations for significant decisions. A key contribution religious life brings to the church is experience with communal discernment. Communal discernment is most often used at significant moments in a congregation, such as a general chapter at which time there is direction setting for the congregation and determining leadership. Communal discernment requires both individual commitment and communal participation in together seeking the Spirit's movement for the direction of a congregation, through one's charism and in light of the cries of the world and church. It requires prayer, deep listening to the Spirit in the individual, the community gathered, and the world around us and sacred conversation to together hear directions calling. The processes of communal discernment used by religious congregations can serve as helpful examples for local churches. The Ignatian process of communal discernment is excellent and perhaps most widely used. At the same time, as the body of Christ is diverse and there are many charisms, there is an urgent

---

[26] See, for example, *Catholic Ethicists on HIV/AIDS Prevention,* ed. James Keenan, with Jon Fuller, Lisa Cahill, and Kevin Kelly (London: Continuum, 2000); Daniel Fleming, James Keenan, SJ, and Hans Zollner, SJ, "Doing Theology and Theological Ethics in the Face of the Abuse Crisis," *Journal of Moral Theology* 3 (CTEWC Book Series 3) (March 16, 2023): i–374.

[27] Daniel Bogner, "Journeying Together: Does a Synodal Church Improve Respect for the Human Person?" in Fleming, Keenan, and Zollner, "Doing Theology and Theological Ethics in the Face of the Abuse Crisis," 176.

need today for religious congregations across charisms to articulate their way of communal discernment and share this with the church.

Co-Creative Collaboration

A third necessary dimension of synodality is co-creative collaboration. On the local and global level, co-creative collaboration is first a reminder that God is creating something new all the time, and is doing so with us. Many congregations already collaborate. Women religious in the United States, for example, have for decades worked together with others in common mission. What has shifted throughout these decades is the attitude underneath this transformation. Formerly the practice of collaboration with laity might be presented as necessary "because we do not have enough sisters," or there might have been an attitude that "religious" hold the charism for the institutions and others join in. This new moment is telling us that we are working together *because this is how the Spirit is moving among us.* We need one another. Together is our only way forward.

Synodality requires both willingness and practice in co-creative collaboration. Co-creative collaboration means we create together and each person is needed for the new creation. No longer does one person or group create while others are merely invited to join the vision. Synodality reminds the church that the Spirit works through all and that the insights of all are needed, particularly where the local is lived. The same is true in religious life. As each offers the gifts given, new possibilities emerge. Much more is possible together, on local and global scales.

Charism is vitally important, and we cannot yet fully see what will emerge as we intentionally work across charisms for the sake of mission. We must trust that responding to unmet needs together will only enhance our individual charisms. New dimensions of each charism will come forth as we find ways together that we could not separately. Perhaps these experiences can help in dioceses where parishes must merge or in other cases where realities demand reshaping ecclesial communities. In all, we build webs of relationship so that no one falls through the cracks of care and so that the earth might also have opportunity to heal. This is a necessary public witness in our world. This co-creative collaborative attitude and response must also live in our institutions and ministries. There can be no group or institution that waits for others to fall and fail. In co-creative collaboration, individuals and groups work together, learn from and with one another, and meet unmet needs. I offer two examples here.

In Padua, in 2006, Catholic Theological Ethics in the World Church (CTEWC), founded by Keenan, held its first gathering, bringing four hundred theological ethicists together for scholarly community and sharing. It was the first time many of us had the opportunity to meet moral theologians outside of our national communities. Together we listened to voices that widened our horizons on poverty, medical ethics, HIV/AIDS, and fundamental moral theology. The theological insights came from local contexts and influenced our own contexts, offering a more global vision. Conversations and relationships ensued through the opportunities to think, hear, and imagine together. There have been two further large gatherings as well as several regional gatherings to build on those networks, and the CTEWC monthly newsletter also includes essays from across the globe on key ethical issues.

More recently, in January 2023, an international conference on synodality at Dharmaram Vidya Kshetram (Pontifical Athenaeum) in Bangalore, India, was organized by a team led by Shaji George Kochuthara, CMI, in association with Chavara Central Secretariat (Congregation of Carmelites of Mary Immaculate). Participants included theologians, bishops, priests, and laity, including women and men religious. A number of theologians present were members of CTEWC. While focused on the Asian and particularly the Indian context, the conference intentionally invited and held spaces for eighty participants outside of India and even Asia. The circles of encounter widened as theologians, bishops, and practitioners listened, dialogued, and shared meals. The context provided a profound space for both Asian participants and the widening international community to learn together, share calls and challenges of synodality, and generate ideas for co-creative collaboration.

The call to interculturality reminds us there is still and always room for growth in our journey together.[28] Recognizing the gift of diverse perspectives and experiences, growing numbers of religious congregations are working toward becoming intercultural communities. This ongoing process requires education (formation) and practice. The cultural diversity present in our parishes and communities offers a rich opportunity to engage one another across cultures (ethnicity, age, gender, and so on) as we encounter the Spirit's movements through our cultures. As people are welcomed and the diversity of gifts is recognized, we can also more easily work together in response to unmet needs.

Witnessing and modeling gender equality are areas of interculturality and co-creative collaboration to which religious congregations, the academy, and the church are urgently being called. A beginning for women and men

---

[28] For an understanding of interculturality, see, for example, Anthony Gittins, *Living Mission Interculturally: Faith, Culture, and the Renewal of Praxis* (Collegeville, MN: Liturgical Press, 2015); and Maria Cimperman and Roger Schroeder, eds., *Engaging Our Diversity: Interculturality and Consecrated Life Today* (Maryknoll, NY: Orbis Books, 2020).

religious would be intentionally building synodal spaces for co-creative collaboration. This synodal dimension will require vulnerable, respectful, mutually responsive listening and sacred conversation to create a new way together. This is also a call to theologians, who are not all clergy but are certainly capable of participating in upholding clericalism, as Keenan has pointed out.[29] Even today, vigilance is needed on planning teams to model the equality about which we speak in our gatherings. The ITC reminds theologians:

> "As is the case with all Christian vocations, the ministry of theologians, as well as being personal, is also both communal and collegial." Ecclesial synodality therefore needs theologians to do theology in a synodal way, developing their capacity to listen to each other, to dialogue, to discern and to harmonize their many and varied approaches and contributions.[30]

The virtue of synodality calls forth the dispositions and practices of listening, sacred conversation, and co-creative collaboration. Francis tells us that as we, the people of God, walk together on the synodal journey, we will see that its purpose is to "plant dreams, draw forth prophecies and visions, allow hope to flourish, inspire trust, bind up wounds, weave together relationships, awaken a dawn of hope, learn from one another and create a bright resourcefulness that will enlighten minds, warm hearts, give strength to our hands."[31] As the church learns from consecrated religious how to practice sacred conversation and the virtue of synodality, one exemplar in this work is Keenan, a Jesuit for more than forty years. He is always in the midst of reality and calling us to the prophetic edges. Synodality and sacred conversation are our call whether we are in religious life or not. So we go—together—on the synodal path!

---

[29] See Maria Cimperman, *Religious Life for Our World: Creating Communities of Hope* (Maryknoll, NY: Orbis Books, 2020), 106.

[30] International Theological Commission, *Synodality in the Life and Mission of the Church*, no. 75. The opening quotation in the extract is from International Theological Commission, "Theology Today: Perspectives, Principles, and Criteria" (2012), 45.

[31] Preparatory Document for the 16th Ordinary General Assembly of the Synod of Bishops. "For a Synodal Church: Communion, Participation, and Mission," September 7, 2021.

20.

Radical Relationality

A Preferential Option Embracing Vulnerability

Mary Jo Iozzio

Vulnerability has become a key interest for many in philosophical and theological anthropology. Ethicists too have begun to engage vulnerability in their work on disability, ethnicity, immigration, LGBTQ+ experience, and nondominant-race precarity. James F. Keenan, SJ, has recently turned in earnest to vulnerability and its fundamental place in ethics and the moral life. This essay builds on his work. My contribution addresses the radically dependent nature of human beings inclusive of the dependence we often fail to notice in the grandeur and simplicity of both divine and human creation that surrounds and challenges each of us every day, that is, our dependence on God, the world, and its inhabitants.

Vulnerability, a natural state of dependence on others journeying from life to life, can be successful only when each of us preferentially embraces our dependence and, thereby, our vulnerable need of and for one another as an inherent condition of our humanity. By *preferentially* I mean without shame or embarrassment when I, for example, recognize my dependence on others for most activities of daily life—from intimate to social—as well as dependence during personal or social crises and local, regional, or global catastrophe. Thus, by embracing my own dependence, I can develop an explicit, sympathetic preference for my neighbors when I respond to my neighbors' needs and vulnerability as my own. We are foolish, I argue, to think otherwise (that is, to see myself as a "super-hero" or invulnerable and to see my neighbor as fodder when in fact we both exist in radical, dependent, and vulnerable need of each other without exception).

Through the lens of Catholic social teaching on the *imago Dei*, human dignity, preferential option for the poor and vulnerable (especially with regard to intersecting oppressions), and the common good, I engage some of Keenan's insights on the risk-taking examples of vulnerability that God takes on our behalf. I hold that we are all vulnerable and in need of both intimate and social support. These supports are communal by nature and inclusive of each of our needs for and dependencies upon others to be, to "get by," and to thrive, as well as our dependencies upon impersonal physical and social infrastructures.

The essay unfolds in five parts: basics of vulnerability; disability; divine passibility and the disabled God; vulnerability and the precarity of chance; and our response to our own and our neighbors' encounters with precarity and encounters of hope.

Basics of Vulnerability

Unsurprisingly, the *Oxford English Dictionary* defines *vulnerability* through the lens of military engagements as (1.) "Having the power to wound; wounding. *Obsolete, rare*"; . . . (2.a) "that may be wounded; susceptible of receiving wounds or physical injury;" (2.b) "open to attack or injury of a non-physical nature; esp., offering an opening to the attacks of raillery, criticism, calumny, etc." Somewhat surprising, though understandable, the *OED* presents war, de facto resulting in wounding, as the principal cause of vulnerability to both combatants and noncombatants. As part of the *OED*'s 2012 *Draft Additions*, vulnerability is defined as "designating a person in need of special care, support, or protection (esp. provided as a social service) because of age, disability, risk of abuse or neglect, etc."[1] Further, *Oxford Reference* defines *vulnerability* as "a state of relative disadvantage, which requires a person to trust and depend upon others."[2]

Given these definitions, we can envision expressions of bravery, courage, and grit in the military model of vulnerability as told by historical characters (the victors far more than the victimized) in the never-ending engagement of war instigated over resources, lands, and peoples. However, since the pursuit of war fails on almost every level in achievement of its ends, it is essentially senseless given the numbers of civilian and military dead; survivors with emotional, physical, and social disability; and collateral

---

[1] *Oxford English Dictionary*, "Vulnerable, *adj.*," and *Draft Additions 2012* (Oxford, UK: Oxford University Press, 2023).

[2] *Oxford Reference*, "Vulnerability" (Oxford, UK: Oxford University Press, 2023).

environmental damage left in the wake of modern munitions and chemical warfare. Relatedly, movies and video games both perpetuate the lies that war is good for national self-interest, the veteran, and the economy.[3] Contra this narrative, vulnerability can be extracted from war-makers' hopes for domination and other ulterior motives. As the definitive condition of all living beings, vulnerability is better embraced for its recognition of mutual dependence upon and support of one another as for oneself.

Certainly we can begin to reconceive vulnerability through the lens of those most subjected to violence. However, violence presents in multiple ways and against many individuals and groups identified by a dominant community as untoward and, thereby, unworthy of the social and personal supports of care, civility, and community. In the work of Judith Butler, to which Keenan turns,[4] we find that resistance to violence offers an antidote to this state of affairs.[5] One of Butler's insights points out the interdependence upon which the social order rests: "I depend on you in order to survive and flourish."[6] Denial of this interdependence, if not radical dependence,[7] is foolhardy at best and dangerous in its worst guise.

Alternately, we know from Christian tradition that, given the incarnation, our God is a vulnerable God, "weak in power but strong in love."[8] Divine possibility or, more familiarly, vulnerability, can be denied no longer (at least not since the incarnation). Rather, vulnerability may very well be the Name of God, especially vulnerability to the vicissitudes of life in its human forms. After all, Jesus was born in precarity, a Jewish male in Roman-occupied Judea, a laborer, a teacher, a threat to the powers of religious leaders and the empire, tortured and crucified. God's

---

[3] See Institute for Economics and Peace (IEP), "Economic Consequences of War on the US Economy" (New York: IEP, 2011).

[4] See James F. Keenan, "The World at Risk: Vulnerability, Precarity, and Connectedness," *Theological Studies* 81, no.1 (2020): 132–49; Keenan, "Vulnerable to Contingency," *Journal of the Society of Christian Ethics* 40, no. 2 (2020): 221–36; and Keenan, "Building Blocks for Moral Education: Vulnerability, Recognition, and Conscience," in *Conscience and Catholic Education*, ed. Kevin Baxter and David DeCosse (Maryknoll, NY: Orbis Books, 2022), 17–30.

[5] See Judith Butler, *Vulnerability in Resistance* (Durham, NC: Duke University Press, 2016).

[6] Judith Butler, "Rethinking Vulnerability, Violence, and Resistance," March 20, 2020, versobooks.com/blogs.

[7] See Mary Jo Iozzio, "Radical Dependence and the *Imago Dei*: Bioethical Implications of Access to Healthcare for People with Disabilities," *Christian Bioethics* 23, no. 3 (2017): 234–60.

[8] Leonardo Boff, *Jesus Christ Liberator: A Critical Christology for Our Time* (Maryknoll, NY: Orbis Books, 1978), 27.

self-willed vulnerability is instructive for us as it reveals "the redemptive nearness of God to human vulnerability and brokenness, a nearness of solidarity that does not undo or fix such brokenness but . . . paradoxically embraces it."[9]

As disability scholars and scholars of other nondominant communities have instructed us, recognition is the first step of relationality, while the second step requires recognition of our vulnerability.[10] We human beings depend upon recognizing others and on being recognized in turn. "There is no human 'I' outside of the constant granting of recognition and being recognized in all our vulnerability."[11] Feminist scholars offer similarly liberating ways of recognizing both contingency and vulnerability as an existential turn or "openness towards the complex bonds of sociality that intertwine us with a heterogeneous, plural and unfamiliar plexus of innumerous others."[12] Denying vulnerability serves no good purpose: "Ignorance of vulnerability is produced precisely because we do know and experience our own vulnerability, yet disavow it as formative."[13] Thus, captive to "independence," we refuse to admit the depths and the multiple relationships upon which each of us, without exception, depends.

Disability

Disability in the human community is often presented as the epitome of vulnerability—sometimes rightly, but just as often hastily and wrongly. To live with disability is not, necessarily, an impediment to human well-being and thriving. Denial of the possibilities of a good life lived with disability is, simply, a stricture imposed upon persons with disability and the good

---

[9] Thomas E. Reynolds, *Vulnerable Communion: A Theology of Disability and Hospitality* (Grand Rapids, MI: Brazos Press, 2008), 32. See also Enda McDonagh, *Vulnerable to the Holy: In Faith, Morality and Art* (Dublin: Columba, 2005).

[10] See Turana Burke and Brené Brown, eds., *You Are Your Best Thing: Vulnerability, Shame, Resilience and the Black Experience* (New York: Random House, 2021); Katie G. Cannon, *Katie's Canon: Womanism and the Soul of the Black Community* (New York: Continuum, 1995); James H. Cone, *A Black Theology of Liberation*, 40th anniv. ed. (Maryknoll, NY: Orbis Books, 2010).

[11] Brian Brock, *Wondrously Wounded: Theology, Disability, and the Body of Christ* (Waco, TX: Baylor University Press, 2019), 95.

[12] Ariadni Polychroniou, "Towards a Radical Feminist Resignification of Vulnerability: A Critical Juxtaposition of Judith Butler's Post Structuralist Philosophy and Martha Fineman's Legal Theory," *Redescriptions: Political Thought, Conceptual History, and Feminist Theology* 25, no. 2 (2022), 116.

[13] Erin Gilson, "Vulnerability, Ignorance, and Oppression," *Hypatia* 26, no. 2 (2011), 314.

lives many if not most of them experience. Such strictures have resulted in vulnerability to oppression of many kinds "that give rise to an extraordinary level of violence."[14]

Disability is not a simple phenomenon. The presence of disability exemplifies a set of complex social relations in the human community. Both familial and not, social relations are the key to anyone *and* everyone's success. Each of us depends upon our parents, siblings, and extended family members as well as our teachers, friends, faith communities, employers, coworkers, farmers, harvesters, grocers, medical providers, and keepers of the infrastructure. We are socially related, and we are dependent on these relations, yet most of these relations go unrecognized. However, compared to the nondisabled, the history of relations and relationships that persons and communities with disability experience has been tenuously both kind and unkind in familial, community, and institutional care—kind with love and friendship, unkind with violence. Discrimination and violence against persons with disability are widespread across time and place. Their vulnerability to abuse is institutionalized in explicit and opaque ways. From verbal to physical, sexual, and emotional abuse, to sequestering and bullying, including murderous violence,[15] history reveals scandalous experiences alongside the kind of welcome that is more readily experienced by the dominant and able of the community.

Moreover, disability serves as an experiential trope for the abled. It functions like the symbol of God functions: to liberate or to oppress.[16] Disability can be easily manipulated to serve the cultural practices of the dominant community, using a normate lens to "other" those deemed deviant from the presumed normativity of the nondisabled and too different from the "standards" of capacity, strength, and beauty on account of their vulnerability.[17]

---

[14] James I. Charlton, *Nothing about Us without Us: Disability Oppression and Empowerment* (Berkeley: University of California Press, 2000), 99.

[15] See Dick Sobsey, Don Wells, Richard Lucardie, and Sheila Mansell, *Violence and Disability* (Baltimore: Paul H. Brookes Publishing Co, 1995); Eugenics Archives, eugenicsarchive.ca; and Erika Harrell, "Crime against Persons with Disabilities, 2009–19 Statistical Tables," Bureau of Justice, Statistics (November 2021).

[16] Cf. "the symbol of God functions"; see Elizabeth A. Johnson, *She Who Is: The Mystery of God in Feminist Theological Discourse*, 3rd ed. (New York: Herder & Herder, 2017).

[17] "This neologism names the veiled subject position of the cultural self, the figure outlined by the array of deviant others whose marked bodies shore up the normate's boundaries. . . . The constructed identity of those who, by way of the bodily configurations and cultural capital they assume, can step into a position of authority and wield the power it grants them." Rosemarie Garland-Thomson, *Extraordinary Bodies* (New York: Columbia University Press, 1997), 8.

Norms ultimately function as a means to liberate or oppress.[18] Yet disability is a naturally occurring reality, though its reception is frequently fraught with negative connotations: "Treating disability solely as an exceptional accident of fate veils the relationship between disability and violence, between disablement, domination, and colonialist power."[19] The trope that oppresses is all too common and often harms persons with disability and their support systems.

For example, think about the ways in which genetic testing has become a standard practice in obstetric offices. Recommended for all pregnant women, "reproductive genetic testing offers the opportunity to identify people who are at increased risk for having a child who has a genetic disease or to identify an affected embryo or fetus . . . to detect abnormalities in genes or chromosomes of a fetus before birth . . . [or] at increased risk for a trisomy disorder (such as Down Syndrome) or neural tube defect."[20] Persons with disability are discomforted by much of the rhetoric that surrounds ulterior purposes of such tests, as selective abortion often follows positive test results. Selective abortion expresses negative or discriminatory attitudes about a particular trait, a lack of recognition or tolerance of diversity, and a near explicit declaration that it would be better if persons living with this or that anomaly were never born.[21] Disability scholars conclude that "selecting against embryos or fetuses on the basis of predicted disability reinforces the belief that disability is inimical to a worthwhile life."[22]

Anyone who has firsthand experience with disability of self or a loved one knows precarity and vulnerability expressed in concrete terms. For some (many?) to not have their humanity recognized and respected has led to gross offenses exacerbating their precarity and vulnerability with oppressions and abuse against them.[23] Although both oppressor and oppressed

---

[18] See Mary Jo Iozzio, "Norms Matter: A Hermeneutic of Disability/A Theological Anthropology of Radical Dependence," *ET-Studies* 4, no. 1 (2013): 89–106.

[19] See Julia Watts Belser, "Violence, Disability, and the Politics of Healing," *Journal of Religion and Disability* 19, no. 2 (2015): 191.

[20] National Academy of Sciences, *An Evidence Framework for Genetic Testing* (Washington, DC: National Academies Press, 2017), 3.

[21] See Erik Parens and Adrienne Asch, "The Disability Rights Critique of Prenatal Genetic Testing," *Hastings Center Report* Special Supplement (September–October, 1999); see also Mary Jo Iozzio, "Genetic Anomaly or Genetic Diversity: Thinking in the Key of Disability on the Human Genome," *Theological Studies* 66, no. 4 (2005): 862–81.

[22] Adrienne Asch and Dorit Barlevy, "Disability and Genetics: A Disability Critique of Pre-natal Testing and Pre-implantation Genetic Diagnosis (PGD)" (Chichester: John Wiley and Sons, LTD: *eLS* Science and Society, 2012), 1.

[23] See Michel Foucault, "The Subject and Power," in *Power*, trans. Robert Hurley et al. (New York: New Press, 1994); and Bruce G. Link and Jo C. Phelan, "Conceptualizing Stigma," *Annual Review of Sociology* 27 (2001).

are in fact created in the image of God, these oppressions confound the humanity of both the perpetrators who harm the persons they identify as undeserving of the designation of being created in the *imago Dei*, as well as those oppressed with often deadly consequences.

Divine Passibility and the Disabled God

Kenosis may be defined as God's own freedom to embrace susceptibility to the vicissitudes of human life with all its hopes and imperfections, its vulnerability and precarity. In the incarnation God becomes vulnerable by means of reducing Godself from potency to act. In free enfleshment, God is affected immediately by the joys and sorrows that come with skin and bones and blood and muscles and senses and minds through which human beings experience and interpret the world we inhabit. Divine passibility—of joys and sorrows—is surely manifest in love for the world that God has created, not for God's own entertainment but for the superabundant and extravagant love that God bestows upon creation. This love is both God's gift and calling card.[24]

While the annunciation signals a particularly concrete and familiar example of *kenosis*, definitively confirmed in the crucifixion-death-resurrection of Jesus, human understanding of God even before the incarnation both signaled and still confirms God's passibility in relation to the world that came to be "in the beginning" from the singular decision to create the cosmos as we now know it: "Let there be." Once that decision to create was made, God's word was given a voice: "Let there be" earth and sky, light and dark, sun and moon, land and water, creatures in the sea, plants and living creatures on land and birds in the air. Then God said, "Let us make humankind in our image, according to our likeness. . . . Male and female he created them" (Gen 1:26–27). What soon follows this creation narrative is God's delight in what was made. This delight is perhaps the first instance of God's passibility: the expressed ability to emote, akin to being moved and affected by what is seen, heard, and felt. Similarly, God's sorrow over troubling events, like the slaughter of innocents and violence against racial, gender, and disability minorities, is just as surely a manifestation of God's love for what God has created. Sorrow gives passible witness to love of another. The pathos of sorrow points then to virtue: to love, surely, and to restorative, corrective, and social justice. Thus, "if we rule out God's having the capacity for sorrow on the basis of a physiological theory of emotion,

---

[24] See Charles Taliaferro, "The Possibility of God," *Religious Studies* 25 (1989): 217–24.

we also rule out God's having the capacity for happiness"[25] and visceral care for what God has created.

The incarnation may be the sine qua non example of vulnerability in its precarity: God passing from ultimate power to powerlessness, born into the human estate, of humble parentage, a marginalized Jew. The incarnation is God's own embrace of the same precarity "experienced by marginalized, poor, and disenfranchised people who are exposed to economic insecurity, injury, violence, and forced migration."[26] If we had doubts about God's own vulnerability and willing entry into precarity, the incarnation gives the definitive expression of passibility, reminds us of our strengths and frailties, and calls us not only to recognize but to incarnate joyfully the radical nature of our dependencies before, upon, and with one another.

Since the late 1980s the Christian community has benefited from theology by scholars with disabilities and their abled interlocutors. Much of this work exhumed the sometimes positive but frequently appalling history of treatment—exposure of neonates; abandonment of children; emotional, physical, and sexual abuse; institutionalization; and murder—that people with disability have experienced since recorded history began. As Christians, disability theologians have a commitment to the trinitarian God: the Creator, Jesus the Word of God enfleshed as the Christ of Faith, and the Holy Spirit. Among the most provocative of theologies from this community is Nancy Eiesland's *The Disabled God*. Like the contributions of scholars from underrepresented racial communities, the image of God in a "sip-n-puff chair" confirms God's willingness to be vulnerable to the vicissitudes of life in a world of contingency and risk, of vulnerability and precarity, and of disability. Eiesland's insight points to the risen Jesus who was recognized by the scars of the crucifixion; with punctured hands and feet, wounds in his side and head, Jesus is materially the passible God. "Hence, disability not only does not contradict the human-divine integrity; it becomes a new model of wholeness and a symbol of solidarity."[27] Enfleshing God as disabled brings the question of God's passibility to a close.[28] The incarnation surely reveals God in Godself as all in . . . with and for us:[29] this "theology of disability is

---

[25] Taliaferro, 221.

[26] Sharryn Kasmir, "Precarity," *The Open Encyclopedia of Anthropology* (March 13, 2018).

[27] Nancy Eiesland, *The Disabled God: Toward a Liberatory Theology of Disability* (Nashville, TN: Abingdon Press, 1994), 101.

[28] See M. Shawn Copeland, *Enfleshing Freedom: Body, Race, and Being* (Minneapolis: Fortress Press, 2010).

[29] See Catherine Mowry LaCugna, *God for Us: The Trinity and Christian Life* (New York: HarperCollins, 1993).

central to our understanding of what it means to know who God is and to know what it means to be a human being living fully under God."[30]

Moreover, the disabled God liberates the many who have been brought low on account of their difference from the dominant community and its built-in structures of exclusion. The Black church, Brown church, Indigenous Peoples of the Americas, Asian church, and African church have recorded their voices and experiences in ways that resemble as well as intersect with the experiences of people with disability.[31] That resemblance is liberated by the disabled God of precarity and vulnerability to the forces of empires, nations, and systems designed to disadvantage, exclude, and oppress.

The disabled God offers vulnerable communion as an antidote to hubris, bullying, shaming, mocking, and abuse that minoritized peoples have long suffered. "Vulnerability and weakness carry a secret power because they radiate with divine plenitude, a surplus of love that ruptures conventional categories of instrumental value. . . . Each being is fundamentally relational, open to others in a vast web of interdependency with roots in God's gratuitous love."[32] This enfleshed communion is instigated by the possibility of speech itself, first recorded in the Creator's words of creation, the possibility in the Spirit's songs, and the possibility of the incarnate God's vulnerability in his conception-childhood-ministry-death-resurrection: the constitutive elements of love are vulnerability to the other in the precarities of compassion, empathy, and forgiveness.[33] This vulnerability is an active bending over backwards to accommodate another's need.[34] This vulnerability is God bending low to hear and respond to our precarity.

---

[30] Jon Swinton, "Who Is the God We Worship? Theologies of Disability: Challenges and New Possibilities," *International Journal of Practical Theology* 14, no. 2 (2011): 206.

[31] See, for example, David Endres, ed., *Black Catholic Studies Reader: History and Theology* (Washington, DC: Catholic University of America Press, 2021); Roberto Chao Romero, *Brown Church: Five Centuries of Latino/a Social Justice, Theology, and Identity* (Downers Grove, IL: IVP Academic, 2020); David Endres, ed., *Native American Catholic Studies Reader* (Washington, DC: Catholic University of America Press, 2022); Kwok Pui-Lan, ed., *Third World and Indigenous Women's Theology* (Maryknoll, NY: Orbis Books, 2010); and Agbonkhianmeghe E. Orobator, *Theology Brewed in an African Pot* (Maryknoll, NY: Orbis Books, 2008).

[32] Reynolds, *Vulnerable Communion*, 175–76.

[33] See Roberto Sirvent, *Embracing Vulnerability: Human and Divine* (Eugene, OR: Wipf and Stock/Pickwick, 2015).

[34] See Iozzio, "God Bends Over Backwards to Accommodate Humankind," *Journal of Moral Theology* 6, SI 2 (2017): 10–31.

Vulnerability and the Precarity of Chance

The likelihood of disability in life is almost a given. Some persons are born with disability, and many will acquire a disability over the course of their lives.[35] Both scenarios limit access to the places that the able-bodied or able-minded routinely enjoy.

> Becoming disabled demands learning how to live effectively as a person with disabilities, not just living as a disabled person trying to become nondisabled. It also demands the awareness and cooperation of others who don't experience these challenges. Becoming disabled means moving from isolation to community, from ignorance to knowledge about who we are, from exclusion to access, and from shame to pride.[36]

Vulnerability to acquiring disability increases with age, military service, and limited access to everyday resources.

Vulnerability is intrinsic to life with a body, an existential gift of the human condition expressed in the chance of personal and social relationships, in interdependence with systems and structures, as well as the dangers of abuse and oppression.[37] Here vulnerability and precarity dance with the likelihood of an encounter with danger or accident accompanied by a change in one's self-perception as indomitable. This precarity frightens most, yet persons with disability meet these normate fears of presumed incapacity or loss of loving self-regard with magnanimity, genius, and aplomb, as well as frustration in socially constructed denials of accessibility and welcome.

Precarity is an experience that will more than likely visit all people at some point in their lives. This chance carries the possibilities of understanding oneself ever more clearly as dependent upon others and systems and of finding ways to embrace the vulnerability that is the human condition. And, like the vulnerable God, we can embrace the likely chance of weakness in power and still hold on to being strong in love of ourselves and others.

---

[35] Council for Disability Awareness, "Chances of Disability: Me, Disabled?" (2024).

[36] Rosemarie Garland-Thomson, "Becoming Disabled," in *Beginning with Disability: A Primer*, ed. Leonard J. Davis (New York: Routledge, 2018), 15.

[37] See Amanda Grenier, "Rereading Frailty through a Lens of Precarity: An Explication of Politics and the Human Condition of Vulnerability," in *Precarity and Ageing: Understanding Insecurity and Risk in Later Life*, ed. Amanda Grenier, Chris Phillipson, and Richard A. Setterson, Jr. (Bristol: Bristol University Press, 2020), chap. 4; and Hanne Laceulle, "Virtuous Aging and Existential Vulnerability," *Journal of Aging Studies* 43 (2017): 1–8.

Encounters with Precarity and Encounters of Hope

Hope is one of the theological virtues that serves as trust in the future to recognize the promises that God has made to us and those supporting us in our daily affairs.[38] Experiences of precarity can destabilize the status quo in expressions of resistance that signal hope for change: "Besides trouble, precarity movements flip vulnerability upside down in such a way that experiences of insecurity and dispossession lead to initiatives of collective agency and organized resistance."[39] Organized resistance presents hope for the futures of persons vulnerable to abuse, being left behind, invisible, nugatory, undeserving. Ontologically prior to changes in the structures of oppression, resistance ignites the individual and social imaginaries of change. Those imaginaries leading to that change will be attentive to precarity and dependent on the hope of transformative justice to expose encounters with precarity and move toward a sustainable future. On a global level the United Nations Universal Values expose what is mostly anonymous precarity in discriminatory laws, policies, and social practices that leave behind those who are vulnerable on account of limited access to the means of basic human functioning.[40] Encouragingly, the UN recognizes that an "important outcome of meaningful participation is participants' strengthened empowerment, which can be defined as their capacity to exert control over their lives and to claim their rights."[41] In these initiatives hope abides as vulnerability and precarity subside.

Precarity challenges the dominant sense and imposition of control, and vulnerability challenges the ways we navigate structures of sin and grace. Both challenges require a radical rethinking and embrace of God's passible and willing precarity and vulnerability as God loves creation into being, in the incarnation, and in the Pentecost descent of the Holy Spirit. Created in God's image, we too, then, are subject to the precarity of things unseen and unknown that surround us. Thus, as *kenosis*, scandal, and vulnerability become the normative way that the symbol of God functions, so the disabled God navigates the world in radical dependence through mutual relationality and the precarity of life enfleshed. This passible, vulnerable God is in, with, and for us—so must we be for others.

---

[38] See Thomas Aquinas, *Summa Theologiae* II.II.17c.

[39] Maribel Casas-Cortés, "Precarious Writings: Reckoning the Absences and Reclaiming the Legacies in the Current Poetics/Politics of Precarity," *Current Anthropology* 62, no. 5 (2021): 511–12.

[40] United Nations, "Universal Values: Principle Two: Leave No One Behind" (2023), unsdg.un.org.

[41] United Nations Sustainable Development Group, "Operationalizing Leaving No One Behind" (March 2022), 61.

Importantly, radical relationality offers insight into vulnerability and precarity in times past, present, and future. As Keenan instructs, "When I recognize that the word *vulnerable* does not mean being or having been wounded but rather means being able to be wounded, then it means being exposed to the other; in this sense vulnerability is the human condition that allows me to encounter, receive, or respond to the other."[42] As the discipline of moral theology is dedicated to identifying the rightly ordered life and facilitating rightly ordered action with the guidance of scripture, reason, and faith, so, as Keenan reminds us, we are enjoined to embrace the reality that "vulnerability is the human condition that allows [us] to hear, encounter, receive, or respond to the other even to the point of being injured."[43]

---

[42] Keenan, "The World at Risk," 139.

[43] Keenan, "Preparing for the Moral Life: Vulnerability, Recognition, and Conscience," St. Ignatius Loyola Parish, New York, January 30, 2022.

21.

Keenan's Visionary Project of Bridging Moral Teaching with Pastoral Practice

Reception of Amoris Laetitia by Australian Catholics

AI PHAM, SJ

Introduction

Followers of James Keenan's work may recognise the prevailing terms *bridging* or *building bridges* that appropriately describe his ongoing zeal in teaching and writing theological ethics. His academic vocation and pastoral ministry aim to build bridges between distinct areas in theological ethics: morality and spirituality, theological ethics and scripture, and between ethical perspectives (or ethicists) in different contexts or cultures. He has also written many articles and books to bridge the church's moral teaching and pastoral applications. Focusing on bridging moral teaching and pastoral practice, I examine: (1) Keenan's bridging project in his teaching, writing, and academic work; and (2) connecting Keenan's method to efforts to build a bridge between moral teaching and pastoral practice in the reception and implementation of the Apostolic Exhortation *Amoris Laetitia* by Australian Catholics.[1]

---

[1] Pope Francis, *Amoris Laetitia* (March 19, 2016). The exhortation is hereafter cited in notes as *AL*.

Bridging Moral Teaching and Pastoral Practice:
James Keenan's Visionary Project

After three years of pastoral ministry in South Australia, I came to Weston Jesuit School of Theology asking how I could apply the moral teaching of the church to particular pastoral contexts such as parishes and migrant communities in Australia. Keenan initially guided me to consider Norbert J. Rigali's approach for bridging morality and spirituality in Christian living. Among Rigali's writings, a few noticeable ones argue for a unity of moral and pastoral truth.[2] This early and useful step has guided me into a moral-pastoral path with three key steps: primacy of charity-love, defending the conscience, and enhancement of moral discernment.

The Primacy of Charity-Love

Keenan's textbook *Moral Wisdom* begins with a chapter entitled "Love." He argues that this point of departure in moral theology is grounded in scripture, tradition, theology, spirituality, arts, and lived human experience.[3] Vatican II has retrieved the importance of charity-love in moral theology. In the process of conscientious discernment, love motivates our search for a truth in order to love rightly or justly; love prompts our search for a freedom for a greater love; love drives, animates, and moves our action in our longing for union. Charity-love also highlights the social dimension of Christian conscience. As Josef Fuchs remarks: "Certain worldly human factors enter into the exercise of the various other virtues, but in exercising charity man gives himself in person."[4]

Conscience

Keenan has defended the primacy of conscience.[5] Turning to contemporary theologians, he proposes a notion of "a socially informed and collectively

---

[2] E.g., Norbert J. Rigali, "The Unity of the Moral Order," *Chicago Studies* 8 (1969): 125–43; "Christian Ethics and Perfection," *Chicago Studies* 14 (1975): 227–40; "The Unity of Moral and Pastoral Truth," *Chicago Studies* 25 (1986): 224–32.

[3] James Keenan, *Moral Wisdom: Lessons and Texts from the Catholic Tradition*, 3rd ed. (Lanham, MD: Rowman & Littlefield, 2016).

[4] Josef Fuchs, *Human Values and Christian Morality* (Dublin: Gill and Macmillan, 1970), 25.

[5] E.g., James Keenan, "Compelling Assent: The Magisterium and the Conscience," *Irish Theological Quarterly* 57 (1991): 209–27; "Examining Conscience: Ancient Wisdom on Judgment, Justice, and the Heart," *America* 214, no. 11 (April 4–11, 2016): 15–17; "The Call to Grow in Love" and "Examining Conscience in Light of Scripture," in *Conscience at Work*, ed. Kristin E. Heyer and Karen K. Kiefer (Boston College, MA: C21 Resources, Fall 2016); "Called to Conscience: Americans Must Recognize Their Own Capacity for Evil," *America* 216, no. 1 (January 2, 2017): 14–18.

engaged conscience."[6] In this respect he develops the notion of *sensus fidelium* referenced by Pope Francis at the 2014 Synod.[7] It is, as Keenan notes, "the instinct of faith that all the faithful share." Its process involves mutuality and communality. Its judgments come "only by deep, prayerful, conscientious struggle."[8] In addition, Pope Francis recently called for a church of synodality, centred on mutual listening, learning, collegiality, and solidarity. This notion of conscience involves a process of moral discernment.[9]

Moral Discernment

Keenan has enhanced individual, communal, and social moral discernment based on Ignatian spirituality.[10] Moral discernment, as Keenan sees it, is the "trademark" of Pope Francis. In *Amoris Laetitia* the pope couples it with the guidance of the Holy Spirit and the Christian conscience. Moral discernment, as Keenan elaborates Pope Francis's teaching, locates the moral life of Christians in relationality rather than in merely personal-individual decision-making. Moving from an Ignatian understanding of discernment, Keenan further develops the notion of moral discernment drawn from *Amoris Laetitia* into a definition as "a social practice used in a variety of relational ways to determine a pathway of living out the summons of the gospel."[11] He sees the Spirit, accompaniment, compassion, and prudence as constitutive of moral discernment.[12] Prayer, listening, consultation, and discussion involving all levels of the faithful as shown in the journey of two extraordinary synods and the 2015–16 year of mercy may serve as the best examples of communal, social discernment.

---

[6] James Keenan, "Redeeming Conscience," *Theological Studies* 76, no. 1 (May 2015): 133.

[7] Pope Francis, "Speech at the End of the Synod," *Vatican Radio*, October 18, 2014.

[8] Keenan, "Redeeming Conscience," 131.

[9] See, e.g., Pope Francis, "Ceremony Commemorating the 50th Anniversary of the Institution of the Synod of Bishops: Address of His Holiness Pope Francis," October 17, 2015; Keenan, "Redeeming Conscience," 135–46; John Honner, "Cathedrals and Caravans," *Eureka Street* 33, no. 3 (February 27, 2023). For a helpful view of bridging moral teaching and pastoral practice in the Christian conscience, see Martin M. Lintner, "The Notion of Conscience in *Amoris Laetitia* and Its Significance for the Divorced and Remarried," European Forum, Catholic Theological Ethics in the World Church (CTEWC), May 5, 2016.

[10] James Keenan, "Moral Discernment in History," *Theological Studies* 79, no. 3 (2018): 668–79.

[11] Keenan, 668.

[12] Keenan, 676.

Pope Francis has repeatedly mentioned those moral tools in his teaching, particularly in *Amoris Laetitia*,[13] in which the pope has emphasised the need for bridging moral teaching and pastoral application. Keenan investigates various ways of reception, development, and implementation of *Amoris Laetitia* in different cultural contexts. Only a few US bishops have received *Amoris Laetitia* to the extent of most other bishops' conferences, which Keenan characterizes as "a lot of innovation and acknowledgment that the pope's summons is challenging but necessary."[14] Keenan affirms that "relationality, listening, accompaniment, and prudential guidance" make up the proper process of moral discernment toward the teaching in *Amoris Laetitia*. "But before attending to all this," he adds, "we must remind ourselves that there is a subject, the agent, the Christian who seeks to discern his or her trajectory before God . . . the Christian who needs to make a decision—a prudential one as a Christian—in the church, with the Holy Spirit."[15] This comment echoes Pope Francis's words: "We have been called to form consciences, not to replace them" (*AL,* no. 37).

In fact, Keenan has practiced what he preaches. Along with his writings on *Amoris Laetitia*, he has worked to bring bishops and moral theologians and other wise and grounded laypeople together to implement its teaching.[16] Joining in this significant project, other ethicists in places like Africa, China, India, Philippines, the United States, and beyond have examined how *Amoris Laetitia* has been received and implemented.[17] Next I investigate how

[13] Caleb Bernacchio, "Pope Francis on Conscience, Gradualness, and Discernment: Adapting *Amoris Laetitia* for Business Ethics," *Business Ethics Quarterly* 29, no. 4 (October 2019), 437—60.

[14] Interview of James Keenan by Sean Salai, "The Moral Theology of Pope Francis: Questions for Jesuit Ethicist James Keenan," *America* (April 28, 2017).

[15] Keenan, "Moral Discernment in History," 679.

[16] See, e.g., James Keenan, "Receiving *Amoris Laetitia*," *Theological Studies* 78, no. 1 (March 2017): 193–212; "What I Learned from Organizing, Participating in Boston's 'Amoris Laetitia' Event," *National Catholic Reporter*, October 9, 2017; "7 Takeaways from Hosting 'Amoris Laetitia' Theology Seminars for 47 US Bishops," *National Catholic Reporter*, March 1, 2018; *Amoris Laetitia: A New Momentum for Moral Formation and Pastoral Practice*, ed. with Grant Gallicho (Mahwah, NJ: Paulist Press, 2018); "Eight Ways that *Amoris Laetitia* Is Being Received and Promoted around the World," *Marriage, Families and Spirituality* 28, no. 1 (2022): 4–17.

[17] E.g., George Therukaattil, "Pope Francis' Moral and Pastoral Approach in *Amoris Laetitia*," *Jnanadeepa* 22, no. 1 (January–June 2018): 112–30; Emily Kerama and Eunice Kamaara, "*Amoris Laetitia* and the Pastoral Challenge Facing the Family in Africa Today," in *Love, Joy, and Sex*, ed. Stan Chu Ilo, 156–81 (Eugene, OR: Cascade Books, 2019); Romulo G. Valles (Catholic Bishops Conference of the Philippines), "Pastoral Statement on the Year 'Amoris Laetitia Family,'" March 19, 2021; Simeiqi He, "Love and the Social Mission of Marriage in China," *CTEWC Forum*, September 2, 2021; Emily Reimer-Barry, "*Amoris Laetitia* at Five," *Theological Studies* 83, no. 1 (2022): 109–32.

the local church in Australia has also received, developed, and implemented the teaching in *Amoris Laetitia*.

Australian Reception of *Amoris Laetitia*

In general, the Australian church has received *Amoris Laetitia* positively, as a challenging but necessary innovation, and worked hard to bridge the moral teachings of the church presented in *Amoris Laetitia* and the pastoral complexities of the Australian contexts. I examine the reception of *Amoris Laetitia* by Australian laypeople, theologians, and bishops. These voices consistently discern Keenan's three themes of charity-love, conscience, and moral discernment within the text of *Amoris Laetitia* and as key for the Australian church's implementation of it. I show how these themes emerge in three key areas of concern for the Australian church: bridging the ideal and the reality of marriage and family life today, holy communion for divorced and civilly remarried Catholics, and recognition of same-sex couples.

Bridging the Ideal and the Reality of Marriage and Family Life

In bridging between the ideal and realistic complexities, Peter Johnstone, president of Catholics for Renewal Inc., reminds the bishops of the *sensus fidelium* and asks for implementation of this spirit of Vatican II by listening to the "people of God." He recommends the way of discernment exercised by the church in leading the Synods of Bishops' Assemblies on the Family according to the pope's direction in *Amoris Laetitia.*[18]

Shawn and Branka van der Linden, a married couple with four young children, who represent the Australian Catholic Marriage and Family Council, welcome the exhortation: "To have a church document that speaks in a realistic way about the practicalities of family life is a great encouragement and relevant to our lived experience."[19]

Brendan Nicholls, a high-school liturgy coordinator, also notices an ideal in *Amoris Laetitia*: "an insight into the beauty of true love that sacramental marriage offers and how such love transcends the world in which we live." To actualise that ideal of marriage and family love in the reality, Nicholls asks Australians to be aware of the complexities of the modern world and thus to support marriages and families in difficulties with "fullness of

---

[18] Peter Johnstone, "The Synod on the Family—The Start of Major Reform?" address to a group of Pumphouse SIPs (Spirituality in the Pub) at St Carthage's Parish, Parkville, Victoria, May 4, 2016.

[19] Australian Catholic Bishops Conference (ACBC), "Pope Francis Encourages Marriage and Family Life, Mindful of Ideal and Reality," April 8, 2016.

compassion and pastoral care." Supporting those with special needs, the sick and the elderly, even at personal cost, is a way for all Australians to respect the sanctity of life, and it is clearly an expression of charity-love.[20]

For Garry Everett, a lay educator, contact is a practical way of bridging the ideal and the reality. He welcomes *Amoris Laetitia* with this observation: "Jesus healed the leper by contact. Therefore *Amoris Laetitia* invites all the faithful to a journey of contact which engages 'inculturation and appropriate devolution of decision-making' as well as 'communication and charity so that together we can strengthen the bonds of marriage and its basis in love.'"[21] This observation points to social, conscientious moral discernment.

Noel Connolly, a Columban missionary priest and missiologist, sees a possibility of bridging the ideal and the "concrete situations and practical possibilities of real families" (*AL*, no. 36) by properly exercising conscience and moral discernment. He claims that Pope Francis has confidence in the competence and maturity of the faithful, quoting the pope's words: "Not all discussions of doctrinal, moral or pastoral issues need to be settled by interventions of the magisterium" (*AL*, no. 3). Connolly encourages pastors to undertake three tasks in discernment as accompaniment: "understand the difficulties people face; offer spiritual nourishment, encouragement and a positive vision; and form consciences and help people to discern." With this practice of discernment, the faithful will grow in personal maturity, that is, "the ability to make faith decisions and a mature friendship with Christ." Reaching this level of discipleship, the church will be a "more adult, discerning, decentralised and consultative church."[22]

Australian senior theologian Gerald O'Collins acknowledges a creative fidelity with the papal teachings after Vatican II and a creative balance between doctrinal tradition and pastoral accompaniment. He notes:

> Francis makes quite clear his two central convictions. On the one hand, he insists that the church must continue to "propose the full ideal of marriages" (*AL*, no. 307) and "clearly express her objective teaching" (*AL*, no. 308). On the other hand, to those who press for "a more rigorous pastoral care which leaves no room for confusion" (*AL,* no. 308), the pope responds that if "we put so many conditions

[20] Brendan Nicholls, "In '*Amoris Laetitia*: Families—Love and Marriage,'" *Australian Catholics*, May 5, 2016; cf. *AL*, no. 164.

[21] Garry Everett, "Much to Admire about *Amoris Laetitia*," *The Good Oil* (April 2016).

[22] Noel Connolly, "Pope Francis—A Church 'Called to Form Consciences,'" *Columban E-Bulletin* 9, no. 4 (May 17, 2016).

on his [God's] mercy that we empty it of its concrete meaning and real significance," we will be indulging in "the worst way of watering down the Gospel" (*AL*, no. 311).[23]

Archbishop Mark Coleridge, who attended the 2015 Synod in Rome, remarks on bridging the ideal of the moral truth and pastoral practice:

Of course he [Pope Francis] says the church must speak the truth. But that isn't enough. If that's all we do, then we run the risk of turning the great truths of Christianity into stones that we hurl at those we want to condemn. We also need to walk with people, all kinds of people, especially those who are struggling in their marriage or family life.[24]

By saying this, Coleridge also calls for pastoral accompaniment, which is strongly emphasised in *Amoris Laetitia*:

To walk with people, whoever they are, means to enter into dialogue with them. That means we listen to people, whoever they may be and however far they may fall short of the ideal. For Francis, the *ideal* does matter; the vision must be kept clearly focused. But, if we speak only of it, then we can *drift off into some abstract no-sphere* that doesn't breathe *the air of reality.*[25] (Emphases added)

The Australian Catholic Bishops Conference (ACBC) as a body, as well as many dioceses, developed pastoral implementation projects with the goal of accompanying married couples, especially the newly married and those experiencing complex situations, and improving marriage preparation.[26]

Pastoral Practice on Admitting Divorced and Civilly Remarried Catholics to Holy Communion

Theologian Thomas Ryan, SM, clarifies the implications of chapter 8 of *Amoris Laetitia*, which deals with complications surrounding marriage and

---

[23] Gerald O'Collins, "The Joy of Love (*Amoris Laetitia*): The Papal Exhortation in Its Contexts," *Theological Studies* 77, no. 4 (2016): 920.

[24] Archbishop Mark Coleridge, "The Joy of Love: Pope Francis Sets Out a Human Journey," ACBC Media Blog; the article was first published in *The Weekend Australian*, April 9, 2016.

[25] Coleridge.

[26] See ACBC, *Plenary Meeting*, May 4–11, 2017.

occasioned significant, sometimes controversial discussion.[27] Ryan notes the pope's clear and specific guidance toward a prudential process of pastoral discernment. He shows how aligned *Amoris Laetitia* is with Keenan's moral principles when he quotes Keenan, saying: "From an anthropological foundation (the human person as relational and responsive), *Amoris Laetitia* uses traditional moral categories and the theology of grace (in its 'fruits') to evaluate 'irregular' situations concerning marriage. Importantly, it is not about compromising teachings. It is rather seeing that they are 'actually greater than we have imagined.'"[28]

From a biblical perspective, Francis Moloney suggests that the church "reflects upon its biblical and ecclesial tradition in dialogue with an ever-expanding body of knowledge and experience."[29] Hence the possibility of admitting the divorced and remarried to the sacraments not only reflects divine mercy and compassion but is grounded on the teaching of "the *authentic Tradition* generated within the Spirit-filled formative decades of Christianity."[30]

Gerald O'Collins also takes the authentic tradition of the church into consideration in dealing with admitting the divorced and civilly remarried to the sacraments, especially the Eucharist. He interprets that Pope Francis dictates neither yes nor no to that question. But the pope leaves room for a responsible discernment on an individual basis in "some, justifiable circumstances" and "the immense variety of concrete circumstances" (*AL*, no. 300) to seek appropriate access to the sacraments of reconciliation and the Eucharist for those divorced and civilly remarried. This discernment involves not only the couples themselves but also their bishop, parish priest, and/or other spiritual guides.[31]

Archbishop Timothy Costello of Perth responded to *Amoris Laetitia* in a pastoral letter. He noted "more positive and creative ways of strengthening and encouraging couples and families in difficulty," and "a strong appeal to pastors to help such individuals and couples find their proper place in Catholic parishes, and to accompany each one with patience, discernment, and above all compassion." In multiple pastoral letters he assures the

---

[27] Thomas Ryan, "'Weakness, and Wounded and Troubled Love' in *Amoris Laetitia*: Pope Francis as Pastor," *Australasian Catholic Record* 94, no. 2 (2017): 131–47.

[28] Ryan, "'Weakness, and Wounded and Troubled Love' in *Amoris Laetitia*," 132 and 146–47 respectively; ref. Keenan, "Receiving *Amoris Laetitia*," 202.

[29] Francis J. Moloney, "A New Testament Hermeneutic for Divorce and Remarriage in the Catholic Tradition," *The Australasian Catholic Record* 92, no. 3 (July 2015): 287.

[30] Moloney, 287.

[31] O'Collins, "The Joy of Love (*Amoris Laetitia*)," 918–20.

faithful in his archdiocese that "it was never the Pope's intention to change Catholic teaching on divorce and remarriage, or on same-sex unions."[32]

Recognition of Same-Sex Couples

On same-sex unions Pope Francis writes: "We would like before all else to reaffirm that every person, regardless of sexual orientation, ought to be respected in his or her dignity and treated with consideration" (*AL*, no. 250). Developing this instruction, Nick Miller, a morning news editor at the *Guardian Australia* and a frequent commentator on Catholic issues, notes the erotic dimension of love in *Amoris Laetitia*. The exhortation states: "The erotic appears as a specifically human manifestation of sexuality. It enables us to discover 'the nuptial meaning of the body and the authentic dignity of the gift'" (*AL*, no. 151). The union of love involved in conjugal love "combines the warmth of friendship and erotic passion, and endures long after emotions and passion subside" (*AL*, no. 120).[33]

With a more forthright voice, Dr. Ron Pirola and his wife, Mavis, married for fifty years and members of the Pontifical Council for the Family, view sex as an essential foundation for their relationship. Spirituality as sexual attraction brought them together and has sustained their marriage for more than half a century. They told two hundred bishops around the world at the Vatican's Synod on the Family: "That attraction that we first felt and the continued bonding force between us was basically sexual. The little things we did for each other, the telephone calls and love notes, the way we planned our day around each other and the things we shared were outward expressions of our longing to be intimate with each other." Their experience did not stop them from calling for inclusion of homosexuals in the church, though not for official recognition of same-sex unions. This would be a "model of evangelisation" for parishes around the world and a new way to touch the hearts of the faithful.[34]

Former New South Wales premier and practising Catholic Kristina Keneally responded: "The Australian sense of honesty and frankness is

---

[32] Catholic Archdiocese of Perth, "Archbishop Costello Responds to Apostolic Exhortation *Amoris Laetitia*, The Joy of Love," April 8, 2016; Timothy Costello, "Pope Francis Apostolic Exhortation *Amoris Laetitia*—Address to the Dawson Society," at Rosie O'Grady's Northbridge, March 28, 2017, Catholic Archdiocese of Perth.

[33] Nick Miller, "*Amoris Laetitia*: Pope Francis and the 'Erotic Dimension of Love,'" *The Sydney Morning Herald*, April 9, 2016.

[34] Jenna Clark, "Australian Couple Explains the Joy of Sex to Pope Francis," *The Sydney Morning Herald*, October 8, 2014.

a welcome gift to the Catholic Church. Ron and Mavis Pirola have said what many Australian Catholics have been saying for years regarding divorced people, single parents, and homosexuals who also want to have a relationship with God."[35] Keneally views it as "amusing and depressing" to hear about sexual union from a long-married couple rather than the more frequent commentary from celibates who may be presumed to have little relevant experience. Reading *Amoris Laetitia* on taking the ideal and the reality of families with pastoral sensitivity, Gerald O'Collins wonders if *Amoris Laetitia*'s teaching recognises a complementary, permanent, and exclusive relationship between two freely consenting gay or lesbian adults. Considering same-sex unions as a remote analogy to marriage unions between men and women, he opens up further consideration: "One might well agree that such unions 'radically contradict' the 'ideal' of Christian marriage (*AL*, no. 292). But does that rule out a remote analogy to such marriage?"[36]

Archbishop Anthony Fisher of Sydney reads hope and joy for the future of marriage into *Amoris Laetitia*.[37] Against any proposed legal recognition in Australia of same-sex marriages conducted overseas, Fisher defends "historically understood" marriage, as "building a civilization of life and love." For this, he recalls a respect for conscience guided by the gospel and the church in hearing and responding to the call of discipleship, though he does not recognize that conscience might expand our view of marriage and not necessarily point toward the traditional definition of marriage.[38] Elsewhere Fisher calls for a pastoral approach of compassion and inclusion, namely, to treat those in failed marriages like "Christ the Good Samaritan and to learn from him how to be a field hospital for all."[39]

While other responses to *Amoris Laetitia*'s discussion of same-sex couples touched on themes of charity-love, discernment, and accompaniment,

---

[35] Clark.

[36] O'Collins, "The Joy of Love (*Amoris Laetitia*)," 913.

[37] Anthony Fisher, "*Amoris Laetitia*—The Joy of (Marital) Love," keynote address at the Renaissance of Marriage Conference at the University of Technology, Sydney, October 21, 2016.

[38] Anthony Fisher, "Building a Civilisation of Life and Love," *The Australasian Catholic Record* 92, no. 3 (July 2015): 289–97; also "Conscience, Relativism, and Truth: The Witness of Newman," Conference on Newman the Prophet: A Saint of Our Times, Pontifical University of St. Thomas (Angelicum), Rome, October 12, 2019.

[39] Anthony Fisher, "Between Ideal and Reality: What Future for Marriage in Australia?" Address to the John Paul II Institute in Australia, *Catholic Weekly,* August 11, 2017.

the ACBC focused on the consequences of changing the classical, traditional definition of marriage between a man and a woman.[40] Archbishop Anthony Fisher even quoted Pope Francis's earlier positions on same-sex marriage legislation as Archbishop of Buenos Aires in a blog post opposing the same legislation in Australia.[41] However, in recommending a pastoral approach to clergy, the bishops followed *Amoris Laetitia*'s guidelines of charity-love when they recommended their priests and pastors both speak the truth and show mercy to people. At the same time they invited them to accompany those in complex situations through the external and internal forum that involves a process of moral discernment and a well-formed conscience.[42]

Two bishops in the ACBC took a different and more open attitude toward civil same-sex marriage. Bishop Vincent Nguyen Van Long of Parramatta observes LGBTI people as a sign of the times. They have not been treated with acceptance and respect by the church. He suggests that Catholics reach out to those people, "affirming their dignity and accompanying them on our common journey towards the fullness of life and love in God."[43] The late Bishop Bill Wright of Maitland-Newcastle took a similar stand. He used the common good argument in supporting same-sex legislation as he said: "In our pluralist society, it does more for community peace and harmony for gay couples to have a place in the recognized structures than for them to be excluded."[44]

Alan Hogan, a retired Catholic lawyer based in Sydney, supported legalization of same-sex marriage through an approach that comports with *Amoris Laetitia*'s message of accompaniment in complex situations. He observes: "A substantial number of people in the community have already entered into homosexual relationships, monogamous and intended to be permanent, or will do so. Some of them will break down, as do heterosexual relationships. Disputes will arise about matters such as property, maintenance, and custody of and access to children." Admitting that reality, he argues: "It would be for the common good if there were one set of laws for all Australians who suffer a relationship breakdown, and one set

[40] ACBC, *Don't Mess with Marriage: A Pastoral Letter from the Catholic Bishops of Australia to All Australians on the "Same-sex Marriage" Debate,* November 24 2015.
[41] Inés San Martín, "Australian Bishop on Same-sex Marriage: Listen to 'Signs of the Times,'" *Crux* (September 17, 2017).
[42] ACBC, *Plenary Meeting,* May 5–11, 2016.
[43] "Bishop Vincent's [Nguyen Van Long] Pastoral Letter on the Same-sex Marriage Postal Survey," *Catholic Outlook* [Diocese of Parramatta], September 13, 2017.
[44] San Martín, "Australian Bishop on Same-sex Marriage."

of specialist courts to deal with disputes arising from such breakdowns, especially where children are concerned."[45]

Conclusion

Christian morality can be understood as the person's response to God's call by discerning in conscience a pathway of living out the Christian life following the summons of the gospel. Without Keenan's vision being referred to or implemented in *Amoris Laetitia*, however, there are clear resonances between Keenan's framework and what we see in *Amoris Laetitia* and applied in different contexts. In the document Pope Francis directs all the faithful to a process of discernment in the form of accompaniment. This moral-pastoral approach aims to strengthen family bonds, prepare couples for their marriage commitment, and promote a culture of inclusive church. Marriages and families in turbulence and complexity are included with a discerning consideration of admission to the sacraments. Instead of giving a simple yes or no answer to a complex question that demands a differentiated answer, *Amoris Laetitia* has opened up new possibilities in pastoral practices for the local church, including reception of sacraments by the divorced and remarried. Australian Catholics have received *Amoris Laetitia* as an opportunity for church renewal and have developed and implemented its instructions, particularly with regard to charity-love, conscience, and discernment.

Keenan noted those resonances of *Amoris Laetitia* with his moral-pastoral framework in seven terms: *pastoral, local church, discernment, Holy Spirit, conscience, accompaniment*, and *mercy.*[46] Assisting the American bishops and theologians in implementing *Amoris Laetitia*, he realized that they have well comprehended those key terms. He remarked after hosting the 2017 *Amoris Laetitia* Symposium at Boston College: "Using Francis's terms like 'the church as field hospital,' 'the irreplaceable conscience,' 'accompaniment,' and 'authentic discernment,' we became for 36 hours a bit more forgetful of ourselves and more mindful of the papal exhortation on our families. It was a refreshing moment."[47] He added after the 2018

---

[45] Alan Hogan, "A Common Good Argument for Legalising Same-sex Marriage," *Eureka Street* 26, no. 17 (August 31 2016).

[46] James Keenan, "Regarding *Amoris Laetitia*: Its Language, Its Reception, Some Challenges, and Agnosticism of Some of the Hierarchy," *Perspectiva Teológica, Belo Horizonte* 53, no. 1 (January/April 2021): 41–60.

[47] Keenan, "What I Learned from Organizing, Participating in Boston's 'Amoris Laetitia' Event"; Keenan, "Eight Ways that *Amoris Laetitia* Is Being Received and Promoted around the World."

theological seminar in Santa Clara: "The language and imagination of Francis were present. Terms like discernment, accompaniment, gradualism, growth, freedom and conscience became the language of the conference. . . . In a way, the discussion was animated by mercy with an appreciation of its healing balm."[48]

In this respect Keenan and his companions have also applied the teaching of Vatican II:

> The Church guards the heritage of God's word and draws from it moral and religious principles without always having at hand the solution to particular problems. As such she desires to add the light of revealed truth to mankind's store of experience, so that the path which humanity has taken in recent times will not be a dark one. (*Gaudium et Spes,* no. 33)

---

[48] Keenan, "7 Takeaways from Hosting 'Amoris Laetitia' Theology Seminars for 47 US Bishops."

Contributors

Maria Cimperman, RSCJ, is both professor of theological ethics and consecrated life at Catholic Theological Union in Chicago and synodality coordinator at the International Union of Superiors General in Rome. Author of several books, she participated in the Synod on Synodality as a non-voting expert.

Daniel J. Daly is the founding executive director of the Center for Theology and Ethics in Catholic Healthcare. He is also associate professor of moral theology at Boston College's Clough School of Theology and Ministry. His monograph *The Structures of Virtue and Vice* (Georgetown University Press, 2021) was awarded first place in the theological and philosophical studies category by the Catholic Media Association in July 2022.

Craig A. Ford, Jr., is an assistant professor of theology and religious studies at Saint Norbert College in De Pere, Wisconsin, and on the faculty at the Institute for Black Catholic Studies at Xavier University of Louisiana. His current projects are a monograph, *Works of Art: Sexuality, Gender, Race, and a New Theology of Embodiment*, under contract with Fortress Press, and an edited volume on the future of theology told exclusively from the perspectives of queer Catholic theologians of color.

Eric Marcelo O. Genilo, SJ, is an ordained minister and a member of the Society of Jesus, Philippine Province. He is currently a professor of moral theology at Loyola School of Theology and a formator of diocesan seminarians at San José Seminary in Quezon City, Philippines.

Mark Graham is an associate professor of theological ethics and director of the undergraduate program at Villanova University. He is the author of *Josef Fuchs on Natural Law* (Georgetown University Press, 2002), and *Sustainable Agriculture: A Christian Ethic of Gratitude* (Pilgrim Press, 2005), and is currently finishing a monograph on Catholic environmental ethics.

Mary Jo Iozzio is professor of moral theology and *professora ordinaria* at Boston College's Clough School of Theology and Ministry. She is the author of *Self-Determination and the Moral Act* (Peeters, 1995), *Disability Ethics/Preferential Justice* (Georgetown University Press, 2023), and *Radical Dependence: A Theological Ethics in the Key of Disability* (forthcoming, Baylor, 2024).

Michael P. Jaycox is an associate professor in the Theology and Religious Studies Department at Seattle University. His research and teaching engage ethical questions about systemic racism and white supremacy, sexuality and gender, emotions, and bioethics, and his articles have been published in *Political Theology, Religions, Horizons, The Journal of the Society of Christian Ethics, Health Progress,* and *Developing World Bioethics.*

John Karuvelil, SJ, is a Jesuit priest and a professor of moral theology at Pontifical Athenaeum, Jnana Deepa (JD), Institute of Philosophy and Theology, in Pune, India. At present he is the dean of the faculty of theology. He specializes in biomedical ethics.

Conor M. Kelly is an associate professor of theological ethics at Marquette University in Milwaukee, Wisconsin. He is the author of *The Fullness of Free Time* (Georgetown University Press, 2020) and *Racism and Structural Sin* (Liturgical Press, 2023), and coeditor, with Kenneth R. Himes, of *Poverty: Responding Like Jesus* (Paraclete Press, 2018) and with Kristin E. Heyer, of *The Moral Vision of Pope Francis: Expanding the US Reception of the First Jesuit Pope* (Georgetown University Press, 2024).

Joseph J. Kotva, Jr., is a former Mennonite pastor, avid cyclist, lifelong photographer, climate-change advocate, and grateful husband (to Carol) and father (to Joseph and Matthew). He codirects the Scholarly Concentration in Ethics, Equity, and Justice at the Indiana University School of Medicine—South Bend and is the coeditor, with M. Therese Lysaught, of *On Moral Medicine: Theological Perspectives on Medical Ethics* (Eerdmans Publishing, 2012, third edition).

Vincent Leclercq, AA, is a medical doctor, the secretary general for formation of the Augustinians of the Assumption (Assumptionists), and an associate professor of ethics at the Pontifical John Paul II Institute in Rome. He is the author of *Blessed Are the Vulnerable: Reaching Out to Those with AIDS* (Twenty-Third Publications, 2010) and *Fin de vie—Pourquoi les chrétiens ne peuvent pas se taire* (Éditions de l'Atelier, 2013).

Xavier M. Montecel is an assistant professor and the theology graduate program director at St. Mary's University in San Antonio, Texas, working in areas including liturgy and ethics, fundamental moral theology, and Catholic social thought. His writings have appeared in the *Journal of the Society of Christian Ethics*, *Religions*, and the *Journal of Moral Theology*, among other venues.

Megan K. McCabe is an assistant professor of religious studies at Gonzaga University. Her work centers on issues related to sexual violence and moral responsibility for social changes.

Ai Pham, SJ, is currently an adjunct lecturer at Catholic Theological College, Honorary Fellow of the Loyola Institute at Australian Catholic University, and doing pastoral ministry in Melbourne, Australia.

Cristina Richie is a lecturer on the ethics of technology at the University of Edinburgh and the joint editor of *Global Bioethics*. Richie is the author of two monographs, *Principles of Green Bioethics: Sustainability in Health Care* (Michigan State University Press, 2019) and *Environmental Ethics and Medical Reproduction* (Oxford University Press, 2024) and over fifty articles in journals, including *The Lancet*, *American Journal of Bioethics*, and the *Hastings Center Report*.

Kathryn Getek Soltis is director of the Center for Peace and Justice Education and associate teaching professor of Christian ethics in the Department of Theology and Religious Studies at Villanova University. She has served as a lay Catholic prison chaplain in Boston and a volunteer minister in the Philadelphia Department of Prisons.

Osamu Takeuchi, SJ, a native of Japan, is a professor of moral theology/ Christian ethics at Sophia University in Tokyo. He is the author of *Conscience and Culture: A Dialogue between the West and the East concerning Conscience* (LAP Lambert Academic Publishing, 2010).

Edwin Vásquez Ghersi, SJ, is a Jesuit priest from Peru. He has taught moral theology and bioethics for several years at Universidad Antonio Ruiz de Montoya in Lima, published articles, and coedited a book in bioethics. Currently he is the president of San José High School in Arequipa, Peru.

Christopher P. Vogt is associate professor of theology and religious studies and a senior fellow of the Vincentian Center for Church and Society at St. John's University in New York. He is the author of *Patience, Compassion, Hope, and the Christian Art of Dying Well* (Rowman & Littlefield, 2004). He is currently working on a book on Catholic higher education and the common good.

Kate Ward is associate professor of theological ethics at Marquette University in Milwaukee, Wisconsin. She is the author of *Wealth, Virtue, and Moral Luck: Christian Ethics in an Age of Inequality* (Georgetown University Press, 2021) and is completing a book on work in Catholic social thought.

Ronaldo Zacharias has a doctorate in moral theology (Weston Jesuit School of Theology—Cambridge/USA), a post-doctorate in democracy and human rights (University of Coimbra—Portugal), and coordinates the post-graduate course in sexual education at the Salesian University Center (São Paulo, Brazil). He is author and coeditor of many books on moral theology in English and Portuguese.

Index

Black Fantastic, 209
Bogner, Daniel, 235
Bordeyne, Philippe, 125
Buber, Martin, 167, 168–69
Burggraeve, Roger, 89, 184
Butler, Judith, 89, 91, 241

Cahill, Ann J., 186, 187
Cahill, Lisa Sowle, 130, 166, 177
Callaghan, Tonya, 35
caritas, 205, 209
Casaldáliga, Pedro, 172
Casti Connubii papal encyclical, 6
casuistry, 28
    bioethics, grounding in, 132, 133, 181
    casuistry principles, Keenan
        interpreting, 36, 181–82
    in Catholic moral theology, 5, 126–
        27, 129
    high casuistry, 26, 129, 182
    Keenan's scholarship in, 25–27, 109,
        128
    moral discernment and, 33–36
Catechism of the Catholic Church
        (CCC), 20, 29, 33
Catholic Health Association (CHA), 152
Catholic moral theology, 27, 31, 48,
        49–50, 97, 123, 127, 129, 161
Catholic moral tradition, 4, 25–26, 100,
        176
Catholic social teaching, 66, 81, 129,
        166, 184, 207, 240
Catholic Theological Coalition on HIV/
        AIDS Prevention, 27
Catholic Theological Ethics in the World
        Church (CTEWC), 67, 161, 184,
        236–37
Catholic Theological Society of America
        (CTSA), 175, 183
celibacy, 128, 215, 218–19, 260
Centers for Disease Control and
        Prevention (CDC), 138, 150
Chan, Yiu Sing Lúcás, 27, 38, 98, 102–3
character formation, 20, 49, 55, 97
charisms, 230, 231, 235–36
charity, 9, 31, 60
    bioethics and, 130, 152
    charity-love, 252, 255, 256, 260–61,
        262

commitment to, 105
    fraternal correction as an act of
        charity, 80–81
    scandal as a sin against, 28
    as a virtue, 72
chastity, 128, 214, 217–18, 220
Childress, James, 154
Choudhury, Kumar, 88
Church (journal), 111
Clark, Meghan, 4
climate change, 53, 171
    climate education and health, 145–46
    environmental crisis, addressing via
        bioethics, 162
    health effects of climate change,
        149–50, 153
    ideal health as impossible due to,
        147–48
    lower-carbon healthcare systems,
        152–55
    vulnerability and, 165
Coblentz, Jessica, 37–38, 42, 43, 44, 46
co-creative collaboration, 227, 230,
        236–38
Coleridge, Mark, 257
common good, 67, 104, 137, 202
    in bioethics framework, 151, 153, 166
    in Catholic social teaching, 129, 240
    justice as part of, 205
    organizational virtue and, 68–69
    in preferential option for the poor, 130
    relationality and, 201
    in same-sex legislation argument, 261
    sin as harmful to, 80
    in a virtuous parish, 64
communal discernment, 228, 230,
        235–36
condom use, 7, 26, 28, 127, 181–82
confraternities, 61, 65, 67
Congregation for Catholic Education
        (CCE), 30, 33, 35
Connolly, Noel, 256
conscience
    call to growth as coming through,
        113–14
    conscience formation, 16, 114, 192,
        193
    European theology of conscience,
        185, 189–92, 193

Milton Keynes UK
Ingram Content Group UK Ltd.
UKHW011820070924
447949UK00006B/56

9 781626 985957